AF608127

ANTHONIUS MARGARITHA AND THE JEWISH FAITH

ANTHONIUS MARGARITHA AND THE JEWISH FAITH

Jewish Life and Conversion in Sixteenth-Century Germany

Michael T. Walton

W

Wayne State University Press   Detroit

16 15 14 13 12 5 4 3 2 1

Library of Congress Cataloging-in-Publication Data

Walton, Michael Thomson, 1945–
Anthonius Margaritha and the Jewish faith : Jewish life and conversion in sixteenth-century Germany / Michael T. Walton.
p. cm.
Includes bibliographical references and index.
ISBN 978-0-8143-3800-1 (cloth : alk. paper) — ISBN 978-0-8143-3801-8 (ebook)
1. Margaritha, Anton, 1490–1537. 2. Christian converts from Judaism—Germany—Biography. 3. Judaism—Relations—Christianity. 4. Christianity and other religions—Judaism. 5. Judaism—History—Medieval and early modern period, 425–1789. I. Title.
BV2623.M38W35 2012
284.1092—dc23
[B]

2012001065

Typeset by BookComp, Inc.
Composed in Warnock Pro and Meta

To Phyllis

Contents

Illustrations

Acknowledgments

I thank Matt Goldish, Yaacov Deutsch, and Andrew Gow for reading early drafts and suggesting many improvements.

I am grateful to the librarians of the Klau Library for their extraordinary competence and helpfulness, especially for approval to use illustrations from their collections. The librarians at the University of Chicago Regenstein Library, the Andover-Harvard Theological Library, and the University of Utah Marriott Library have shown me many kindnesses.

I owe a great debt to Harris Lenowitz for encouraging this project. He also helped find many obscure materials without which this book could not have been written. Finally, thank you to several anonymous readers and to Ray B. Waddington and Dawn Hall for their editorial efforts, which, no matter how great, can never fully expunge my many faults.

Preface

Anthonius Margaritha was perhaps the best-known Jew of his generation in Germany to convert to Christianity. Born in the 1490s, Margaritha was the grandson, son, and brother of noted rabbis.[1] His conversion in 1521 had the effect of making him in his own eyes two people, a Jew by flesh and a Christian by rebirth. The "new man" wrote several polemics on the errors of Judaism. The most popular was his *Der gantz Jüdisch glaub* (The entire Jewish faith) (1530). In it, he described the Jewish life cycle and provided the first translation of the Hebrew prayer book into German. *Der gantz Jüdisch glaub* influenced Martin Luther's attitude toward Jews and embroiled Margaritha in a controversy with Rabbi Joseph (Josel) of Rosheim, Emperor Charles V's advisor. The importance of his family, his own notoriety, and his autobiographical comments provide information about Margaritha that is not available for other sixteenth-century converts.

With the rise of "scientific" history and *Wissenschaft des Judentums* (the scientific study of Judaism) in the nineteenth century, Margaritha's story and his work supplied important data for study. The noted historians Leopold Zunz, Ludwig Geiger, Heinrich Graetz, and Harry Bresslau mentioned Margaritha, his work, *Der gantz Jüdisch glaub,* and incidents from his life in their works. Geiger's studies of Reuchlin and the study of Hebrew in early modern Germany refer to Jacob Margoles and Anthonius. Zunz cited Margaritha concerning the liturgy and agreed with some of his opinions. Graetz described Margaritha's disputation with Josel of Rosheim as well as using him elsewhere as a source of information on Jews and Judaism in the sixteenth century.[2]

What might be called the biography of Margaritha was not written in the nineteenth century. He was treated as a source for ethnography, as a type for the converts from Judaism to Christianity, and as a commenter on the Jewish liturgy. It was not until 1916 that Josef Mieses published a study of Margaritha and his prayer book translation.[3] Mieses produced a biography of Margaritha to place his prayer book translation in a historical context. He corrected previous errors, correcting the assumption that Jacob Margoles was Margaritha's father, whereas he was, in fact, his grandfather and Samuel was his father. Mieses also drew attention to the importance of Margaritha's *Isaiah Commentary*. Nonetheless, Mieses had a poor opinion of Margaritha's Hebrew skills and Jewish scholarship, a judgment that seems to have been a reaction, in part, to Margaritha's conversion and his composition of anti-Jewish polemics.

Margaritha remained an anti-Jewish exemplar for scholars until contemporary times. Raphael Straus mentioned him in his study of Regensburg.[4] Selma Stern's biography of Josel of Rosheim recounted the famous disputation but added little to the picture of Margaritha painted by others, especially Mieses.[5] Beginning in the 1970s, some historians became interested in detailing questions about liturgy, anti-Jewish polemics, and conversion. Critical editions of sources that mention Margaritha became available, such as Chava Fraenkel-Goldschmidt's editions of Josel's *Sefer ha-Miknah* and his historical writings.[6] Hans-Martin Kirn and R. Po-chia Hsia furthered the study of anti-Jewish polemics.[7] Stephen Burnett produced articles and a study of Johann Buxtorf that highlighted the significance of Margaritha's work for the study of sixteenth-century Jewish ethnography.[8] Elisheva Carlebach, among her other fine studies, produced an insightful and detailed work on Jewish converts to Christianity, in which Margaritha played a prominent role.[9] Peter von der Osten-Sacken devoted an entire volume to Margaritha and Martin Luther.[10]

Two younger scholars, Maria Diemling and Yaacov Deutsch, have dedicated their considerable talents to placing Margaritha and his thought into a historical context. Diemling, for her doctoral thesis on Christian ethnographies and converts, discovered new details about Margaritha's travels, teaching, and family life.[11] Among other things, she discovered documents that referred to his wife, children, and poverty, including an accounting of property after his death. The information in her articles has aided the analysis of his writings.[12] Yaacov Deutsch has focused on the Jewish perception of and response to Christians, an area in which Margaritha provides some information. Building on Burnett's work, he coined the term "polemical ethnography."[13] My own brief article on Margaritha was intended to test Margaritha's trustworthiness as an ethnographic source, a paper that grew out of a conversation with

Stephen Burnett about Mieses's negative assessment of Margaritha's skills.[14]

Given the many fine studies listed above, the question arises, "What does the present effort hope to add?" The answer is straightforward. All treatments of Margaritha analyze his person and his works in the context of specific issues; those issues, and not Margaritha himself are their focus. In this work, I hope to use Maria Diemling's archival research combined with Margaritha's own writings and previously known material to tell the story of his life and examine his ideas, in part, for their own sake. It seemed (and seems) to me that a biography of Margaritha—although sources are limited—might yield an understanding of him as an individual rather than as a type.

Margaritha's compositions provide perspective on his motivations and attitudes, which were not necessarily the same as those of other converts. I have also tried to use the publications of other scholars to illuminate Margaritha, without distorting their original purpose. By assembling many of the materials on Margaritha, including making translations of some of his work, I have attempted to present a more complete study of the man. I have sought to place him in the Jewish and Christian contexts of the late-fifteenth- to mid-sixteenth century.

Margaritha lived in a particular context, or, rather, in several contexts, and to understand him as a man, not a type, it is necessary to examine those contexts. His conversion to Christianity owed something to his studies and the Jewish society of his youth and young adulthood. His wife probably came from the same society. In spite of his embrace of Christianity, he seems to have never fully cut himself off from his Jewish family. His writings give glimpses of his feelings and reasons for becoming a Christian, but they also reveal some confusion about his choice and the nature of Christianity. Although his understanding of Judaism and Christianity changed over time, his love of his family and his rejection of their faith remained constant. As a convert who wrote polemically about his old faith, however, Margaritha was a force harmful to his brothers and sisters of the flesh. In this, he was part of a select group of converts, including Victor von Carben and Johannes Pfefferkorn, who fostered and reinforced anti-Jewish attitudes among German Christians. To fully make use of facts known about Margaritha, I shall divide his life into *before* and *after* conversion. His genealogy and Jewish observance in a Christian Germany underlay *Der gantz Jüdisch glaub.* Many other extant materials provide a detailed picture of Jewish life in Germany in general and of the places where his family lived in particular. His life after conversion, as a Hebrew teacher, polemicist, and *paterfamilias*, can be traced through various sources. The appendices provide additional details and analyses of issues raised in the chapters. When assembled, the materials reveal a man who converted out of genuine conviction, but whose life thereafter must have been sadly different from what he had initially anticipated.

1 The Margoleses of Bavaria

Anthonius Margaritha was born into a family of rabbinic scholars. The family's rabbinic tradition may have extended to his great-grandfather and beyond, but can be solidly dated to his grandfather, Jacob (c. 1430–1501). Jacob Margoles [Margolith] spent most of his life in Germany—Schwabia, Württemberg, and Bavaria. He is remembered as an expert on Jewish divorce and as the last chief rabbi of Nürnberg before its expulsion of the Jews in 1499. Jacob's place of birth and education are not certain. His parents were probably Moses and Margoles (a feminine name); his surname derives from his mother's name, a common practice.[1] Jacob's early life and education may have been connected with the city of Worms, which had been a center of Jewish life and learning for centuries. His siblings and stepsiblings lived in the Bavarian town of Nördlingen. Perhaps he spent youthful days there. Although he was born and raised in Germany, as a Jew, Jacob could not be a German citizen of any city or principality. He lived and worked as a teacher and rabbinic judge in enclaves permitted to Jews. He, his children, and his grandchildren were members of a tolerated minority, subject to civic sanctions and expulsions by the German Christian majority, who believed that they as Christians had replaced the Messiah-killing Jews as God's chosen people.

I

Jewish communities were often quite small, restricted in part by the Christian cities and states limiting or forbidding Jewish immigration. The organization of the Jewish community, when possible, consisted of a council, at least one rabbi, a synagogue, a school, a cemetery, and a ritual bath. The "Memory Books" of various communities reveal not only the deaths and births in the community but also the customs and the social structures that formed Jewish life. (Anthonius Margaritha mentions memory books in *Der gantz Jüdisch glaub* [1530], iiiT.) Customs, which varied from place to place, bound the members of individual communities together. The rabbis and prosperous men were the leaders of the community.[2] Larger communities employed several rabbis as teachers and judges. Jacob Margoles appears in records as a teacher of students in *cheder,* or elementary schools, and in yeshivas, or secondary schools. More advanced yeshivas produced rabbis.

Jacob taught and gave rabbinic judgments in Ulm, Württemberg, before 1460.[3] The city of Ulm had granted civic rights to some Jews in the fourteenth century, but in the fifteenth century, the Jewish community suffered from increased taxation and restrictions on money lending. When the community hired Jacob as a rabbi, he was allowed to live in the city under an exception. In 1457 the city expelled those Jews who had not been granted civic rights,[4] and Jacob likely left at that time, for his name appears in the records of Giengen, north of Ulm, around 1460.[5] In 1499, Ulm gave the Jews still resident in the city five months' notice to leave, after which the city was legally *Judenrein,* Jewfree.

Because of its proximity to Ulm, Giengen became a place of refuge for at least some of the 1457 expellees. It was also a stop on the life journey of Jacob Margoles. By 1465 he was in Schwäbish Gmünd, northeast of Giengen. He moved from there to Luchau and finally to Nürnberg in 1480. After the expulsion of Jews from Nürnberg, he became the rabbi of Regensburg in 1499.[6] During his frequent moves, Jacob seems to have spent time with relatives in the town of Nördlingen, a short distance from Nürnberg. His brothers, David, Jesse, Elias, and Noe, and his sister lived in Nördlingen, along with his stepbrothers, Jacob the Elder, Samuel, Jesse, and his stepsisters.[7] Nördlingen was significant also because when Jacob's first wife died, he returned there to marry again in 1475. His second wife was the widow of Aaron of Neresheim. Both of Jacob's wives had children from previous marriages. In some documents, Jacob is called the son-in-law of Joseph of Nördlingen, who was also known as Joseph of Donauwörth.[8] Because Joseph lived in Ulm in 1453, he was probably the father of Jacob's first wife.[9]

Jacob's stepbrothers, David and Samuel, moved from Nördlingen to Italy, where they married in 1488.[10] This move established family contacts in Italy, which made future trips there easier for Jacob's children and grandchildren. The Nördlingen connection, that is, the family connection to Jacob's father-in-law, Joseph of Nördlingen, may indicate that Jacob served as rabbi in the town. Joseph's son Schmael (Samuel) of Donauwörth converted to Christianity in 1462. Schmael identified himself as the brother-in-law of the rabbi of Nördlingen.[11]

Jacob Margoles's second wife died in Nördlingen in 1486.[12] It is difficult to determine whether Jacob's sons were born to his first or second wife. His three natural sons were Isaac (d. 1525), Samuel (d.1551), and Shalom Shakhna (d. 1573). Samuel, who succeeded Jacob as rabbi in Regensburg, may have been Isaac's full brother, but the much younger Shalom Shakhna most likely was not. Isaac lived in Nürnberg at least until 1495. After that date, he moved to Prague, where he served on the rabbinic court of Jacob Pollock, his father's former student. Isaac prepared his father's study on the laws of divorce, *Sefer ha-Get,* for printing, which never took place. Samuel, as noted above, succeeded his father in Regensburg. Shalom Shakhna worked in Prague and edited another unpublished manuscript of *Sefer ha-Get* (MS Bodleian 803).[13]

If the travels of Jacob Margoles and his family are difficult to track, his stature as a rabbinic scholar is not. He lived before the publication of Joseph Karo's authoritative codification of Jewish law, the *Shulchan Aruch* (The prepared table). Without such a universally accepted guide, rabbis had to rely on their personal studies of legal sources and local customs. During his nearly nineteen-year tenure in Nürnberg (1480–99), Jacob established himself as an eminent scholar. He participated in legal disputes, the most famous of which was with his student, Rabbi Joseph Pollock, on the topic of the betrothal of underage girls.

Anthonius Margaritha discussed this debate with familial pride in his *Isaiah Commentary,* written after he had become a Christian.[14] The problem in the case turned on a technical issue regarding betrothal (*erusin*), known as *miun,* or refusal. The parents of an underage girl (the age of consent being twelve) could betroth her, but she could refuse to marry the intended bridegroom when she reached her majority. About the year 1490, Rabbi Pollock's mother, Raschko, had betrothed her underage daughter to an older man, Rabbi David Zeller. Raschko regretted the betrothal. Because a betrothal was virtually a marriage, Raschko asked Rabbi Zeller to give her daughter a bill of divorcement (*get*), but he refused. Rabbi Pollock gave a rabbinical judgment that in the case of *miun* a bill of divorcement was unnecessary; the betrothal was annulled, an action that did not require the prospective bridegroom's consent. Rabbi Margoles and most other German rabbis who considered the question decided to the contrary.

Rather than accept the judgment of these rabbis, Rabbi Pollock ignored them. His teacher, Rabbi Margoles, then issued a ban on Rabbi Pollock's rulings unless he withdrew his opinion on *miun.* Rabbi Margoles died in 1501, with the ban still in place. Rabbi Judah Mintz of Padua ordered Rabbi Pollock to go to his teacher's grave and beg his forgiveness, something that Rabbi Pollock either would not or could not do.[15]

In 1569–71, more than half a century later, Moses Isserles published his *Mappah,* glosses on the Sephardic work *Shulchan Aruch* based on Ashkenazic custom. In it he followed his teacher Rabbi Pollock's opinion on *miun.* Rabbi Jacob Margoles's ruling was preserved as a significant contrary authority.

In light of the stresses of Jewish life in Germany in general and in Nürnberg in particular, the attention then paid to Jacob Margoles's scholarship may seem anomalous; it dealt with an unusual problem that had little effect on the lives of most Jews. In Nürnberg, Jews were vexed by taxes and threats to their persons. In the fifteenth century, authorities compelled Jews to attend Christian missionizing sermons, including those by famous preachers such as Giovanni da Capistrano in 1454 and Peter Schwartz (Petrus Nigri) in 1478. Schwartz, a Dominican Hebraist, preached these sermons in order to "help" the Jews to understand that "our Lord Jesus Christ [is] the true Messiah" and to acknowledge "the curse of Jewish unbelief."[16] Schwartz managed to make some converts, yet, for the most part, the people, guided by their scholarly rabbinic leaders, such as Margoles, remained committed to Jewish life, law, and custom.

Schwartz also gave sermons in the churches, which were meant to and did inflame the Christians, the "body of Christ," who loathed having the cursed Jews among them. The anxiety that many Christians felt about the Jews being in their midst was especially strong in light of debts owed to Jews. The Nürnbergers' feelings about Jews were articulated in drama by the master barber and playwright Hans Folz (1435/41–1513). In *A Play about the Duke of Burgundy,* Folz depicted Jews living in misery because of their false and unfulfilled messianic expectations. Jewish suffering caused them to hate Christians and murder Christian children. The Jews in his drama bemoan the fact that:

We have been in misery now
For fourteen hundred years
And in that time
Suffered a great deal at the hands of Christians

. . . If only they knew
What great curses, what hatred and envy
We have always harbored for them.
How much we have stolen from them,
How many whose lives we have spoiled,
Of those to whom we were physicians:
How many young children
We have stolen from them and killed.[17]

A rabbinic leader such as Jacob Margoles was the official liaison between the Christian and Jewish communities. An exchange between Margoles and the humanist Hebrew scholar Johannes Reuchlin illustrates his role. Reuchlin was no particular friend of the Jews, but he believed that their literature, especially kabbalistic books, contained valuable truths. About 1497, Reuchlin asked Rabbi Jacob to obtain some kabbalistic texts for him. Margoles replied that the texts were not available in Nürnberg.[18] This may have been a dissimulation, made to prevent Christian access to the kabbalah. In fact, part of Reuchlin's interest in using theoretical and divine-name kabbalah was to provide evidence of the truth of Christianity.[19]

Margoles seems to have been acquainted with the kabbalah popular in German rabbinic circles. That kabbalistic tradition descended from the thirteenth-century Hasidei Ashkenaz. At root, it involved meditative, sometimes theurgic, exercises. Margoles may have taught kabbalistic prayer meditations to Rabbi Naftali Hirtz Treves, who later became a cantor in Frankfurt am Main.[20]

In Nürnberg, Jacob Margoles was the leader of a community on the edge of extinction. In 1499, by order of the civic authorities, all Jews were expelled from the city. Rabbi Margoles and his family moved to the approximately eight-hundred-member Jewish community of Regensburg in Upper Bavaria, where he served as chief rabbi until his death in 1501. The Margoleses' settlement in Regensburg may have been related both to Jacob's renown as a scholar and to his son Samuel's marriage to the daughter of Saidia Straubinger, a wealthy resident of the city.[21] The Straubingers were part of the old Regensburger family, the Veiflins, a family wealthy enough in 1411 to pay one-half of the community's assessed taxes.[22] In 1419, in order to extract tax payment from him, authorities in the town of Straubing arrested Michel Veiflin, and he was thereafter referred to as Michel of Straubing.[23] Saidia, Samuel's father-in-law, was probably Michel's descendant. Saidia's second daughter married Rabbi Eisik Stein, and Saidia's son Isaak is referred to in the records as "master," a term for rabbi.

Samuel Margoles married while the family was still living in Nürnberg, and it is likely that there in the 1490s his wife gave birth to his son Anthonius. (Anthonius's Hebrew name is unknown, but the consonants of his Latin name suggest it may have been Nathan or Yonathan.) Two other children, Baruch and Moses Mordechai, were born either in Nürnberg or later in Regensburg. Saidia and the prominent Straubing-Veiflin family probably welcomed the arrival of their notable in-laws. Anthonius's brothers became Jewish professionals—Baruch a cantor in Regensburg and later in Italy and Moses Mordechai a rabbi in Cracow. The Margoles family, fortunate in its religious and scholarly occupations and in its marital connections, could live comfortably in Regensburg.

II

The city of Regensburg and its Jewish community were very much like the other German towns and cities in which the Margoleses lived. Jewish life in late-fifteenth- and early sixteenth-century Regensburg informed Anthonius's education and social experiences before his conversion. The Jewish community dated to the eleventh century. It had undergone persecutions from Crusaders (the entire community was forced to convert in 1096), host desecration charges, blood libels, and accusations of spreading plague. During the thirteenth century, under Rabbi Judah the Pious and his Hasidei Ashkenaz, the city became a center of Jewish piety. Princes and prelates valued Regensburg's Jews, or rather Jewish loans and taxes. By protecting the Jews, economic advantage accrued to the Duke of Bavaria and to the emperor, for they levied taxes on the interest collected by the Jews. The presence of the Jews allowed them to derive financial benefit from their Christian subjects without having to tax them directly. The usefulness of the Jews frequently caused these rulers to try to ameliorate anti-Jewish pressures, but the Christians' unremitting distaste for the Jews at all levels of Regensburg society made life difficult, even with official protection.[24]

Raphael Straus's study of Regensburg indicates that by the mid-fifteenth century, the Jewish community was in economic decline.[25] Loans, which had formerly generated interest rates of 43 1/3 percent to 86 2/3 percent, depending on the term, were no longer being made to the nobility, burghers, and merchants. The community was not able to keep current with its taxes. This placed it in danger, especially given that the city council saw the Jews as "by day and night . . . working for their own advantage [against the Christians' interest]."[26]

During the fifteenth century, the city fathers adopted various rules against the Jews. In 1452, Christian midwives were forbidden to help with

Jewish deliveries. Jewish purchase of fish was restricted in 1456 and again in 1459. Jews were charged with conducting business contrary to the law during Easter in 1463. Jewish brides from other localities were not allowed to settle in the city in 1461.[27] In part, such anti-Jewish actions arose from the Christians' perception that the Christian community was the body of Christ (*Corpus Christi*).[28] How was it proper for devout Christians to allow the killers of Christ, the stiff-necked and rejected Jews, to dwell among them, even, or especially, for economic gain? Ritual murder accusations in 1470 and 1473–76 highlighted the danger of allowing an incongruous Jewish presence in the midst of the earthly body of Christ. The belief in Jewish perfidy was part of folk belief as well as of theology. Sermons, such as those Peter Schwartz delivered, reinforced common belief. Only by becoming Christians could Jews be rendered harmless.

Charges of Jewish ritual murder of Christians, especially children, were common and their validity was often unquestioned by Christians. They formed part of Schwartz's call to action. He claimed,

> The Jews . . . eat Christians, by taking the whole [body] for the part [blood] . . . they kill innocent people and the children of Christians and eat their blood in matzot, that is, unleavened bread, and drink it by mixing with wine in the *paza*[*sic*], that is the paschal meal, as a trial has brought to light with regard to the holy martyr Simon in the city of Trent.[29]

The murder of Christians, who were part of the body of Christ, was among the most inflammatory charges laid against the Jews. Jews, it was claimed, had sacrificed many Christians, not just poor Simon of Trent in 1475. The 1473–76 charges of ritual murder in Regensburg were in part the result of Simon's death. A wandering Jew named Israel was arrested in Trent on suspicion of Simon's murder. Under interrogation, he begged for baptism and confessed to being party to a ritual murder in Regensburg seven years earlier. Israel, his Christian name now Wolfgang, implicated seventeen of Regensburg's most prominent Jews in the act, including Rabbi Eisik Stein, Saidia Straubinger's son-in-law. The Jews Wolfgang identified were then arrested. Thus began complicated negotiations among the Duke of Bavaria-Landshut (Ludwig IX), the Regensburg civic authorities, and the Holy Roman Emperor (Frederick III). Any interest in actually investigating the charges became secondary to the question of controlling the Jews and their assets. In the end, the prisoners were released on payment of 10,000 gulden to the emperor and 8,000 gulden to the city, and a promise to continue payment of various fees. The duke and his successors eventually dropped out of the blood libel competition to milk the Jews.[30]

Such successful extortions helped to undermine the Regensburg Jewish community. Throughout Germany, the Jews' economic and demographic position declined steadily from the fourteenth century. In the second half of the fourteenth century, there were about 7,000 Jews in the Holy Roman Empire. That number had declined to 2,500 by the beginning of the fifteenth century.[31] Because wealthier Jews paid taxes for entire communities, they were granted limited rights to live in cities and towns, but poorer Jews were merely tolerated and could be easily expelled.[32] Restricted in opportunity, they became an economic drain on their richer coreligionists. It is estimated that between a quarter and a half of the Jews of Erfurt and Nürnberg lived in poverty by 1489.[33] As time went on, truly indigent Jews wandered from community to community, living on charity.

Anthonius Margaritha described this itinerant class in his *Der gantz Jüdisch glaub*. He recounted the attitude of established Jews, whom he reported were hard on their poor wandering coreligionists. When in search of charity, such individuals came to Regensburg from other towns in Germany and from even farther afield, and they were required to obtain rabbinical permission before begging.[34] Some beggars went to other places, such as Prague, where Margaritha had an uncle. Margaritha recounted how the poor there and elsewhere were treated:

> Where, however, many Jews live together, as in Prague and similar places, their poor have to suffer a lot; on Fridays and on the eve of holidays they need to go into the houses [to beg], on holidays they beg for bread and for leftovers in front of the houses. They have the custom not to sing, as do our [Christian] students, when they beg in front of the houses, neither do they demand [alms] for God's sake, as do our beggars, but they shout, "Schnap!"[35]

While requesting rabbinic permission to beg hardly seems harsh, what Margaritha depicts are communities in economic crisis. Communal financial issues and power struggles among the prosperous marked Regensburg in Margaritha's youth. The incident that most troubled Margaritha by his own account involved a Jew named Moses Wolf who settled in Regensburg about 1505. Wolf challenged the lay establishment for control of the community and when rebuffed, enlisted the aid of the Christian authorities.[36] *Hauptman* Siegmund von Rohrbach, the local imperial authority, had ridden through the Jewish community, stimulating the local wits who lacked Wolf's restraining hand, to refer to him as Haman, the villain in the story of Esther. Wolf made a report to Rohrbach (Margaritha calls him Rorbeck), who then had three Jewish leaders arrested. Margaritha's father, Rabbi Samuel, obtained their release and placed Wolf under *haerem,* a form of excommunication. Rohrbach sided with Wolf, elevated him to a position of leadership, and fined all the parties (including Wolf). Eventually Wolf and his "wolf pack" were driven from the Jewish community.[37] The incident illustrates the narrow base of communal leadership, the role of wealth in a generally poor community, and the precarious position of even leading Jews.[38]

III

Tenuous financial status and pressure to support the poor were in large measure the result of civic and imperial policies. The presence of Jews with enough money to lend was a necessary evil, because Christians were forbidden to take interest from one another. The occupations of poorer Jews who were not moneylenders were of little interest to policy makers. The need for money justified the existence of the Jewish community in Regensburg. The decline in the community's financial health coincided with a change in lending patterns, with Jewish moneylenders making more loans to Christian tradesmen, lesser merchants, and minor officials.[39] The economic problems that forced regular citizens to seek loans from the Jews only increased their resentment. Preachers, such as Schwartz, relied on the resentment of greedy moneylenders to enflame anti-Jewish attitudes. Regensburgers who were indebted to Jews had even more reason to detest outsiders who seemed a disease in the Christian body.

Representative of the day-to-day consequences of the hatred of Jews in Regensburg was the issue of bread. The Jews did not own their own bakeries and relied on Christians for that staple. The Christian bakers often refused to sell bread to Jews. In 1499 the Jewish community complained to Duke Georg of Bavaria-Landshut that "no baker will sell us any bread, a situation our small children have long had to endure."[40]

Duke Georg communicated to the Regensburg council that he would suffer financially if the Jews were forced to leave the city. He directed the council not to do "this [not sell bread] or any other injury that might drive out the Jews."[41] Emperor Maximilian I also asserted his financial interest in the Jews, requiring bakers to sell bread to them.[42] One can only imagine how the citizenry resented the self-serving and counter-Christian dictates of the duke and emperor (although some of the bakers may have appreciated having an excuse for selling product to the despised Jews).

The records are largely silent about how the Jews regarded their life as members of a barely tolerated minority. Anthonius Margaritha's account is one exception. A report about the Christian Hebraist Johann Böschenstein (1472–1540) may say something about how Regensburg's Jews interacted with Christians. Böschenstein complained about his salary at the University of Wittenberg before he left that institution. Philipp Melanchthon related the complaint thirty years later:

> 30 years ago we had a Hebrew professor here who said what should I do? I can arrange to live where I can have it better. I asked which place he had in mind. He answered, I could have lived for free with the Jews of Regensburg [c. 1517–19]. One morning I went on my constitutional to their temple. There an old lady gave me a coin (*Batzen*) and bid me say a mass for her [Böschenstein was a priest], in like manner a second and a third. I could earn six coins a week.[43]

What significance the women attached to the priest's masses is difficult to answer; nevertheless, they treated him with respect. The antipathy shown by Christians to Jews was not openly returned to Christian visitors to the Jewish quarter. Böschenstein remembered and recounted his experience, an experience that may have led him to regard Jews more favorably than did most Christians. So unusual was his mild tolerance of the Jews that it led some to question whether this member of the minor nobility was actually of Jewish descent.

IV

In the midst of Christian animus, the Jews of Regensburg and the rest of Germany had to contend with messianic expectations proclaimed by a Jewish herald from Italy. Asher Lemlein, originally from Reutlingen, appeared in Venice in 1500/1501. He preached repentance and the imminent coming of the Messiah. Messianic fervor swept through the Jewish communities of Germany. Describing the incident later in the sixteenth century, Rabbi David Gans wrote of the hope engendered among the dispirited Jews:

> Rabbi Lämmlen [*sic*] announced the advent of the messiah in the year 1500/1, and his words were credited throughout the dispersion of Israel. Even among the Gentiles, the news spread and many of them also believed his words. My grandfather Seligman Gans, of blessed memory, smashed the special oven in which he baked *matzzot*, being firmly convinced that the next year, he would bake *matzzot* in the Holy Land. And I, the writer, heard from my old teacher, R. Eliezer, head of the Bet Din in Frankfurt, that the matter was not without basis, and that he

had shown signs and proofs, but that perhaps because of our sins, he [the Messiah] was delayed.[44]

When the Messiah failed to materialize, some Jews left the faith. Even before the Lemlein messianic fervor of the sixteenth century, conversions in Regensburg were not uncommon. The cantor Kalman converted to Christianity in 1470; when he later returned to Judaism, the Christian authorities punished him with execution.[45] In 1456 a husband and wife converted with their children,[46] as did Samuel Kupferberg. Samuel gave his wife a *get* when she refused to follow him.[47] The utter devastation of the hopes Lemlein raised led many to question their faith and look to Christianity. In Cologne, a butcher, Johannes Pfefferkorn (1469–1523), concluded that the Messiah had already come as Jesus Christ. He converted with his wife and children about 1504. Pfefferkorn became one of the most vociferous literary opponents of the Jews in the early sixteenth century. His *Der Juden Spiegel* (The Jewish mirror) of 1507 stressed Lemlein's failure:

> It is written that in 1502 a Jew called Lemel arose in Italy who preached to you and sat a half year long to do a certain penance and to prepare himself for the immediate coming of the messiah. And when that half year and the penance passed, a fiery pillar with a dark cloud would surround all Jews, as at the time of pharaoh, and then they would again go to Jerusalem, rebuild the temple and make sacrifice. And he gave a sign, that the Christian Church would pass away and collapse, therefore such a great and severe penance could occur, such as your forefathers never saw. Oh, how you are always deceived![48]

Pfefferkorn, although a radical example, surely reflected the feelings of many Jews whose daily suffering was not met by a promised redemption. His German text, which was also translated into Latin, was available throughout Germany, including Regensburg. After the publication of Pfefferkorn's *Mirror,* Regensburg's Jews had to contend in 1516 with a new anti-Jewish priest, Balthasar Hubmaier. He, like Schwartz, often singled out the "idle, lecherous, and greedy" Jews in his sermons. He stressed the ills, especially usury, that the body of Christians suffered from the presence of Jews. His opinion corresponded to that of a Franciscan friar who wrote to the Duke of Bavaria in 1506, recounting the story of a Regensburg baker who had borrowed six gulden from a Jew and had to supply the lender with bread for a year.[49] Hubmaier tapped into the discontent of Regensburgers.

The issues of bread and usury were part of a 1518 petition to Emperor Maximilian, asking for the expulsion of the Jews from Regensburg. The city asked permission to remove every Jew in the city, with the exception of fifteen families who were under imperial protection. This was an attempt to offer a compromise between the emperor's financial interests and the citizens' desire to purify the city. In their response, the Jews complained to the emperor that the bakers of Regensburg refused to sell them bread. The expense of constructing and heating ovens, as well as the danger of fire they presented, meant that most bread was baked in bakeries and not in the homes of individuals.[50] Because the bakers would not sell to them, the Jews were forced to import bread from the surrounding territory of Duke George (the emperor's rival). The emperor denied the city's petition, but the tensions between the citizens and the Jews were not ameliorated and remained extreme.

Emperor Maximilian died in January 1519. Until a new emperor was elected, the city of Regensburg was under the sole control of its own council. Taking advantage of the interregnum, the council, with Hubmaier's encouragement, moved swiftly to destroy the synagogue on February 22 and within days to expel the six hundred to eight hundred Jews then living in the city.[51] The Jews argued against their expulsion, citing the long history of the Jewish community in Regensburg, going back to the time of Jesus. A letter purportedly sent to Regensburg from "a Jew from Jerusalem" at the time of the Passion described "how a prophet was killed who had claimed he was the son of God." The letter had been used before as proof that the Jews of Regensburg were not responsible for the death of Jesus.[52] Neither the arguments, nor the letter, nor the employment of legal counsel availed the community. After the Jews were forced out of the city, a church dedicated to the Virgin Mary was built on the site of the destroyed synagogue, and Hubmaier became its priest (fig.1). Jewish headstones were removed from the cemetery and used for building materials.[53]

The expulsion of the Jews from Regensburg appears to have been the result of traditional but intensified Christian hostility. Two Jewish sources, however, point to conflict within the Jewish community as a major factor contributing to the exile of the city's Jewish residents. Such divisions may have prevented concerted Jewish action. Anthonius Margaritha, in his *Der gantz Jüdisch glaub,* attributed the preexpulsion strife to the efforts of Moses Wolf and his minions to seize the leadership of the Jewish community. The origin of that contretemps occurred no later than 1511, the year of Rohrbach's death.[54] The Wolf family and its supporters, however, may have persisted in their efforts for some years. Margaritha alleged that the animosity within the community actually resulted in the expulsion of the Jews from Regensburg. "There was such disunity among them [the Jews] that they were expelled. Had they been unified they would have avoided such an expulsion."[55]

Bild 7: Außenansicht der mittelalterlichen Synagoge zu Regensburg.
(Nach einer vermutlich von Altdorfer stammenden Skizze.)

Figure 1. Synagogue in Regensburg from a sketch attributed to Albrecht Altdorfer, in Isaak Meyer, *Zur Geschichte der Juden in Regensburg* (Berlin: Louis Lamm, 1913). Courtesy Klau Library, Hebrew Union College–Jewish Institute of Religion, Cincinnati, Ohio; also in Raphael Straus, *Regensburg and Augsburg* (Philadelphia: Jewish Publication Society, 1939).

Margaritha's judgment that factors within the Jewish community contributed to its inability to resist expulsion was supported by Rabbi Joseph of Rosheim. Rabbi Joseph, also known as Josel, defended Judaism and Jews before Emperor Charles V against the charges made by Margaritha in *Der gantz Jüdisch glaub,* as will be discussed in a following chapter. In his *Sefer ha-Miknah,* Rabbi Joseph attributed the expulsion to the actions of two traitors (*mosrim*) who divided the Jewish community. "Note that the destruction of Regensburg did not begin except by two informers."[56] Rabbi Joseph is probably referring to Moses Wolf and Anthonius Margaritha.

> The two traitors who instigated the sin came to an evil society [a circumlocution for conversion]. The one with his entire progeny and the other with his fiancée [*erustho*] even though they were of distinguished lineage their merit did not protect them.[57]

Josel indicated that Margaritha was the traitor who converted and took his fiancée with him. He described "that one man" as he who caused problems for "the entire Diaspora" by "publishing heretical books," which charged the Jews with cursing the gentiles, mocking Jesus, and circumcising proselytes.[58] These were the issues Josel and Margaritha debated before the emperor. Josel's charge that Margaritha was one of the informers in Regensburg who had caused the expulsion of the Jews appears to be unwarranted. It is unlikely that Margaritha was actually involved in the expulsion, except as a victim, because he converted two years after the event; moreover, there is nothing in *Der gantz Jüdisch glaub* that suggests he played any role. Nonetheless, at the time of the famous debate, knowledgeable Jews probably had made Josel privy to certain matters in Margaritha's background. His reference in *Sefer ha-Miknah* to "the traitor's" fiancée is not contradicted by what we know about Margaritha. Margaritha was in his twenties, of marriageable age, and, as the son of a prominent rabbinic family, likely to have been betrothed to a woman from a distinguished or relatively wealthy background before he converted to Christianity. By 1521 the couple probably had married. It thus appears that Margaritha's wife was Jewish and that she followed him into the Christian world, whether she herself converted or not.[59] Although Margaritha refers to his wife, he never gives her name nor explicitly says that she is a Christian. He refers often to his own "rebirth."

Both Margaritha's and Josel's explanations of the expulsion from Regensburg place blame upon the Jews. Their accounts reflect Jewish attitudes toward suffering in which personal and communal trials were understood to be God's punishments for sin and disunity. No matter how unjustified were the actions of Christians, the Jews looked for fault within their own community as the source of their suffering; the tradition of blaming themselves for their troubles went back at least to Isaiah. Josel also saw problems as resulting from Jewish sin.[60] This explanatory idea is seen throughout Jewish history. For example, in the seventeenth century, the Jews of Frankfurt described their expulsion thus: "[They] burned our streets . . . also mishandled these *sifrei torah* [scrolls of the Law] on account of our sins."[61] Whatever the role of Jewish disunity and sin, and whatever the psychological value to the victims of feeling they had some collective control of their fate, the immediate cause of the expulsion from Regensburg was the decision by Christian secular authorities to rid themselves of an alien presence.

Upon their expulsion, Samuel Margoles and his family traveled to Italy, perhaps to sojourn for a time with relatives. Anthonius and his wife may have accompanied them or wandered elsewhere in Germany. The Margoleses spent time in Cremona. Baruch, the cantor, took up a position in Verona. He was one of the major Jewish taxpayers there in 1539–43.[62] Moses Mordechai traveled to Poland and became a rabbi in Cracow. He wrote *Hasdei ha-Shem,* a mystical commentary on the thirteen attributes of God's mercy found in Exodus 34:6–7, and edited *Zohar Chadash* and *Midrash*

Ne'elam. Samuel (d. 1551) went on to become the chief rabbi of Posen, a town in what was then known as Great Poland. Anthonius converted to Christianity in Wasserburg (am Inn) in 1521. The Margoles family, which had played a significant role in Jewish Germany, was scattered, and like so many lesser families, no longer had a place in the fatherland.

The numerous expulsions of the fifteenth and sixteenth century left Germany impoverished with regard to Jewish culture. Only two centers remained after the fall of Regensburg: Frankfurt am Main and Worms.[63] The Margoleses' future lay in the east where Samuel, Moses Mordechai, Isaac, and Shalom Shakhna continued the rabbinic tradition. Only the convert Anthonius remained in Germany, and he had left the Jewish world for the Christian one.

2

"I Will Be Your God and You Will Be My People" —Leviticus 26:12

Anthonius Margaritha's presentation of the Jewish life cycle and its associated customs and practices is the essence of his ethnographical value for most scholars. If one turns from ethnography to Margaritha's own Jewish life, his description reveals his daily and cyclical routines and observances. What he did and how he eventually came to understand Jewishness help explain his conversion to Christianity. Although it cannot be absolutely proven that the customs and practices he described in his first work, *Der gantz Jüdisch glaub,* were those followed by the Margoles family, Margaritha's repeated references to differing observances in other Jewish communities are a strong indication that the greater part of his presentation reflected personal experience.[1]

Margaritha, as a scion of a rabbinic family, lived a commandment driven, structured Jewish life. The belief that custom and ritual had been revealed at Sinai and transmitted through the generations served to create a socioreligious community, which viewed itself as God's treasured people. Reflecting the position of the biblical prophets, the Jews looked to their past and present sins for the origins of the problems and persecutions they endured. They found comfort and purpose in the prescribed life cycle and hope for redemption in tradition. Margaritha was a member of a *kehillah,* or community. In some ways the *kehillah* resembled a coeducational monastery, where daily observances sanctified the mundane and led to a portion in the world to come. Jewish law did not so much focus on spiritual experiences as a way to connect with the divine, but rather on the daily actions and the yearly and occasional events that distinguished and defined Jews as God's people. The observances that characterized Jewish life were powerful boundary markers, which defined Margaritha and his fellows as holy. The *kehillah* created a sense of intimacy with God through the Sinaitic covenant as expressed in the rabbinic formulation of laws and practices derived from the Pentateuch.

As a child and young man, Margaritha learned from his teachers that although the written Hebrew Bible was a divine communication, the oral tradition provided the details for living a Jewish life. It was known to scholars, and certainly taught to Margaritha, that before the destruction of the temple in the first century CE, various sects held different understandings of the meaning of the law. Only the rabbinic (Pharisaical) tradition, with its oral law, survived the revolts against Roman authority. The rabbinic formulation of Jewish law was set down in the *Mishnah* in the second century CE. The *Mishnah* was elaborated in the *Gemara* in various academies into the sixth century and the two formed the *Talmud.* Further, scholarly treatises, rulings, and local custom guided each community. The result was a flexible yet defined holy life that unified the Jews according to the prophetic statement, "You only have I known of all the families of the earth" (Amos 3:2). Each Jew counted, and communal life had both secular and eternal consequences.

Several codifications of Jewish law, such as Maimonides's *Mishnah Torah* (Repetition of the Torah, c. 1170) and Rabbi Jacob ben Asher's *Arbaah Turim* (Four columns, fourteenth century) prescribed and shaped Jewish observance before the sixteenth century. In 1542, the year of Margaritha's death, Joseph Karo produced his commentary on the *Arbaah Turim,* which he called the *Shulchan Aruch* (Prepared table). It would become the definitive code of Jewish practice. Margaritha and the men in his rabbinic family learned from the *Talmud* and studied the available compilations and tractates, which formed the bases for Joseph Karo's work. Rabbis referred to these written works and local traditions to answer questions and solve disputes regarding correct Jewish behavior. Of course, even after the publication of *Shulchan Aruch,* local custom and scholarship continued to control much of communal life.[2]

There were disadvantages to living in a rigorous, defined community. Not everyone flourishes under the stringent rules set out for the monk, nun, or observant Jew. Following the prescribed minutiae of daily life could be difficult and stressful. Margaritha and others who left the faith complained that many practices seemed far removed from biblical prescriptions. Outside pressures and "commandment" fatigue occasioned frustration, which helped overcome the familial, social, and religious inertia that may have held some doubters to the *kehillah.* Sometimes the discontent led to conversion to Christianity, however, many Jews returned to the fold after experiencing life outside the *kehillah.* Because return was dangerous and potentially fatal, the willingness or need of the prodigals to rejoin Jewish society argues for the attractions of such a Torah-based life. Johannes Reuchlin told the story of Rabbi Moses Zoret of Ulm. The rabbi converted to Christianity, but returned to Judaism and then fled to Turkey to avoid execution by German authorities.[3] The existence of many women who refused to convert with their husbands also testifies to the draw exerted by the *kehillah,* a life with familiar people, where one had female family and friends, well-known practices, and language.[4] The famous convert Victor von Carben reported that his wife and children remained Jews, while he became a priest. Some perceived converted Jews to be so likely to falter in their Christianity that Conrad von Magenberg, a priest, compared them to "sparrow excrement," which "comes out hot but cools rapidly."[5] There were also Jews who converted repeatedly for legal and financial reasons, as the enactment of laws against multiple conversions demonstrates.[6]

The requirements and rhythms of Jewish life in Regensburg defined Anthonius Margaritha's existence before his conversion. As a rabbi's son, he was trained in the law and lived it with care. In *Der gantz Jüdisch glaub,* he describes how he came to believe that the rabbinically mandated life was unscriptural, indeed a perversion of scripture.[7] When Margaritha's biases and anti-Jewish asides are disregarded, his account of Jewish practices in *Der gantz Jüdisch glaub* becomes an ethnographic treasure. More importantly, it is a window into his life as a Jew in Regensburg and in the other cities he visited. Careful reading of his comments and criticisms reveals some of the reasons why he left Judaism and his privileged place among God's "treasured people" (Deuteronomy 14:2).

I

Jewish observance encompassed daily rituals, life cycle events, such as birth and death, and communal days, such as the Sabbath, Passover, and Yom Kippur. Daily practices defined male and female roles and distinguished Jews from non-Jews. They could provide a sense of holiness. Jewishness fostered a self-contained life of separation (*kodosh,* or holy) from the non-Jewish world. Jewish awareness intensified at special times, such as on festivals. In theology, or more correctly orthopraxy, there were no profane aspects of life, only levels of holiness associated with week days compared to the Sabbath or other divinely commanded days in the year.

Margaritha thus was enveloped in the Torah and its commandments, especially as his rabbinical family led the *kehillah* and trained him for community service. The brief ethnography in *Der gantz Jüdisch glaub* that precedes the German translation of the daily prayer book indicates the scope of his education. In it he described how he lived and reacted to the life of holiness. His education gave him insights into observances and their relation to scripture and tradition. His account tends to describe the custom of Regensburg, which followed Austrian custom.[8]

Margaritha began with the obligation to bless God one hundred times each day.[9] The number one hundred, he explained, was derived by the rabbis from Deuteronomy 10, where the letters *mem* and *hey* are seen as a shorthand or a defective spelling of the word one hundred, *mem aleph hey.* He also gave a *kabbala,* in this usage a received tradition, not a mystical teaching. The hundred blessings represent an ordering of the alphabet with the first letter paired with last, the second with the penultimate, and so on. The immediate source of the hundred blessings was the commonly used Book of Rules (*Sepher Middoth*) according to Margaritha.[10] The essential message of Jewish life transmitted by such a rabbinic work was stated in Leviticus 18, "Keep my law." The process of reciting one hundred blessings surrounded one with an awareness of God and His law.

Each morning on arising, a good Jew, such as Margaritha had been, thanked God for restoring his soul to the body after sleep. He immediately put on a garment in order to prevent seeing himself naked. He blessed God for separating day from night. He also put on a four-cornered garment with fringes (*tzitzit*), which Margaritha was taught warded off evil spirits, and covered his head to honor God.

In relieving himself, the Jew used his left hand. (As in other cultures, the left side was associated with negative forces.) After performing his early morning functions and completing his dressing, he went to the synagogue to study and pray. Only after morning prayers did he break his fast. Before eating, he washed his hands and spoke no words until the bread was blessed. After eating he recited a blessing that contained an expression of hope that he would see the Messiah. Margaritha emphasized the frequent references to the Messiah in daily life, highlighting the fact that Messianism was essential in creating his new Christian identity. As a Jew, he, like many others, was taken up in the hope of redemption. The frustration of that hope within Judaism moved him toward Christianity.

When Margaritha, or any other Jew, left the home, he would touch a box (*mezuzah*) on the doorpost that contained scriptural passages. Among the passages was the *shema,* beginning with the words "Hear O Israel the Lord is our God, the Lord is One."[11] On the street, Jews called each other not by their first names but, rather, by their last names. In their conversations, they welcomed each other in God's name and were forbidden to say negative things about other Jews. Christians, however, were impure and objects of fear; they were not greeted in God's name.

Along with the other men of the community, Margaritha would have again entered the synagogue for afternoon and evening prayers. Any competent male, including Anthonius himself and not just the cantor or the rabbi, could serve as prayer leader. Retiring at night, and signifying his complete devotion to God, he would again recite the *shema* with its 248 words corresponding to the 248 members of the body. Before going to sleep, he should have forgiven anyone who may have wronged him. Margaritha made special mention that married men ought not to have marital relations until so doing.

Without explanation, Margaritha did not include certain common practices, such as hand washing upon rising, but his account of daily life, especially as it applied to himself as a man, is accurate. He gave little attention to the practices of women, who had many of the same obligations as men, but were not required to perform rituals associated with specific times, such as wearing a four-cornered garment and praying three times a day. For the most part, Margaritha was describing his own life and the rabbinic rationalization behind its defining customary actions.

Margaritha discussed and explained the rabbinic interpretations of the dietary laws. For example, Exodus 23 forbade seething a kid in its mother's milk. The rabbis had extended the prohibition to mixing meat, including fowl, and milk products. The rabbis treated fowl as if it were meat because it might be mistaken for meat. They required two sets of dishes to be sure that milk and meat did not mix. After eating meat, Margaritha's community waited one hour before eating milk, the usual western European custom. Community rabbis answered questions about food and its preparation. An example of such a question was whether it was permitted to eat food that had been contaminated by forbidden food, such as pork or food prepared by Christians falling into the cooking pot. In the hypothetical, if the impure food comprised one-sixtieth (1/60) or less of the volume of the permitted food, the rabbi would rule that a Jew could eat from the pot.

Margaritha described the care with which meat and fowl were made kosher. Two experts, the slaughterer (*schochet*) and the inspector (*bodek*), ensured that animals were killed properly and that their corpses did not exhibit forbidden blemishes. He went into technical detail on their work. A *schochet* worked with a sharp knife that had a blunt end. He slaughtered an animal with one stroke and covered its blood with earth. The *bodek* then examined the heart, liver, and lungs, looking for irregularities that would disqualify the animal. The meat was salted and washed to remove any remaining blood. Women knew the rules of cooking. They were responsible for the level of ritual purity in the home. They maintained proper vessels for cooking and for eating, and they inspected foods other than meat. For example, they would not use eggs that had any spot of blood, and when they washed vegetables and fruits they were careful to remove insects. Margaritha does not mention it, but many communities also maintained communal kitchens and dining halls, with facilities for making utensils kosher for Passover.[12]

II

Other converts to Christianity may have come from lowly circumstances, as did Pfefferkorn the butcher, but Margaritha came from one of the most distinguished Jewish families in Europe. As rabbis and cantors, his family officiated at both joyous occasions, such as betrothals, weddings, and circumcisions, and at poignant or grievous ones, such as divorces and funerals. Most of the *kehillah* attended public events, but Margaritha, as his father's son, may have been particularly well placed to note the legal and customary details. The betrothal (*erusin*) was a quasi-marriage with the prospective bride and groom entering into agreement. Those present then celebrated with blessings and a joyous meal. So serious was the covenant that a bill of divorce was required to break it. Margaritha's account takes on a personal meaning in light of his own betrothal. When Josel of Rosheim revealed that Margaritha and his betrothed were from distinguished families, he was stating what would have been the case for the son of almost any rabbinic family, for spouses were chosen for social suitability. That his betrothed left the Jewish community with him underlines both the seriousness of *erusin* and the personal relationship between Margaritha and his fiancée.

Margaritha described how marriage followed betrothal. The bride visited the ritual bath before the wedding ceremony; a monthly immersion would become an integral part of her childbearing years.[13] The marriage contract (*ketuba*) spelled out the couple's obligation to build a Jewish home. On his wedding day, the groom, who had been fasting, gave his consent to the contract, which had been written by the rabbi and then signed by two witnesses. The ceremony of reading the contract (Margaritha called the contract a *Brief*, that is, a letter.) took place out of doors, under a covering (*huppah*). Margaritha described how the cantor (such as his brother) sang "Blessed is he that comes" as the groom approached. The bride walked around the groom three times (other customs dictated seven circuits). The contract was read and blessings were said over a cup of wine. The groom placed a ring on the bride's finger. Prayers were said for the return to Zion. The groom broke a vessel, a cup, whereupon the onlookers called out "good luck" (*mazel tov*). A festive meal was served.

Circumcision was the means whereby a male child became a part of God's covenant people. The eight days of uncircumcised life were a dangerous, liminal period. On the night before the ceremony, most European Jews kept watch over the child to protect him from malevolent forces. Margaritha remarked that "much magic" accompanied circumcision.[14] An expert called a *mohel* performed the actual procedure (*britmilah*). In Regensburg, a member of Margaritha's family may have been the *mohel.* Members of the community purchased the right to perform functions at the ceremony, the most prestigious of which was that of the *sandach,* the one who would hold the child. Margaritha noted that the *mohel* prepared the circumcision knife and an oil-soaked wrap to cover the wound. A blessing was made over a cup of wine. *Der gantz Jüdisch glaub* records the blessing, which mentions the covenant of circumcision. After removing the foreskin, the *mohel* sucked a drop of blood from the wound, an addition to the circumcision ceremony that Margaritha found unscriptural and painful for the child. The ritual concluded with the father's prayer and, of course, a festive meal. The mother was not present, for she did not rejoin the congregation until the end of a period of ritual impurity, a practice that Margaritha noted followed the prescription of Leviticus 12.[15]

Margaritha also outlined the writing of a bill of divorce and the procedure (*chalitzah*) for avoiding Levirate marriage (Deuteronomy 25). (Divorce seems to have become a specialty of the Margoles family, beginning with Rabbi Jacob.) A rabbi supervised the bill of divorce to ensure that it conformed to the technicalities of traditional law. The frequency of divorce is not known, but it was especially important when one spouse converted. Without a divorce, a woman remained married or "chained" (*agunah*) to her absent husband. Within the community, some women seem to have forced their unwanted husbands to grant a divorce by threatening to convert. This created a serious issue, because a divorce was valid only if a husband granted it freely. Rabbi Jacob Margoles mentions one such case in his tractate on divorce.[16] The woman converted to Christianity and later returned to Judaism. In the interim, her husband divorced her. Rabbi Margoles's account does not tie the divorce to her threatened conversion, but that act certainly provides a subtext to the husband's action.

Related to questions of divorce was the biblical command for a brother to marry his deceased brother's wife if the deceased died without children from the marriage. The rabbis had done away with the practice by essentially requiring the parties to avoid the obligation. Nevertheless, the widow and brother had to undergo a biblically prescribed ceremony for rejecting the obligation. Under the rabbi's oversight, the man, wearing a special shoe the community kept for this purpose, ritually stated his refusal to marry his brother's widow. The woman then unlaced the shoe and spat upon the man. The rabbi dictated to her the precise words, which she repeated, charging the brother with failing to keep the commandment. She was then free to marry again—but not free to marry the brother. Margaritha claimed that the process, as mandated by the rabbis, was a perversion of scripture, a rabbinic nullification of a biblical commandment.[17]

Margaritha presented a particularly detailed account of the customs that surrounded death and burial. As a rabbi's son, he was involved in his father's guidance of such rituals. (Later Christian writers, such as Buxtorf, seem to have found his text useful.) A mortally ill person arranged his estate and "confessed" to the rabbi. The confession included a statement of belief in the coming of the Messiah and recognition that death was a recompense for sin. Margaritha noted that a dying person would pray that his death would atone for his sins. He did not mention the customary requirement of reciting a final *shema,* if possible. A candle was left burning day and night next to a dying person. With customs surrounding death and burial, Margaritha illustrated the superstitious aspects of Judaism. He recounted a Jewish tradition, reportedly going back to King David, that Satan, bearing a sword, appeared to people as they lay dying. To alleviate the suffering of the mortally ill, the rabbis of the Talmud bound Satan, restricting his power.

After death, the body when cold was taken to a place where it was washed with warm water and anointed with wine. A male corpse was dressed in the white garment, called a *kittel,* which was worn in life on holy days, and then wrapped in a prayer shawl. Those who tended the body before burial wrote their names on a candle, which was lit and placed near the corpse, and recited prayers and psalms. The body was placed in a coffin, carried to the open grave, and placed inside. The mourners threw dirt on the coffin and departed quickly. According to Margaritha, the speedy withdrawal was occasioned by the (superstitious) belief that a mouse would enter the grave and bite the deceased on the nose. The pain of the bite was so great that the dead cried out. Anyone who heard the scream would die within thirty days.[18]

After a burial, the community gathered in the foyer of the synagogue, which Margaritha termed a *kirche* (church), washed their hands, turned around three or four times and then sat down in mourning. The immediate family sat barefoot on the earth for seven days. People sent the family food, including eggs, a symbol of life, to feed and comfort them. The family neither bathed nor participated in joyous activities for thirty days. During the mourning period, Jews bore witness to one another that each person must die.

III

Margaritha mentioned certain customs he had come to believe were mere superstitions, unscriptural, or even counterscriptural; he included among those washing hands before using holy books and the anonymous confession of sins. The latter was a custom whereby a sinner placed an unsigned confession in a book on the rabbi's desk in the synagogue. The rabbi would write a reply, leaving it in the book for the sinner to retrieve. Margaritha recounted that not only his father but also his uncles in Prague handled confessions in that way. Such customs are instructive as to his family's rabbinic practices.

Important in Margaritha's description of customs is his discussion of the festivals, or holy days (*festen*). The Sabbath was the primary and indeed the most frequently observed holy day, the focus of the week. Jews called all other days of the week by number, first through sixth, but the Sabbath had a proper name. Each Jew tried to procure the best fish, meat, and other good foods in honor of the day on which he was a king and his wife a queen.

Margaritha recalled how Jews would fast from Friday midday until the beginning of the Sabbath in the evening. Pre-Sabbath preparations included cutting nails and bathing. The women of the house lit candles. On the Sabbath, Jews drank wine and ate three meals that included bread. The Jews of Regensburg needed the bread baked by the recalcitrant Christian bakers not only for physical but also for spiritual sustenance. No wonder they were willing to petition the duke and emperor when the local bakers and council made it difficult to obtain. They required bread to keep the commandment of the Sabbath.

Margaritha's description of Sabbath preparations included his recounting the traditional story of angelic visitors. Two angels, one good and one bad, visited the home before sunset, as the Sabbath began. If the house had been put in order and properly prepared, the good angel said, "May it always be so," and the bad angel had to answer, "Amen." If the household was unprepared, the bad angel said, "May it always be so," and the good angel would have to say, "Amen."[19] Margaritha's mother must have encouraged her family to prepare their home in order to find favor with the good angel and earn his blessing.

In the evening, before the first meal, the men and boys welcomed the Sabbath at the synagogue. When the father returned from prayer, he blessed the children; the boys were blessed to be like Ephraim and Manasseh and the girls to be like Sarah, Rebecca, Rachel, and Leah. The meal began with the father's blessing over wine, recalling the six days of creation and God's rest. After the wine, the father blessed the bread. Everyone drank the wine and ate the bread. As he wrote about the evening meal, did Margaritha remember his mother telling him about the two angels and his father blessing him; did he recall the taste of the wine and bread?

When he wrote about the morning meal, Margaritha mentioned that the washing of hands preceded the eating of bread, and although he does not say so, this was the practice for all meals when bread was served, including the Sabbath evening meal. In addition to Sabbath bread, Margaritha referred to a "pastry," *kugel,* which was eaten in memory of the *mana* sent to the wandering children in double portion before the Sabbath.

Margaritha also told how the Jews in the *kehillah* hired non-Jews to perform work that Jews were forbidden to do on the Sabbath, such as milking cows, lighting candles for illumination in the synagogue and home, and helping with meals.[20] On the Sabbath, he explained, Jews were forbidden to walk more than two thousand paces, discuss business, buy and sell, or do various other kinds of work. Among the superstitions that Margaritha associated with the Sabbath was the belief that just as earthly Jews rested, so Jews in "hell" were released in order to observe the Sabbath. "Hell" was Margaritha's rendering of *gehennom.* Souls of the dead were punished or purified in *gehennom* for up to twelve months after death, before they passed into the "world to come."

The Sabbath Margaritha described was characterized by eating three times, in the evening, after morning services, and, in the afternoon, the "third" meal. Each Jew believed that he received an additional soul to help him fully enjoy the Sabbath in prayer, Torah study, food, and song. The day ended late, with evening prayers, which began, "He who is merciful." After prayers, the family distinguished the Sabbath from the coming week by making special blessings on wine, spices, and a multiwicked candle. The spice blessing acknowledged the savor of the holy day, and the candle's light was used to create shadows on the flesh and nails of the fingers. The light and shadows were likened to the difference between the Sabbath and the days of the week. Margaritha explained that after the Sabbath ended, in another superstitious practice, the tablecloth was quickly removed, an act that symbolized payment for sins.

Margaritha discussed other greater and lesser holy days, the New Month, New Year for Trees (*Tu Beshvath*), as well as Purim and the postbiblical Chanukah. He explained the fast days, which commemorated the destruction of Jerusalem and the two temples. Each holy day had special prayers and rites. He paid special attention to the major festivals, Passover, Weeks, and Tabernacles, along with Rosh Hashanah and Yom Kippur. He admitted that the Passover rules were so complicated that even a large book could only just touch upon them. His goal was to express the basics of the Jewish holidays.

Margaritha began his essential Passover account with the fast of the firstborn, and then moved on to the removal and burning of leavened products. He discussed *matzah* (unleavened bread) baking and the beauty of the Passover Table (a fond memory?). Before the ceremonial meal, three *matzahs* were placed under a cover. During the meal, part of the middle *matzah* was hidden, and, when found later in the evening, used as dessert. Passover was a protected moment for the Jews within an alien, insecure Christian environment. In recounting the story of the exodus from Egypt, they remembered and assured themselves of God's saving power. At one point during the ritual meal, one of the participants opened the door and invited Elijah, the harbinger of the Messiah, to enter. By Margaritha's account, an actor dressed as Elijah entered. (Later rabbinic sources, Joseph Yuzpah Habin [1570–1637] and Yair Hayyim Bachrach [1638–1701] confirm this playacting custom, which has fallen out of practice.[21]) At the end of the meal, the participants asked God to pour out his wrath on the persecutors of the Jews.

Margaritha noted that the meal did not include eating a Paschal Lamb, as scripture required. The rabbis had deleted what seemed to be an essential part of Passover, the lamb, and replaced it with three *matzahs.* The Jews performed an "imaginary" (*erdichte*) ceremony instead of sacrificing a lamb as commanded in the Bible. The lamb symbolized Jesus, who is the Lamb of God, now absent from the Jewish ritual. In another alteration of the holy days, the rabbis had mandated that Jews who were living outside the land of Israel had to observe biblical festivals for two days rather than one. These two changes were unambiguous illustrations, in Margaritha's opinion, of how the rabbis had turned the Jews away from scripture.

On the second day of Passover, the Jews began to count the seven weeks before what had been the offering in the temple of the first of the barley crop in the spring, the Feast of Weeks (*Shavuot*). *Shavuot,* the Christian Pentecost, celebrated not only the barley harvest but also the theophany on Mount Sinai. The Jews marked this time of joy, expanded by the rabbis from one day to two, by eating milk products. Margaritha described a seven-layer cake that was traditionally served in his home, which represented the seven heavens and Mount Sinai.

In autumn, the Jews celebrated the New Year festival, Rosh Hashanah. The men of Regensburg began preparations for the holy day by fasting and

Figure 2a. Woodcut from *Der gantz Jüdisch glaub* (1530 and 1531). Courtesy Klau Library, Hebrew Union College–Jewish Institute of Religion, Cincinnati, Ohio.

digging a pit until they struck water. The pit's sides were plastered. The pit was not the town's ritual bath. The men of the community immersed themselves in the pit in a rite of purification. The pre–New Year immersions mimicked that of the angels, who descended into the mythical river "Dina" 365 times before singing God's praises.

On the afternoon before the New Year began at sundown, every male went to the regular ritual bath, dressed in white, and wished one another a good year. Men and women then attended the rabbi's sermon. Margaritha must have been recalling the efforts of his grandfather, father, and brothers as they devised sermons that were designed to show their erudition. Interestingly, he seemed to disparage the effort that went into preparing the sermons and the resultant congregational admiration of their rabbi.

Figure 2b. Woodcut from *Der gantz Jüdisch glaub* (1530 and 1531). Courtesy Klau Library, Hebrew Union College–Jewish Institute of Religion, Cincinnati, Ohio.

After the sermon, people ate apples and honey, which symbolized a desire for a sweet new year. In the synagogue, by the light of many candles, the Torah scrolls were taken from their resting place in the Holy Ark. The ram's horn (*shofar*) was blown thirty times. After services, the congregation repaired to a stream, or to a windy place if no stream were available, and the members symbolically cast away their sins by throwing away detritus from their clothing. (This custom, *tashlich,* is found neither in the Bible nor in the Talmud, but developed during the Middle Ages. The first unambiguous reference to it is in the early fifteenth century.) Margaritha used *tashlich* as an example of the Jewish misunderstanding of the concept of atonement (Appendix C). One of the woodcuts in the book illustrated its foolishness (fig. 2b).

Figure 2c. Woodcut from *Der gantz Jüdisch glaub* (1530 and 1531). Courtesy Klau Library, Hebrew Union College–Jewish Institute of Religion, Cincinnati, Ohio.

Rosh Hashanah began the ten days of repentance that culminated on the Day of Atonement (Yom Kippur), a fast day. Numbers 29 and Leviticus 23 describe the Day of Atonement in temple times. Margaritha outlined the solemn preparations in his community. The day before Yom Kippur, a young boy acted as cantor, his innocence symbolizing the purity of the congregation. Each man, woman, and child performed *kapporoth,* waving a live rooster or hen, as appropriate, over his or her head three times and proclaiming that the fowl received their sins (fig. 2c). Margaritha revealed that some wits would ask Christians on the street to be their *kapporoth.*[22] The ceremony included the verses from Leviticus 16 where the priest removes Israel's sins. Fathers read Psalm 107 and Job 33 over each family member. It was also customary to go to the cemetery and pray for

Figure 2d. Woodcut from *Der gantz Jüdisch glaub* (1530 and 1531). Courtesy Klau Library, Hebrew Union College–Jewish Institute of Religion, Cincinnati, Ohio.

forgiveness from the dead. In a flagellation ritual, men were lashed thirty-nine times, the limit set in the Talmud, for their sins (fig. 2d). The illustration in *Der gantz Jüdisch glaub* depicted these observances.

Before evening services and before the fast began, family members ate a meal. Large candles, lit in remembrance of the dead, were carried to the synagogue. Margaritha had been taught that if these "soul" candles burned to the end of the festival, the bearer's life would continue for a year. If not, his life was in danger.[23] Upon entering the synagogue, people asked each other for pardon for any offense they may have given. The service then began with an annulment of vows (*Kol Nidre*) so that God would not count unkept promises as sins. During *Kol Nidre*, an earthly court of rabbis

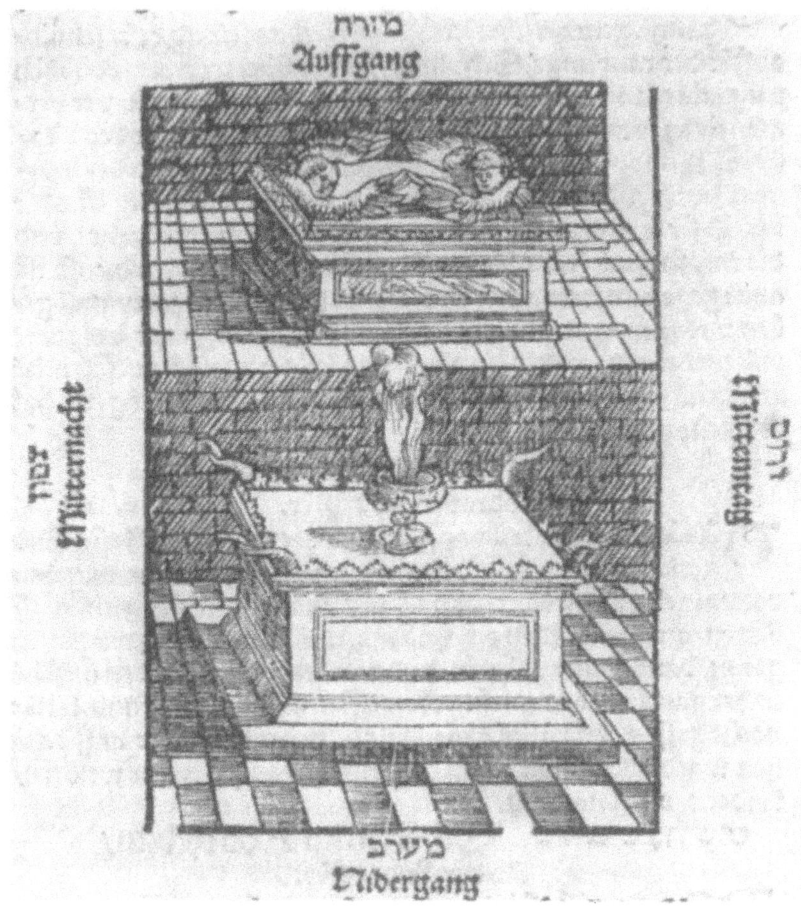

Figure 2e. Woodcut from *Der gantz Jüdisch glaub* (1530 and 1531). Courtesy Klau Library, Hebrew Union College–Jewish Institute of Religion, Cincinnati, Ohio.

and learned community leaders holding the Torah scrolls stood in the synagogue and, for their community, reflected the heavenly court meeting above. After *Kol Nidre* and the evening service, many men remained in the synagogue all night. Marital relations were forbidden.

The next day during services, the Torah scrolls were removed from the ark four times. The *kehillah*'s priests, the hereditary class with few other functions since the destruction of the temple, blessed the congregation and for a few minutes became holy men (fig. 2d and Appendix C). The long day of affliction (about twenty-six hours) ended with a final blast of the ram's horn that signaled the sealing of each person's fate for the coming year. Some left candles in the synagogue; others committed to keep a candle burning continually in the building, an eternal flame (*ner tamid*).

The introspection, repentance, and fasting of Yom Kippur was followed by the autumnal harvest festival of Tabernacles (*Succoth*), which commemorated the deliverance of Israel in the wilderness after leaving Egypt. Margaritha interpreted Tabernacles in light of its strong messianic tone. He mentioned its observances only incidentally and passed over the four species of plants—palm frond, willow, myrtle, and citron—that are regarded as central to this harvest festival. He focused on the messianic expectation epitomized in the cry of the participants to "Save us now!" The great *Hoshannah,* Save Us, which concludes the festival, could lead to the final redemption. Margaritha, normally so disdainful of rabbinic interpretation, accepted the Talmudic association of *Succoth* with the coming of the Messiah. He rejected as superstition, however, the belief that if a person saw his shadow on the clear moonlit night of *Succoth,* he would live another year.

Simchat Torah (Rejoicing in the Torah) immediately followed *Succoth.* Margaritha mentioned several customs associated with the day, including giving three "pennies" to the poor before the holiday and dancing with the Torah scrolls. In dancing with the scrolls, the men, certainly including Margaritha, gave vent to the fervent hope that at any moment the Messiah might come, restore them to the Land of Israel, bring peace to the world, and cause all nations to recognize the greatness of the Torah and of the Jews.

IV

Margaritha's outline of daily life and holy days illustrates how law, ritual, and custom worked to create the cohesive community in which he grew up. His attitude toward Jewish life after his conversion reveals how observance weighed on him. At some time he came to believe that rabbinic enactments incorrectly superseded the Bible, God's clear word, and actually led Jews away from a godly life. In *Der gantz Jüdisch glaub,* he explained, and criticized, his life as a Jew. His informed but critical analysis of Jewish observance reveals how he changed from a Jew to a Christian.

A significant, perhaps the primary, motivation in Margaritha's shift in faith was his evolving understanding of Messianism, the subject of the next chapter. Other Jewish teachings and practices, however, helped facilitate his conversion and acceptance of Christianity as the true biblical religion. Two perceptions of Judaism were crucial to Margaritha's rethinking of the faith. He railed against nonbiblical and superstitious customs and the rabbinical extensions of biblical law that obscured its spiritual meaning. The categories of custom and extended laws often overlap. This fact only highlighted for Margaritha how the Jews were trapped in a misleading and useless religion that was far removed from that of Moses and the prophets.[24]

Many of the "foolish superstitions" Margaritha identified may seem minor matters, but their cumulative effect overwhelmed him. How could the speedy removal of the Sabbath tablecloth lead to a forgiveness of sins? Was it reasonable that counting the number of seeds in an apple after December 15 predicted the number of years left in one's life? Do the forbidden practices of going bareheaded after age thirteen or using the right hand for personal cleansing after defecating really dishonor God? Could the length of time a "soul" candle burned be related to matters of life and death? Who would not see the sucking of blood by the *mohel* as a superstitious perversion of the law?

Margaritha saw the custom of *kapporoth* as one of the most blatant and bizarre of Jewish superstitions. The sacrificial rooster bore human sins; in Margaritha's view, an idea that was a distortion of the fact that Christ bore men's sins. Margaritha suggested that an ape would be a better *kapporoth* sacrifice than a chicken. His proposal disregarded the traditional reason for using a rooster, a reason that he undoubtedly knew. The Hebrew word *gever* can mean either man or rooster; therefore, a rooster was an appropriate sacrifice for a man's sins. Margaritha went on to couple anti-Christian behavior with the foolishness of *kapporoth* by telling his readers how some Jews offered a coin (*groshen*) to a Christian to be their *kapporoth.*[25]

Margaritha correctly asserted that *kapporoth* was not scriptural, nor was it Talmudic. The Geonim first mentioned it in the ninth century CE. The distinguished Sephardic rabbis Solomon Abraham Adret, Nachmanides, and Joseph Karo deemed the ritual to be superstitious.[26] Margaritha used the practice as proof that contemporary Judaism was a rabbinic invention; it was not the divine faith of Moses or the Judaism of Jesus. Yet, he argued, the fact that some Jews offered Germans money to be their *kapporoth,* even if the offer was made in jest, proved that they recognized the possibility that one man could take upon himself the sins of another. Why then did they deny the redemptive act of Jesus?

Margaritha was convinced that all Jewish life had been built on rabbinic extensions and fictitious interpretations of biblical law. Among these were nonbiblical fasts and complicated dietary laws. Particularly burdensome was the addition of a second day to biblically mandated festivals. Such presumptuous legislations removed the Jewish people from God and placed them under the hegemony of the rabbis. The rabbis had deliberately obscured the plain meaning of scripture for their own purposes.

Margaritha's discussion of Passover, which he called Easter in German, shows how he argued that the rabbis had perverted the holidays. Rabbinic law abolished the biblical requirements of the festival, especially those connected to the Paschal Lamb, and attached other ceremonies that obscured its spiritual importance. For example, Jews spent enormous effort in ridding their houses of leaven, a mere physical entity. The finding and burning of leaven, according to Margaritha, should be understood spiritually, as the burning of Satan in the last days, a position many Kabbalists held. But the poor misled Jews focused on external cleanliness rather than on internal purity.

Margaritha faulted the Jews for believing that nothing bad could befall them on Passover night. Although they appropriately thanked God for the redemption from Egypt, they did many things at the meal that are not found in the Bible. When they opened the door for Elijah, they cursed the Christians. Indeed, the custom of having an Elijah actor was nonscriptural. If the Jews took the Passover seriously, they would not make a game of the appearance of Elijah. They would treat his coming to announce the Messiah, the Redeemer of Israel, with respect. Margaritha's perception was that all Jewish holidays and observances, not just Passover, were a confusion of the Bible and rabbinism and that the Jews had lost true worship, observance, and spirituality in a false and superstitious mixture.

V

Margaritha's disenchantment was hardly unique. As noted in the preface, Pfefferkorn and Carben presented similar criticisms of Judaism. In many respects, their anti-Jewish polemics were part of a well-established literary form. Beyond the polemic itself, they had a goal of revealing embarrassing and subversive Jewish secrets. The revelation of such privileged knowledge at one level fed a Christian desire to penetrate the defenses of a secretive and devilish people. It also allowed the convert to proclaim his independence from his former coreligionists. The poem under the title of Pfefferkorn's *Judenbeicht* ended, "that indeed I am not part of the Jews (Doch des ich den Juden nit werde zũtayl)." He, like Carben and Margaritha, found salvation outside Judaism.

Victor von Carben's (c. 1422–1515) *Juden Buchlein* (Cologne, 1508/9) was intended to show how he came to the Christian faith. The book concentrated mostly on Jewish beliefs and practices that he found objectionable. Margaritha's *Der gantz Jüdisch glaub*'s promise was to present "all the [Jewish] customs, ceremonies, prayers, private and public (allersatzungen / Ceremoniē / gebetten / heymlich und oeffentlich)." "Private (*heymlich*)" in the context of the ethnography and the prayer book could also mean *secret*. Whatever he meant by private, Margaritha willingly exposed many embarrassing Jewish secrets. Thus Pfefferkorn, Carben, and Margaritha each discussed Jewish practices in the framework of his separation from Judaism and constructed a polemic to bolster his new faith.[27]

Pfefferkorn's *Juden Beicht* runs only twenty-four pages, giving a mere glimpse of Jewish practices. Given its author's status as a lay Jew, its limitations are understandable. Still, he revealed several secrets about the Jewish practices of atonement before Yom Kippur and described ritual immersions, *kapporoth,* and *tashlich.* He focused on practices he considered superstitious. More seriously, Pfefferkorn argued for increased hostility to the Jews, claiming to expose the fact that Jews cursed gentiles when they prayed. He interpreted the off-spoken Hebrew phrase "may his name be blotted out" as referring to holy Christian names, such as Jesus and Mary. He also criticized Jewish business practices, especially usury, that harmed Christians and attributed Jewish hostility to Christians to the evil Talmud. Many Jews would convert to Christianity, he asserted, but the Jewish community held them back. He recommended forbidding the practice of usury and forcing the Jews to do honest work, which would create an incentive for them to become Christians.

Victor von Carben claimed to have been a rabbi. His description of Judaism in *Juden Buechlein* was similar to Margaritha's, only much more explicitly anti-Jewish. Did Margaritha have access to his work in writing *Der gantz Jüdisch glaub*?[28] Carben's presentation of Judaism was written two decades before Margaritha's conversion. Yet both Carben and Margaritha give detailed descriptions of similar Jewish practices. This may have resulted from their common experience of German Judaism. We know very little about the actual process of Margaritha's leaving his natal faith. We don't know what Christian books he read. Nonetheless, even if Carben and Pfefferkorn directly or even indirectly influenced Margaritha, *Der gantz Jüdisch glaub* is a more scholarly, systematic, and accurate work than theirs.

Carben's apologia, more detailed than Pfefferkorn's, is an important source for understanding the perceptions of rabbinic practices that moved him, and probably others, to convert. He pointed out the Jews' many superstitions. He included the story (also recounted by Margaritha) of the magical Sambat[y]on River, which protected the Lost Ten Tribes from discovery.[29] Unlike Margaritha, Carben misreported the details of certain Jewish customs. This brings his Jewish learning into question. In chapter 10 of *Juden Buchlein,* he stated that Jews "must wait at least 9 hours" after eating meat before eating milk products; a purported custom known from no other source. Margaritha accurately reported the one-hour German practice, and that Sephardic Jews kept six hours.

In Carben's discussion of New Year and Yom Kippur, he spent much time on *kapporoth.* He claimed in chapter 16 that poor men who could not afford a rooster waited for Christians on the street. When they saw one, they said "secretly" the words, "God give you this year as my *kapporos.*" Poor Jewish women also sought out Christian women whom they "cursed" and directed that they "should die" for the poor women's sins. Because the Jews spoke silently, the Christians were unaware of what transpired. Carben revealed the secret. Carben's quietly cursing Jews are different from Margaritha's flippant youth, who spoke audibly, and his report carries more sinister connotations.[30]

Carben gave an insight into Jewish society when he wrote in chapter 19 that women were less likely to convert than men. He stated that wives kept their husbands from becoming Christians. Carben, like Margaritha, mentioned the betrothal ceremony. He used contemporary Jewish practice to flesh out the Gospel account of Mary's betrothal; for example, he noted that a ring would have been placed on Mary's middle finger. To impress his readers with the importance of the information in his work, he argued that learning rabbinic customs added to Christian understanding of the Gospels. Carben also told the story of the Jew mouse that bit the dead. Unlike Margaritha, he claimed that anyone who heard the cry would die within one year.[31]

Carben revealed the anti-Christian details of the *Toldoth Jesu* (History of Jesus), which was commonly available to Jews. (Margaritha also mentioned the work throughout *Der gantz Jüdisch glaub.*) Carben recounted the *Toldoth* statement that Jesus performed his miracles through the power of the Tetragrammaton, using knowledge he had stolen from the temple (chapter 11).[32] Like Margaritha, Carben tended to describe Judaism using Christian terms. He wrote, for example, that Jews made a "mass" on the Sabbath.[33]

Pfefferkorn's, Carben's, and Margaritha's late fifteenth-and early sixteenth-century criticisms of rabbinic Judaism are similar to those of the author of the "*Kol Sakhol*" (Voice of a fool), probably written in the late sixteenth century. The "*Kol Sakhol,*" which many scholars ascribe to the Venetian rabbi Leon of Modena, is a superior scholar's detailed analysis of rabbinism. It gives the doubts about practice and the suggested reforms of a Jew who, if he were Leon, did not convert, but was content to express "a chain of interconnected doubts about the rabbinic tradition."[34] The *Fool* (Sakhol*)* argued for a simplified Judaism, composed from scripture and certain customs, and based upon a historical theory of the Torah. The theory accepted that the Torah was given to Moses, but argued that it was lost after Joshua, as attested by Jewish behavior in the Book of Judges. In the seventh century BCE, during the reign of Josiah, a scroll of the law was discovered in the temple. Based on that scroll, Josiah made many reforms, but when the Kingdom of Judah was destroyed, the Torah was again lost.

Ezra reestablished the law when he returned from Babylon.[35] After Ezra, disputes arose about how to live according to Torah. This gave rise to various sects and the "oral law" of the Pharisees, the forerunners of the rabbis.

The "rabbinates" argued for protective rules, building a hedge around the Torah with secondary prescriptions, such as requiring the separation of meat and milk. Such regulations protected people from the danger of breaking biblical laws; when a Jew diligently separated meat and milk, he would never transgress the biblical prohibition against seething a kid in its mother's milk. But the *Fool* charged that, in fact, the oral law had changed Jewish law, introducing observances that were unknown to Moses and to the prophets.[36] It was as if

> [the rabbinates] mocked our Sabbaths and our superfluous ordinances, the deeds of babes and suckling, and could not imagine that such a difficult existence and so heavy a yoke could be the Torah of God from on high, and they persecuted us as enemies and made us into slaves. And behold, we are a[n object of] mockery and scorn, derision and ridicule for all the nations, declining further every day and not rising. May God will that it not be like this for thousands of years.[37]

The oral law, as described by the *Fool,* was both unscriptural and a burden to Jews. It led to the commandment fatigue seen in Carben, Pfefferkorn, and Margaritha. The *Fool* argued that the oral law obscured the beauty of the Torah and made the people slaves. The solution to the problem was not conversion, for the *Fool* believed that Christianity was worse than Judaism. Jewish life needed simplifying through a return to prerabbinic Torah observances. The *Fool* advocated briefer prayers and blessings and a return to biblical simplicity in observing the Sabbath and other holy days. Nonbiblical ceremonies, such as blessing the moon, needed to be abolished. The second days of holidays with the burdens that they imposed also needed to be eliminated from the calendar.[38] Levirate marriage, as commanded in the Bible, ought be restored and performed.

Although Margaritha with his conversion went far beyond the reforms argued for by the *Fool,* the criticisms of "*Kol Sakhol*" are of a piece with the complaints in *Der gantz Jüdisch glaub.* Margaritha's reaction to rabbinic Judaism, when compared with those of other converts and the *Fool,* indicates that many early modern Jews may have been discontented with the strictures imposed by the oral law. Frustration with the rabbis as well as Messianism and external pressures may have provided an impetus for some to convert.[39] Converted Jews, such as Carben, Pfefferkorn, and Margaritha, expressed a formulaic sense of relief at leaving the "letter of the law," an expression that echoed the words of St. Paul. The formula, however, seems to have articulated genuine feelings. The *Fool*'s rejection of Christianity and his proposed reform of Judaism indicate that conversion was not a necessary consequence of a negative reaction to the antiscriptural stringencies of rabbinism. Indeed, most Jews remained faithful. The *Fool* did not foment reform (the work was little known) and Margaritha apparently had little success in converting other Jews to his point of view.

Conclusion

Whatever the burdens and difficulties, the organic nature of the *kehillah* and its many customs created a meaningful, God-centered life for most Jews. Judaism was a powerful force that helped Jews to see themselves as God's people. God had decreed exile and He would end it. Women encouraged their husbands to remain firm in the faith. Jews supported and strengthened one another. Some found the burden of Torah too difficult and the hope of Messianic redemption too remote. They looked to another Messiah and road to salvation. Margaritha was one who forsook the Torah of the Jews and embraced the Messiah who had come. The following chapter will examine Margaritha's move to a new faith and his life among a different people.

3

The Messiah Who Has Been Sent

Margaritha emphasized Messianism in his discussion of daily life and holidays as well as in his translation of the Hebrew prayer book. The community's petitions to God and ritual practices designed to bring the Messiah and with him Israel's redemption from her cruel exile shaped his Jewish life. The furor excited by Asher Lemlein revealed the potency of the dream of a golden age for the Jews of Germany.[1] Lemlein arrived from Italy. Like John the Baptist, he was preaching repentance to the Jews of Germany and promising the imminent fulfillment of God's promise. The Jews' endurance of the burdens of the Torah's yoke and Christian persecutions was about to be rewarded as the entire world would acknowledge God and his people.

Jewish Messianism competed with the Christian message that the Messiah had already come. Christians were mystified by the obduracy of the Jews in denying the "plain truth" of Jesus's identity as the promised redeemer. Only Satan's power over the Jews could explain such behavior. When Jews converted to Christianity, they gave up false messianic hopes and accepted the real Messiah. From servants of Satan, they became followers of the true God. Margaritha transformed his Jewish messianic hopes when he accepted Jesus as his savior and the Messiah. As a

Christian, he became focused on the false Messianism of his brothers in the flesh. He wanted to demonstrate to them that the promised Messiah had already come; he was the Christ whom Christians worshipped. The Messiah was not part of dead rituals. He lived and brought forgiveness of sin.

I

Jewish Messianism was rooted in biblical texts and their interpretations. Expectations grew with historical experience and the influence of other religions. Ezekiel, a priest and prophet of the Babylonian captivity, predicted the restoration of the Jewish state under the rule of the Davidic line (Ezekiel 39:15–28). The exiled people would return and rebuild the temple. The Jews did return to Jerusalem after seventy years and rebuilt the temple. As residents in a Persian province, they had no political sovereignty. The prophecy of the advent of a Messiah or anointed king, although not fulfilled in the Persian dependency, became a major theme in continuing hopes of total restoration.

Zechariah, who lived in the impoverished Jewish homeland, spoke of the "clans of Judah" who would become "a blazing pot in the midst of wood." The Lord would pour "the spirit of compassion" on the Davidic king of this new state (Zechariah 12). In the eighth century BCE, Isaiah had prophesied the coming of a spiritualized king. "He shall not judge by what his eyes see . . . but with righteousness" (Isaiah 11:4). Biblical passages describing the ideal king and restored theocratic state became the basis of Talmudic discussions about the Messiah and the redemption of Israel. The Talmud testifies to steps in the rabbinic formation of the Jewish Messianism.

The hope for national sovereignty gave rise to many Messiahs, from Nehemiah to the Hasmoneans, Herod, and Jesus.[2] No one fully fulfilled the role. In the second century CE, Bar Kosiba led a Jewish revolt against Hadrian's Rome. Those who believed that he was the promised Messiah called him Bar Kochba, Son of the Star. The rabbis, all of whom hoped for the Messiah, were divided as to Bar Kochba's status. A passage in the Talmudic tractate *Megillah* summarized some of their expectations:

> R. Simeon ben Yohai says: come and see how beloved is Israel before the Holy one, blessed is He; for wherever they went into exile the Shekhinah [the Divine Presence] was with them. . . . Likewise, when they shall be redeemed in the future, the Shekhinah will be with them, as it is written (Deut. 30:3), "Then the LORD thy God will return with thy captivity."[3]

About the time of Bar Kochba's revolt, a new doctrine of two Messiahs arose. One Messiah, the descendant of Joseph, would lead Israel's armies, defeat its enemies, and be killed in the decisive battle. The second Messiah, the traditional Davidic king, would then rule in a time of peace. The concept of one Messiah of war and one of peace found its way into the Talmud and hence shaped later Jewish Messianism. The Talmud describes God's relationship to the two Messiahs:

> The Holy One, Blessed be He, will say to the Messiah, the son of David (May he reveal himself speedily in our days!), "Ask of me anything, and I will give it to thee, as it is said (Ps. 2:7–8), 'I will tell of the decree; the Lord said unto me: Thou are My son, this day have I begotten thee; ask of Me, and I will give the nations for thine inheritance.'" But when he (Messiah ben David) sees that Messiah ben Joseph is slain, he will say to Him, "Lord of the Universe, I ask of Thee only the gift of life." He (God) will answer him: "Life?—Before you spoke, your father David has already prophesied of you, as it is written (Ps. 21:5), 'He asked life of Thee, Thou gavest it him, even length of days forever and ever.'"[4]

Margaritha rejected the idea of two Messiahs as unbiblical. He correctly identified the idea as a product of rabbinic interpretations in the first and second centuries of the Christian era. He contrasted the complicated post-biblical concept of two Messiahs with the one Christian Messiah who fulfilled scripture.

The Talmud was not merely an important source for medieval and Renaissance Jews; they accepted it as a divine communication, like the Bible. The belief that the written (biblical) and oral (Talmudic) law descended from Sinai made both "texts" definitive for the faithful. Rabbinic ahistoricism saw ancient texts as part of a contemporary dialogue. As the heirs of the Pharisees and of the authors of the Talmud, they rejected the concept of religious innovation. What might appear to be their additions to the Torah were actually only the ongoing discovery of how the law applied to new situations. They not only accepted that Moses's teachings were the same as those of the Talmudists, but that Abraham also knew and kept the entire law as understood by the rabbis.

> Rab said: Our father Abraham kept the whole Torah, as it is said: "Because that Abraham heard my voice [Genesis 26:5]." R. Shimi ben Hiyya said to Rab: Say, perhaps that this refers to the seven laws [of Noah, given to all humankind]. Surely there was also that of circumcision! . . . Raba or R. Ashi said: Abraham, our father, kept even the

law concerning the "erub of the dishes" [a nonbiblical law], as it is said: "My Torahs" one being the written, and the other the oral Torah. (B. T. *Yoma* 28b)

Judaism as Margaritha experienced it assumed that then contemporary practices and legal interpretations were identical with those from the times of Abraham and Moses. The very reason for the success and persistence of his family was its knowledge of law and observance. His grandfather, father, and uncles were transmitters, not innovators, of the Lord's Torah. The Talmud and the distillation of Judaism found in the prayer book were constant companions of rabbinic families like the Margoleses. Moreover, Messianism and redemption were recurrent themes in daily life, part of the daily prayers and underlying myths.

All Jews, of course, shared the prayer book and its messianic passages. "Gather us together from the four corners of the earth," "restore our judges," "return [us] to Jerusalem," and "speedily establish the throne of David," men, including Margaritha, his family, and all Israel, fervently pled three time a day. Children grew up to the sound of these petitions and their mothers' recitation of redemptive psalms. Hope for the ingathering of God's chosen people in the Promised Land, under the Davidic Messiah in a blessed time, enveloped the persecuted people. The intense response to failed Messiahs and messengers of the redemption continued from the Bar Kochba revolt to Asher Lemlein, and beyond. Sometimes it seems that the very failure of the putative Messiahs intensified Jewish desire.[5]

Medieval and early modern Ashkenazic Jews, such as Margaritha, lived in a hypermessianic world. At least from the thirteenth century, there were predictions that Elijah would appear (1226) and that the Messiah would follow (1233). There were migrations of rabbis to the Holy Land in 1210 and 1211 that show messianic hopes.[6] Asher Lemlein's movement was part of a continuum in Ashkenaz. It was as if the answer to daily prayers would be realized at any moment. Individuals and communities seemingly kept their bags packed to hasten the departure to Jerusalem.

Christians scorned the Jews and their imagined redeemer. Christian Messianism grew out of the same basic biblical texts the Jews used, but they knew that the Messiah had already come. The Gospel of Matthew set out the specific ways in which Jesus met the criteria for the Messiah described by Isaiah and Zechariah. He was a descendant of King David and the rightful king of the Jews. He fulfilled the spiritual role of the Messiah. Isaiah in his chapter 53 prophesied that the Messiah would suffer for others' sins. Margaritha and other Christians argued that the rabbis had misinterpreted that chapter, as well as Zechariah 12, as referring to the tribulations of the

Jews. Christians, however, found fulfillment of these scriptures in the life of Jesus. Clearly, the glorious King Messiah was Jesus. With his imminent second coming, he would reign on earth as he did in heaven. Only willful Jewish blindness, rooted in ignorance if not in actual evil, explained their failure to recognize that Jesus fulfilled messianic promises and was the promised king of the Jews.

II

Their shared scriptural tradition and bitter disagreement about the Messiah informed Jewish-Christian discussions in the fifteenth and sixteenth centuries. After they became Christians, converted Jews such as Pfefferkorn, Carben, and Margaritha argued against the Jewish view of the Messiah. Their polemics addressed both Jewish messianic expectations and Jewish anti-Jesus stories. In particular, they often disputed two Jewish written works: the *Toldoth Jesu,* a counternarrative of the life of Jesus, and the *Sefer ha-Nizzahon* by R. Yom Tov Lippmann Mülhausen. The *Nizzahon,* the Book of Victory, is a handbook structured to counter Christian readings of Hebrew Scriptures. It circulated in manuscript form only, understandably since it provided anti-Christian arguments for rabbis to use in debates with Christians and in countering proselytizing efforts directed at susceptible Jews. (Details of its content will be discussed below.)

Pfefferkorn, Carben, and Margaritha shared several key arguments against Jewish Messianism, arguments similar to those that Christian polemists had used for centuries. Each emphasized that although the Babylonian captivity had lasted only seventy years, it had been a millennium and a half since the destruction of the second temple. Why would God wait so long to fulfill his messianic promise? Jesus clearly fulfilled the words of the prophets; the rabbinic corruption of Jewish tradition hid the fact that the Messiah had already come.

Pfefferkorn was an uneducated butcher. It is highly unlikely that he wrote the works published under his name without help, although he was a source of information on Jewish life therein. His Dominican supporters were fervent in proselytizing the Jews. Pfefferkorn composed his *Judenspiegel* (1507) (Jewish mirror) about two or three years after his conversion (c. 1504). On the first page he wrote of "the 1500 years according to which the Talmud says the Messiah should have come."[7] He charged the Jews with failing to understand that the Messiah had come because the devil "had removed their understanding."[8] Christians correctly understood that they, with the apostles, martyrs, and the virgin, were the true Israel.[9] Pfefferkorn also provided a bizarre interpretation of the biblical commandment prohibiting seething a kid in its mother's milk. He believed that the scriptural passages referred to Jesus, who had been conceived without sperm.[10] Although an intellectual connection between Margaritha and Pfefferkorn is not demonstrable, there is a relationship between two of their texts. The publisher of the first edition of Margaritha's *Der gantz Jüdisch glaub* chose to copy the illustrations from Pfefferkorn's book on the Jewish religion, *Judenbeicht* (1508) (Latin edition *Libellus de Judaica Confessione* [1508]). The "Yom Kippur" woodcut in Margaritha is the reverse image of that found in Pfefferkorn (see fig. 2d).[11]

Victor von Carben's critique of Messianism is rambling and unfocused. In his *Juden Buechlein* (1508),[12] he discussed signs of social change, such as comets.[13] He gave the chronology from Abraham to David and David to the Messiah. The chronology proved that the Messiah would come 1,400 to 1,500 years after David, or at the time of Jesus's birth. Carben attacked the Jewish doctrine that it was a physical temple that would be rebuilt. Because Jesus was the tabernacle, the original tent that housed the Ark of the Covenant, the temple would be rebuilt within his believers.[14] In Carben's view, scriptural passages concerning the restoration of Jerusalem actually referred to the heavenly Jerusalem. Carben's proofs that Jesus is the Messiah followed the pattern of the Gospel of Matthew, including the fact that he had entered Jerusalem on a white ass.[15] Carben cited the *Toldoth Jesu* by name, as an illustration of how Jews twisted and perverted the Gospel facts. For example, the Jews slandered Jesus by claiming that he had stolen the divine name and then used it to perform miracles.

III

Margaritha's *Der gantz Jüdisch glaub* is part of the same genre as the works of Pfefferkorn and Carben, but it achieved a great deal more in accurately describing Jewish life. His general approach to the Messiah question and certain specific examples of Jewish belief and life follow their pattern, but his discussion is more detailed, better organized, and more reliable as to Jewish doctrines. He is not explicit about to his own reasons for abandoning Judaism in favor of Christianity, but he makes clear that his discontent with rabbinic observances and textual readings were factors. As a young man, he engaged in intense messianic meditations, kabbalistic exercises, which he mentions in his prayer book translation. These may have been part of a movement emphasizing prayers and meditations for the messianic age that originated in early sixteenth-century Jerusalem. Rabbi Abraham ben Eliezer ha-Levi (c. 1460–1530) wrote letters to European rabbis promoting the use of prayers and vigils for the purpose of bringing the

Messiah, who, he prophesied, would come in 1530.[16] The Margoles family, by its prominence, should have been aware of Rabbi Abraham's efforts, perhaps even receiving letters. The cantor Naftali Hirtz Treves of Frankfurt am Main, who had lived in Nürnberg when Jacob Margoles was chief rabbi, was aware of the letters.[17]

In 1517 Rabbi Abraham described the spiritual exercises that were required to bring the redemption:

> My son, be careful to fast with the men of the vigils and to cry to God, as they do in confessing their sins and those of their fathers, and those of their brethren the House of Israel . . . and to confess the three things Israel rejected in the days of Rehoboam: the kingdom of heaven, the kingdom of the House of David, and the temple, and to request all three. Even without fasting you should pray for all these things.[18]

There is evidence of a native messianic fervor in the Regensburg community. In his comments on the prayer book, Margaritha mentioned singing a part of the liturgy for up to an hour in the summer.[19] The singers praised God as the creator and followed that singing with a meditation, pleading that God would rebuild the temple speedily and in our day (see Appendix D.) Such an effort to bring the redemption from exile caught up the entire *kehillah.* Heartfelt, emotional, even ecstatic prayer fit with Rabbi Abraham's prescription. Margaritha was certainly conditioned to see the world in messianic redemptive terms.

Margaritha undoubtedly believed Jewish messianic teachings until some experience[s] opened his eyes. He does not tell his reader why he personally rejected Jewish messianic belief. The futility of messianic prayer may have caused him to look to Christianity. By the time he wrote *Der gantz Jüdisch glaub* in 1530, Margaritha was convinced that Jesus was the Messiah. In his Christian eyes, the advent of Jesus had shifted the burden of proof to the Jews, who continued to reject him and the clear meaning of scripture. In nearly seventeen printed pages at the end of *Der gantz Jüdisch glaub,* he refuted Jewish Messianism and thus, for himself, the entire Jewish faith (see Appendix A for a translation of the text and the German original).[20]

Margaritha gave many reasons for the Jewish rejection of Jesus, most of which, he argued, grew out of a misunderstanding of history, especially the history of crucial Jewish texts. The rabbis of the early Christian era had deliberately created spurious texts to confuse the Messiah issue and mislead the Jewish people.[21] Although the pre-Christian *Mishnah* was trustworthy, its Aramaic commentary, the *Gemara,* perverted Christian ideas and scripture. Further, Jewish history and proof texts had been twisted to show that the Messiah was still to come.

Margaritha supported the distinction between pre-and post-Gospel Judaism with his recognition that the Talmudic passages that referred to the two Messiahs, one of Joseph and one of David, were post-Gospel.[22] To the Talmudic misinterpretation of prophetic scripture, the rabbis had early added the slander that Christians were idolaters. They also promulgated the lies about Jesus contained in the *Toldoth Jesu.*[23] Margaritha concluded that the early rabbis had deliberately kept simple Jews from accepting the true Messiah.

So well had the rabbis succeeded in obscuring the truth that the Jews were ignorant of their own rejection by God. Although he does not say how he did so, Margaritha considered himself lucky to have broken out of the rabbinic world of darkness. In *Der gantz Jüdisch glaub,* he concerned himself not only with explaining Judaism to Christians but also with instructing his brothers and sisters in the flesh about the flaws he found in Jewish messianic doctrines.

In Margaritha's account, the Jews failed to understand how the words of Moses and the prophets were fulfilled in Jesus (and yet "our fathers crucified him"[24]). They failed to grasp how their own history proved Christianity. The first temple fell, according to a correct Jewish interpretation, because of Israel's practice of idolatry. The subsequent Babylonian exile lasted seventy years. The temple was rebuilt and stood until the people again became sinful—though they were not as bad as the earlier idolaters. The site of the second temple remained desolate, and the people had been in exile for almost 1,500 years. This extreme penalty flew in the face of the ninth chapter of Daniel, which prophesied that the Messiah was to come after seventy weeks, during which time Israel's misdeeds would be removed. "Seventy weeks," according to Margaritha, actually meant seventy times seven years, or 490 years. This reading accorded with the Jubilee and seventh, or *shmitah,* year. Four hundred ninety years was the time between Daniel and Titus; hence, the Messiah should have come, and indeed must have come, during that time period, before the destruction of the second temple. Jesus, who fulfilled messianic prophecies, came before the destruction; therefore, he was the Messiah. The Jews, by not acknowledging him, had sinned the sin of Psalm 118; they had rejected the chief cornerstone of the building.[25]

IV

Given the failure of their own messianic expectations, why did the Jews continue to reject Christianity? Margaritha found the primary reason in the "comforts" they took from the practices of daily life and their reading and interpretation of scripture. He reported that these comforts were reinforced by the rabbinical interpretation of Hosea 8:10, which promised that the Jews would receive favorable treatment by giving gifts to kings and other magistrates. The benefits they received through the bribery of authorities allowed them to believe that they could persist in exile until their "imagined" Messiah came. The Jews also drew comfort when they remembered the glory of the redemption from Egypt. That redemption gave them faith in a final spectacular redemption from their exile among Christians. That redemption would be greater than the one of the Exodus, for God would punish the Christians with a worse punishment than he had visited upon the Egyptians.[26]

Margaritha argued that the Jews took false comfort in their legends. They stressed that as Abraham's children they were heirs of God's promises to him, but Margaritha rejected the Jews' claim that they were descendants of Abraham with the right to his blessings. He stated, as a point of fact, that the Israelites had become so intermixed with the nations that no one could tell for sure if he was the child of Abraham, or an Egyptian, or a Babylonian. Taking the argument further, in an addition to the second 1531 edition of *Der gantz Jüdisch glaub,* Margaritha stated that those Jews who were truly of the seed of Abraham were those who converted or would convert to Christianity. This meant, of course, that his conversion was proof that he and his family were true Israelites (see Appendixes A and C). After undermining the claim of modern Jews to the blessings of Abraham, Margaritha wrote that it did not matter anyway; regardless of the promises made to Abraham's heirs, the redemptions promised in scripture largely concerned the Babylonian captivity, and those promises had already been fulfilled.[27]

Another false and superstitious comfort, he believed, was the legend of the Ten Lost Tribes, which were living beyond the river "Shabbathion." The return of these tribes would be a harbinger of the redemption. (In a letter to his brother dated 1489, Ovadiah of Bertinoro wrote that Muslim merchants knew about the pure and righteous Jews living beyond the Sambatyon [Shabbathion].[28]) Margaritha attacked the legend, arguing that no reliable source recorded anyone actually seeing the river or the lost tribes. He took the position that the northern tribes, the lost ten tribes carried off by the Assyrians in the eighth century BCE, had assimilated into the heathen nations. They were indeed completely lost and many of their descendants were now probably Christians. Margaritha's analysis notwithstanding, there were recurrent rumors in early sixteenth-century Germany that the "Red Jews" were coming from beyond Sambatyon to free the Holy Land. In 1524, David Reubeni, claiming to be an emissary of the lost tribes and meeting with Pope Clement VII in Rome, entreated Christendom to join the tribes in liberating Jerusalem from the Turks.[29]

The greatest or "golden" comfort of the Jews was the promise of Leviticus 26:44 that God would not cast them off. God had fulfilled this promise, Margaritha claimed, with the end of the seventy-year Babylonian exile, the return to the land, and the rebuilding of the temple. Furthermore, he argued, the golden comfort was made naught by the curse of Deuteronomy 28, which promised eternal exile and bondage. Titus and the Romans had fulfilled that curse with the final destruction of the temple. The curse and its attendant exile would never abate as long as the Jews denied the scriptures and Jesus, and continued to follow a false faith.

Margaritha claimed that he was writing fearlessly about the truth of Judaism's errors to "all believing Christians" and to the Jews, his "brothers after the flesh." He did not limit his arguments to a scholarly discussion of history and proof texts, but called for action. Christian leaders bribed or misled by the Jews, ameliorated God's decree. This must stop and Jews must be forced into honest labor. In Margaritha's opinion, Jews did not suffer enough; remove the comforts of exile and they might open their eyes to the truth.[30]

Knowing that his people would curse him for his work, Margaritha concluded it with the affirmation, in Hebrew and German, "My hope is in the Messiah who has been sent."[31] His polemic cannot easily be dismissed as merely the hurtful words of a self-hating Jew who sought to escape the disability of his faith by becoming a Christian. Nor did he slavishly follow earlier Christian and Jewish polemics; he exhibited some erudition and an internalized grasp of Jewish arguments against Christianity. He made a plausible historical analysis in dating the doctrine of the two Messiahs. In light of his criticism of Jewish texts, it is suggestive, although not surprising, that he did not submit Christian scriptures to a similar analysis. If the Jewish Messiah had already come, why had he in his role as the Christians' Messiah tarried so long in his second coming? The early Christians believed, just as did Margaritha's contemporary Jews, that the Messiah's coming was imminent. Margaritha, having made his choice, did not address the question, and perhaps never asked it. He continued, however, to attack Judaism throughout the remainder of his life.

V

Der gantz Jüdisch glaub is best known today for its ethnographic descriptions of Jewish practices. The bulk of the book contains Margaritha's translation of the Hebrew prayer book into German.[32] This translation was the focus of Josef Mieses's study of Margaritha. Mieses dismissed the translation as poorly done, the work of an uneducated man. He criticized Margaritha's mention of kabbalah, asserting that he "did not understand kabbalah," "he did not know" *Zohar* or any source of kabbalah, and "mentioned no word from them."[33] As noted above, these judgments have tended to prejudice the study of Margaritha.[34] Mieses's opinion of Margaritha's scholarship and skill, notwithstanding, the translation and commentary are obviously based upon Margaritha's experience with the daily prayers as an observant Jew and son of a rabbi.

Margaritha began, "The Jewish prayerbook that they pray and sing each day in their synagogues follows."[35] The order of Margaritha's prayer book is similar to the present Ashkenazic *siddur* [prayer book].[36] The initial daily blessings follow the same order. The men thanked God that they had not been made a woman, and the women acknowledged that they were made "according to God's will." Margaritha's comments on the blessings are informed by both rabbinic tradition and his newfound Christian faith. He noted that the eighteen benedictions of the standing prayer (*amidah*) are actually nineteen benedictions; the nineteenth being a malediction against "converts," or heretics.

Margaritha described the *amidah,* recited five times each day (three times silently and twice aloud) as a substitute for the temple sacrifices that could no longer be made. In the *amidah,* the reverently praying Jews ask for forgiveness of their sins. Margaritha found in this prayer an unwitting acknowledgment of the truth of Paul's position in Romans 9 that they stiff-neckedly have rejected the Messiah and thus remain under God's anger.[37]

Margaritha based his discussion of the *amidah,* the central prayer of the liturgy, not only on his Christian critique but also on Jewish attitudes and sources. For instance, there was a tradition that 1,800 angels attended the recitation of the *amidah,* but only if the petitioners prayed with the proper intention. This tradition was based on deriving a numerical value of 1,800 by taking the values of the first letters of the words of the eighteen benedictions of the prayer, 1,770, and adding the values from the nineteenth, that is, thirty.[38] Margaritha was aware that according to the Talmud Rabbi Samuel [the Small] had composed the nineteenth benediction at the request of Rabbi Gamliel.[39]

Margaritha revealed that when the Christian authorities in Venice required the removal of the anti-Christian words in the *Aleinu* prayer, Jews compensated for the omission by adding to their bedtime prayers a plea that former Jews (*meshumad* [convert/heretic/traitor]) be turned over to Satan. He also reported the rabbinic tradition that the prayer addressed to "He who is all Merciful" and recited after the *amidah* had been composed by the scholars Samuel, Joseph, and Benjamin, whom Vespasian had set adrift in rudderless boats on the Mediterranean during the Jewish revolt.[40]

Margaritha's technical knowledge of the prayer book and the traditions associated with its prayers was to be expected of a rabbi's son who prayed daily for more than twenty years, yet Margaritha did not limit his comments to the written text and the oral traditions. He used his commentary to criticize Jewish worship and customs and extol the superiority of Christianity. Illustrating this are his comments on the morning prayers. One of the first prayers is, "Blessed are you God our Lord, King of the World, who sanctifies us with your commandments and gives us a commandment about washing the hands." Margaritha commented:

> I would like it if a Jew would show me where God commanded such. I believe he must search long until he finds it because even though hand washing is not incorrect, one cannot make a commandment of God from it.[41]

Even in those comments in which he does not specifically challenge the prayer book, Margaritha demeaned it and rejected its approach to the worship of God. This is seen in the way he described its components. He headed one section of his work, "What a Jew should do to pray reverently that God might hear him." The tone of the statement implies that God does not hear the prayers of Jews.[42] (A detailed analysis of Margaritha's prayer book is given in Appendix D.)

Margaritha's animadversions on the Jews and their liturgy invited Mieses's criticism of his understanding of his source. His contention that Margaritha's work demonstrated an ignorance of the prayer book and Hebrew is largely untenable given that he was raised in a family of celebrated rabbis, nor was he a child when he converted to Christianity. Nowhere is Mieses's misunderstanding of Margaritha clearer than in his statement that he knew no kabbalah. From the end of the sixteenth century, some Ashkenazic prayer books contained elements from Lurianic kabbalah and the *Zohar,* which had become the essence of Jewish mysticism for many Jews. When Mieses looked at Margaritha's work, he could not help but notice the absence of such *kabbalah.* Margaritha did not include a meditation from the *Zohar, wayyakhel,* which precedes the reading of the Torah in later prayer books, but that meditation was added to the prayer book long after his conversion. *Wayyakhel* does not appear in Naftali Hirtz Treves's prayer book of 1560 (discussed below). Margaritha's failure to mention *Zohar* does not mean, however, that he was unacquainted with kabbalah; it means only that he did not refer to Zoharic kabbalah. Isaac Luria's (1534–1572) synthesis of *Zohar* with earlier kabbalah occurred after Margaritha's death. Isaiah Tishby quotes Rabbi Moses Isserles on the discovery and popularity of the *Zohar* in mid-sixteenth-century Prague.

> Many ordinary people now jump at the opportunity to learn something of kabbalah, for it is a delight to the eyes. And they are particularly keen on the writings of the late [kabbalists] whose books reveal their ideas quite plainly, especially in our own time when kabbalistic works are printed, such as the Zohar, Recanati, and *Sha'arei Orah.*[43]

The *Zohar* was not printed until 1558; therefore, Margaritha could only have known it in manuscript form or through oral tradition.[44] He can hardly be faulted for not using *Zohar* or Lurianic kabbalah. Margaritha's discussion of the prayer book evinces his knowledge of a traditional form of kabbalistic interpretation of biblical passages, which had long been associated with prayer, especially among the Hasidei Ashkenaz. He mentioned angel names, alphabetic interpretations, and meditations known to his family. This tradition fits with a kabbalah of Rabbi Eleazar of Worms (fl. eleventh century), who wrote in his *Commentary on Prayer,* "When [the people of] Israel bless the name of his glory, his glory is augmented."[45]

Moshe Idel has drawn attention to the medieval origins of "theurgical performances of *mizvoth* [commandments]" found in most kabbalistic works. Prayer was a locus of such kabbalistic interest. Idel writes that the kabbalah involved in performing *mitzvoth* has been understudied. Medieval and early modern Jews "analyzed more than any other" the kabbalahs of prayer.[46] Meditations during prayer on the meaning of commandments and of events in Jewish history made use of letters, numbers, and prayer. Isaac of Acre (fl. fourteenth century) wrote that whoever wanted to know about the connection of the soul to the upper world should in contemplation, during prayer as well as at other times, "see before his spiritual eyes the letters of the divine name."[47] Both Jewish and Christian medieval mystics employed the techniques of contemplation and visualization. Recall that during the last years of the Jewish community in Regensburg, there was a meditative messianic movement centered in Jerusalem. Abraham ben Eliezer ha-Levi wrote letters to rabbis throughout the Jewish world. He saw the expulsion from Spain and the other anti-Jewish events as the birth pangs of the Messiah. He called for the proper praying of the liturgy as well as special fasts and prayers, which would bring the Messiah by 1530.[48]

Margaritha presented a kabbalah of prayer in his prayer book, and, as such, it becomes a source for an improved understanding of *mitzvah kabbalah* referred to by Idel. His prayer kabbalah was derived from Exodus 14, read at the end of the prayer service, which refers to the angel of God who went before the Israelites in the desert. He described how the kabbalah worked to provide the prayer with a theurgic meditation on its meaning and the import of its accompanying paragraphs.

> The primary reason I have noted this long prayer so carefully is that [in it] one sees what the Jewish Cabala is: namely the 72 angel names. From the 3 verses above, they count 216 letters. They write that these 216 letters have the same numerical value as the word *Arie* אריה which means Lion. The word "lion" often refers to God, as in Amos 3. In sum, they say that every creature or created thing that hears it must do the will of whoever prays this prayer.[49]

Margaritha taught that a purpose of prayer kabbalah was to control nature by the use of divine names. His kabbalah is squarely in the tradition of meditative theurgic mystics such as Abulafia and the Hasidei Ashkenaz. Such kabbalah was integral to their later successors, including Menachem Recanati. These kabbalists concentrated on words and letters as foci of connection with God's power. This also is a significant aspect of the kabbalah found in the works of the Christians Pico della Mirandola, who owned translations of Recanati, and Johannes Reuchlin. Reuchlin's first kabbalistic work, *De Verbo Mirifico* (The wonder-working word) (1494) was devoted to the powers of the divine names, as was Paul Ricci's *Portae Lucis* (Augsburg, 1516), a translation/summary of Joseph Gikatilla's thirteenth-century work *Sha'are Orah.* Margaritha understood his prayer book kabbalah as a contemplative, interpretive method with magical overtones. The knowledge of the powers of angel names invoked in prayer was derived from events in scriptural history and the Talmud's report of rabbis working wonders through the use of divine names.[50] Margaritha's treatment of the first angel name illustrates this.

> [The Jews] write that the first angel, והו *Vehu,* has the sum 17. This name corresponds to אב זהב *Af Sohov,* which is also 17. . . . *Affsohoff* means father of gold. God is also called by this name because He gave the Israelites the gold and silver of the Egyptians by the sea. What such a holy thing means to the Jews and what is to be thought of such a cabala, each can decide for himself.[51]

Margaritha realized that the kabbalah of connecting words of the same numerical value could lead to hermeneutic problems and even absurdities. "Such [an approach as] I take can make God a devil and a devil a God."[52] In spite of this, he "would not reject the entire Cabala." He thought, as did many Christians, that it contained great truths. He was also aware of Christian kabbalists and their works, some of which exhibited an awareness of *Zohar.*

> The Jews create many other names than these for God the Almighty in the Cabala, as their scholars well know. Others scholars, such as the pious Christian, the very learned doctor Reychlin, who have read the Cabala, also know more names. Among the most important writers on the Cabala are the noble, highborn, and well-learned Count Picus Mirandula, and, in our time, the Christian and most learned doctor Paulus Ricius, whose like in knowledge of Cabala has not lived among Christians and Jews.[53]

Probably Margaritha's kabbalah was an oral tradition, unprinted but with handwritten comments inserted into the prayer books of the cognoscenti. His few statements can be compared to his older contemporary Rabbi Naftali Hirtz Treves's long and detailed kabbalistic prayer commentary.[54] Hirtz Treves is especially relevant because he discussed living and studying in Nürnberg when Jacob Margoles was its chief rabbi. He does not mention Margoles by name but states that he learned "much about prayer [and] *kavanoth* [intentions]" in Nürnberg.[55] That the Margoles family was involved in his study can be inferred from its prominence in the rabbinic establishment of the city. As a Margoles, Anthonius had access to knowledge similar to that acquired by Hirtz Treves during his Nürnberg studies. Although Hirtz Treves's commentary is much longer and of a different order of scholarship than the few statements Margaritha made, both men appear to be part of the same tradition. Several references to the attributes of God in Hirtz Treves's work and especially his advice from *Otzer he Kavod* that some requests should be directed to the "God of Jacob and not the God of Abraham and Isaac"[56] illustrate this point. It was the "God of Jacob" who delivered the Jews from Egypt; hence, invoking God by that appellation addressed His redemptive attribute. Hirtz Treves's commentary was formal and printed, ostensibly prepared from notes he made during many years of leading prayers in Frankfurt. It was also in Hebrew, although his directions for prayer were in Judeo-German, thus showing it was meant for more learned persons. Margaritha, as a rabbi's son, had acquired such prayer lore from his family and teachers. He presented it in German to inform Christians of the complex nature of Jewish meditation during prayer.

Contrary to Mieses's opinion, Margaritha understood and discussed real kabbalah, but the kabbalah of his time, before the advent of the influence of *Zohar* and Luria. His rendering of the prayer book, especially its meditative discussions with kabbalistic commentary, offers interesting material for the scholarly understanding of Jewish prayer in the early sixteenth century. His work may even add to our understanding of the messianic nature of the prayers Abraham ben Eliezer and Naftali Hirtz Treves offered. Kabbalistic meditations on angel names and Messianism may well have influenced Margaritha's search for the Messiah. The failure of kabbalistic theurgy to yield results may have influenced his decision to look outside Judaism for spiritual food, and to accept "the Messiah who has been sent." (For a more detailed discussion of Margaritha's kabbalah, see Appendix B.)

VI

Margaritha focused on the Messiah in several polemics he wrote after *Der gantz Jüdisch glaub.* The most sophisticated in Hebrew knowledge was a commentary on the fifty-third chapter of Isaiah (*Isaiah Commentary,* 1534), a technical assault on Jewish messianic doctrine. He wrote the commentary in "the 13th year of my rebirth."[57] He intended his grammatical analysis to refute Jewish biblical readings and prove that Jesus was the suffering man Isaiah discussed. Isaiah 53 had long been the stock in trade of Jewish converts. Pfefferkorn and Carben touch on it. The question might be asked, "Was Isaiah a text that fostered conversion or justified it after the fact?" In at least one case, it seems to have aided a conversion. In the sixteenth century, Rabbi Isaac the Elder and his son Stephen converted. With the help of the local noble, he forced his wife and other children to follow suit. Stephen became a priest and then a Protestant cleric. In his account of his life and of his father's conversion, he claimed that the study of Isaiah 53 turned his father to the true Messiah.[58]

> While he was a teacher among the Jews, my father—after first invoking the favor of God—began to read and to study most assiduously the fifty-third Chapter of the Book of Isaiah, in which the sufferings of Christ Jesus, our Savior, are plainly described. And after he had pondered all the facts and seen that the contents of said book could not be taken to refer to anyone else but Christ Jesus, he gave honor to God and betook himself to several theologians, conferred with them in greater detail, and was also comforted and strengthened by them in Christ.[59]

Unlike Rabbi Isaac, Margaritha did not claim that studying Isaiah 53 resulted in his own conversion. Quite to the contrary, his 118-page commentary is a postconversion work that confirmed him in his Christianity. Margaritha proposed to strengthen the case that Jesus was the Messiah by refuting Jewish challenges to the Christian interpretation of Isaiah 53. He also included several autobiographical passages, which will be discussed in the next chapter.

Margaritha showed a specific awareness of the Jewish anti-Christian work, the *Nizzahon* of Rabbi Yom Tov Lippman Mühlhausen. The *Nizzahon* was completed in the fourteenth or early fifteenth century. Circulating as a kind of *samizdat,* it has survived in at least forty-four manuscript copies.[60] Learned Jews, such as the Margoleses, guarded their copies from the eyes of Christians, although Johannes Reuchlin and Sebastian Münster, among others, knew of its existence.[61] Mühlhausen's *Nizzahon* shared its name with an earlier anti-Christian work, and scribes may have copied parts of both works in some manuscripts. Münster probably used such a manuscript. In any case, there was some degree of confusion about the content of and access to each work.[62] Margaritha referred specifically to Mühlhausen's text in his *Isaiah Commentary,* mentioning an idea not present in the earlier *Nizzahon.*[63] It is quite possible that the Margoles family owned a copy of the manuscript and that Margaritha had read it before his conversion. It is even possible that he became interested in Christianity through studying its anti-Christian statements. The *Nizzahon* certainly contained a great deal of information about the forbidden religion from a Jewish point of view.

Mühlhausen explained why Jews rejected the Christian idea of a Messiah who had the dual nature of God and man. How could God have physical seed and children? A person's spirit comes from God, but there is no physical body without seed. Virgins do not conceive without seed. Both seed and womb are necessary for the birth of man. Mühlhausen presented his arguments as a commentary on Genesis, "On the day you eat thereof [the fruit of the tree of the knowledge of good and evil] you will surely die."[64]

Margaritha refuted this argument by referring to Exodus 4:23, "Let my son go that he may serve me," and Psalm 99:5, "your generations will be forever" [Vulgate].[65] He seems to have reasoned, "If God does not have seed, why do the scriptures express such thoughts?" The logic of this argument is a continuation of the polemic against Jewish Messianism begun in *Der gantz Jüdisch glaub* of 1530. Margaritha's mention of *Nizzahon* indicates that he read the work while he was still a practicing Jew, for it was not available except in manuscript copies kept within the Jewish communities.

One Christian scholar who noticed Margaritha's work on Isaiah was Johannes Eck (1486–1543), the Catholic opponent of Luther and well-known anti-Jewish writer.[66] Eck's private comments in a 1535 letter to Nickolaus Ellenbog highlight the former Jew's problem in gaining scholarly acceptance.[67] Margaritha's reading of Isaiah, which opposed Catholic tradition, upset Eck.

> Anthonius Margarita has written against the Jews but what rambling [hallucinatur] in words, in persons, in treatment. He claims that the text of Isaiah was corrupted by the Jews. [He says] they put in place of *lo* (lamed waw [meaning "to him"]) *lo* (lamed aleph [meaning "not"]). Therefore, he claims [that the passage] should be read as a positive, which in our Bible and the Septuagint is read as a negation. It is not good when catechumens and new converts write books that are not carefully proofread.[68]

Eck's reading followed established Catholic theology, based on the Vulgate and Septuagint, as well as spellings in the Hebrew text, "In all their afflictions there is no affliction." Margaritha's interpretation of Isaiah was shaped by the Masoretic markings in the margins of the Hebrew Bible, "In all their afflictions he was not afflicted [literally—"to him there is no affliction"]."[69] Eck, in the Catholic tradition, interpreted the passage as referring to Christian trials in this world. The word "not" [*lamed aleph*) was essential to this Christian meaning.

Margaritha's emendation followed the marginal note of the Masoretes, which corrected the *aleph* (*alef*) to *waw* (*vaf*), changing the negative into *to him.* Margaritha believed that the rabbis had replaced an original *waw* with the *aleph,* and he was merely returning the text to its pristine form. He wrote, "In this place, the Jews put in an evil usurpation, namely in place of *lo,* with a *vaf,* they put *lo,* with *alef,* which means 'not,' so the text would be read, 'in all their suffering to them there is not suffering.'"[70] From the marginalia, Margaritha knew that Isaiah intended to say, "In all their affliction he was not afflicted." This was harmonious with the suffering man (Jesus) of Isaiah 53. The rabbis, by the change of a letter, obscured the Messiah and led the Jews from him.

The Jewish convert had a better technical understanding of the Hebrew than did the famous theologian. Margaritha, in his Jewish life, had undoubtedly been taught rabbinic lore concerning the biblical text and how the written letters and words related to the way it should be read. In his explanation of Isaiah 63:9, Margaritha relied upon Jewish tradition. Not only educated Jews but also Christian scholars with access to the Hebrew text and its Masoretic markings understood and probably agreed with his reading.[71] Margaritha's use of the Masoretic markings placed him, ironically, on the side of Jewish tradition and in opposition to Catholic dogma. Eck was astute in perceiving that Margaritha's reading was an artifact of his being a new Christian.

VII

Before or while writing his *Isaiah Commentary,* Margaritha produced a Hebrew translation of the first two chapters of the Gospel of Matthew (1533).[72] This work was a departure from the polemical style of *Der gantz Jüdisch glaub* and the *Isaiah Commentary,* but was nonetheless profoundly Messianistic. Margaritha's Matthew text lays claim to being the earliest printed Hebrew rendition from that Gospel, which sixteenth-century Christian scholars believed was originally composed in that language.[73] The Matthew, although not usually regarded as a polemical work, reveals his understanding of *the* Christian messianic text. The translation, like any translation, is an implied as well as an explicit commentary, in this case reflecting the translator's theology. Before and after conversion, Margaritha appears to have been persuaded by Matthew's use of biblical proof texts.

Margaritha appended the Matthew to his vocalized *Hebrew Psalter* (*Psalterium Hebraicum*). Both texts were prepared while he was teaching in Leipzig. In the Hebrew colophon, Margaritha identified himself as "Antonius man of Margolith from the seed of Israel"[74] (fig. 3). A friend made a Latin translation of the Hebrew introduction, stating that Margaritha was "an instructor of young men in Leipzig."[75] Margaritha's Matthew translation revealed not only his ability to handle Hebrew but also, by his reliance on his friend's Latin introduction, his inability to use Latin. Possibly he prepared the Matthew text from a German translation, and academic colleagues may have helped him use the Vulgate. His promise to produce a complete Matthew demonstrated that he intended the two-chapter translation to test the market for a complete Gospel that was never published.

Although Luther's German Matthew was not readily available until 1522, there were several printings of a medieval German translation from the Latin. Margaritha could not read Latin, but his personal study of the earlier German Matthew may have influenced his decision to convert. On the other hand, his Christian teachers must certainly have used Matthew in his instruction. It is also possible that he had read the verses from Matthew that were quoted in the *Nizzahon,* which then would have had the unintended consequence of stoking his interest in Christian Messianism.

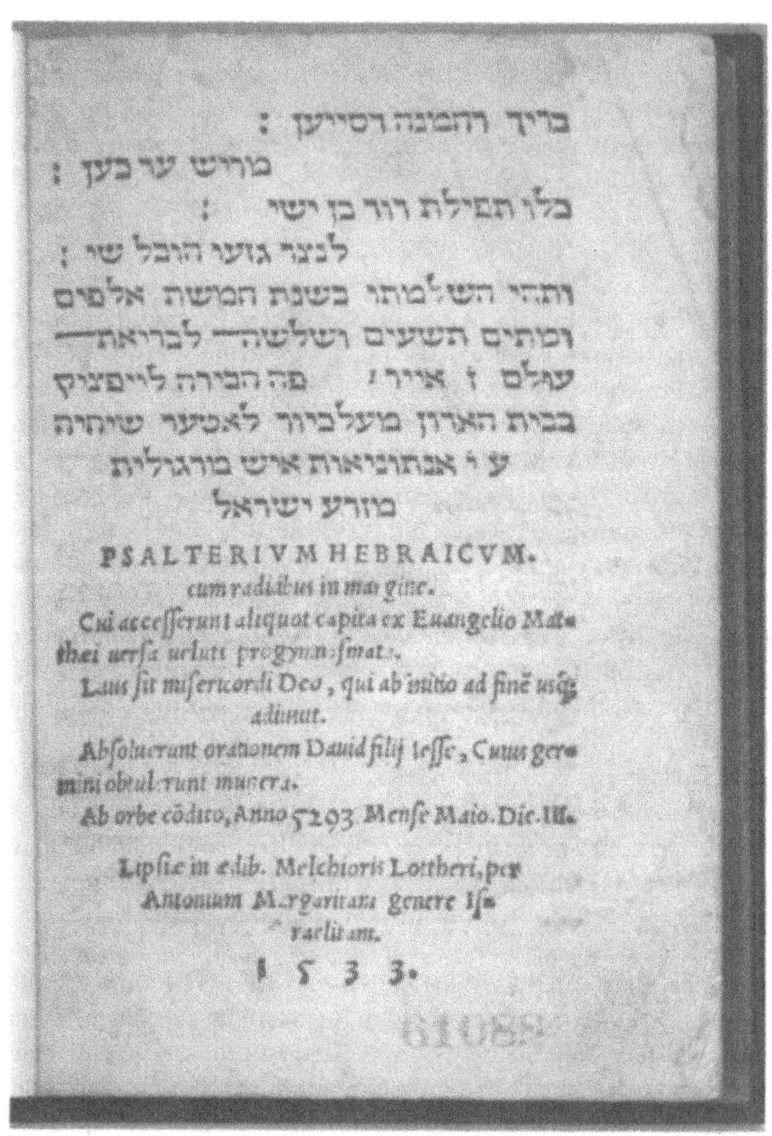

ברוך והמונה רסייען :
מוריש ער כנען :
כלו תפילת דוד בן ישי :
לנצר גזעי הובל שי :
ותהי השלמותו בשנת חמשת אלפים
ומתים תשעים ושלשה — לבריאת —
עולם ז אייר פה הבירה לייפציק
בבית הארון מעלכיור לאטער שיהיה
ע י אנתוניאוס איש מורגליות
מזרע ישראל

PSALTERIVM HEBRAICVM.
cum radicibus in margine.
Cui accesserunt aliquot capita ex Euangelio Matthei uersa ueluti progymnasmata.
Laus sit misericordi Deo, qui ab initio ad finẽ usq; adiuuit.
Absoluerunt orationem David filij Iesse, Cuius germini obtulerunt munera.
Ab orbe cõdito, Anno 5293 Mense Maio. Die. III.
Lipsiae in aedib. Melchioris Lottheri, per Antonium Margaritam genere Israelitam.
1533.

Figure 3. Colophon of *Psalterum Hebraicum* (1533). Courtesy of Klau Library, Hebrew Union College–Jewish Institute of Religion, Cincinnati, Ohio.

Whatever the Book of Matthew's role in Margaritha's conversion, his translation reflected his messianic ideals. It also supported his status as translator. It casts further doubt on Josef Mieses's evaluation of Margaritha's education and linguistic skills.[76] In *Der gantz Jüdisch glaub,* Margaritha admitted that his German was poor. He excused that limitation and even made a virtue of it, claiming that when he translated, he was interested in the meaning and not word for word accuracy.[77] His introduction to the translation of Matthew followed that standard. His Hebrew translations are pedestrian and do not rise to the level of those of Rabbi Mühlhausen.

Margaritha's explicit goal was to present a purified Torah of his new faith. He greeted his readers, "Peace to all lovers of your Torah Lord."[78] The original of his *Psalter* was the traditional Hebrew text, which he may have carried with him from the Jewish world. His source for the Matthew is unclear, but as noted above, perhaps he drew in part on a German text and his Latin-literate helpers.[79]

Margaritha presented his translation of Matthew as a restoration of the Hebrew original.[80] Matthew rendered Jesus's story as the fulfillment of the messianic prophecies found in the Hebrew Scriptures. Christians often structured their anti-Jewish polemic according to Matthew's arguments. Margaritha, a trueborn Jew, presented to Christians and to open-minded Jews the Torah of the Messiah who had fulfilled the words of the prophets. It was no matter that his Hebrew translation evinced some linguistic constructions of German translations and the Latin Vulgate; the Hebrew original would shine through. Of course, Margaritha, the convert, wanted to gain both acceptance and a livelihood from his new Christian brothers. He was not a scholar in the Christian academic sense, but he was able to share his Jewish knowledge and his Hebrew skills. The Psalter and Matthew were produced with several goals in mind as the introductions made clear. Margaritha's obsession with Messianism, however, took precedence, not so much as a polemic, but rather as a statement of faith.

Margaritha's Matthew began with some originality, "This is the book *from* the history [*toldoth*] of Joshua, the Messiah who was the son of David."[81] Margaritha used the pattern of the Hebrew words of Genesis 5, "This is the book of the generations [*toldoth*] of Adam," which is the obvious inspiration for the first verse of Matthew. *Toldoth* means both *generations* and *history.* Margaritha used the preposition "from" with *toldoth;* Genesis does not. In Margaritha's Jewish world, *toldoth* often meant stories, such as in the anti-Christian tract, *Toldoth Jesu.* Therefore, it seems reasonable to understand Margaritha's rendering of the first verse of Matthew as, "This is the book of the history of Jesus Christ the son of David." Margaritha omitted from verse 5 of chapter 1, that Boas begot Obed "from Ruth." It is interesting that he renders verse 23 according to the Hebrew of Isaiah: 15, a "young woman [*alma*]" will conceive, rather than using the word for "virgin" used in the German and Latin Matthew where the Gospel follows the Greek Septuagint. Margaritha omitted from chapter 2:11 the falling down of the wise men before the infant Jesus, translating only "they worshipped him."[82] Such lacunae are not easy to explain because all printed German and Latin Matthews contain the full text.

Margaritha's Hebrew Matthew compares favorably with that of the noted scholar Sebastian Münster, whose 1537 Matthew has long been thought to be the earliest printed Hebrew translation. Neither Margaritha's nor Münster's translations were as clear and idiomatic as the Matthew texts Jewish communities possessed, such as the one Jean du Tillet printed in 1553/54.[83]

More to the theological point, Margaritha presented Matthew, and the rest of the Christian scriptures, as a "second Torah that proceeded from the mouth of God."[84] The Gospels, and especially Matthew, set forth, like the Pentateuch, the essentials for serving God. This service required accepting Joshua (Jesus) and his fulfillment of prophesies, prophesies that the rabbis had misinterpreted. The "Good Tidings" (Margaritha used the Hebrew term *b'sorath*) of Matthew was the Second Torah, because it augmented the Torah of Moses. The Second Torah was the Torah of redemption. It paralleled Moses's saving of the people from Egypt with the gift of Jesus's salvation from sin.

Margaritha offered to complete his translation of Matthew for those who wanted the authentic Hebrew version of the Good News, but there was no ground swell of interest. Christian Hebraists, if they read the Psalter, would have seen the difficulties with the Hebrew and the passages missing from the Matthew. The two-chapter "teaser" offered them little. The few copies that can now be found suggest that it had meager sales. The existence of the translation, however, says something about Margaritha's belief in Christianity as the true Judaism and his belief that the Gospels were a Second Torah, presenting a pure faith unencumbered by rabbinism.

Perhaps the greatest intellectual barrier to conversion that a Jew faced was the Christian doctrine of the Trinity, raising a question: What was Margaritha's theology of the Trinity? Carben was committed to the adoration of the Virgin, but Margaritha seldom mentioned her. He focused on Jesus's status as the promised son of David in the flesh. Such an opinion was not in conflict with Judaism. The Second Torah taught that the Messiah was the only begotten of the father and the savior of humanity. In *Der gantz Jüdisch glaub,* Margaritha presented a fuzzy understanding of the incarnation and did not mention the Holy Spirit. According to him, the Father and the Son were in some way separable in the flesh. They were one being in communion (*gameinschaft*).[85] By the time he published his Psalter and the *Isaiah Commentary,* he had given up such a Judaized view in favor of the orthodox Trinity. He fully acknowledged the Holy Spirit. His intellectual conversion to the doctrine of the Trinity appears to have evolved following his emotional acceptance of Jesus as his Messiah and savior. Whatever his theological development, Margaritha was consistent in emphasizing his rebirth and salvation through the Messiah.

VIII

Margaritha's acceptance of the Christian Messiah required him to defend Jesus against Jewish calumnies. Evidence of the Jews' hatred of Joshua (Jesus's Hebrew name) was found in the *Aleinu* prayer, which closed the three daily prayer services. The prayer originated in the ancient world and incorporated various elements from the Hebrew Scriptures. It thanks God for making the Jews His people and looked forward to a time when all peoples acknowledged Him. It begins, "We are obliged to praise the Lord of all." One ten-word passage quotes Isaiah 45:22, "for they bow to vanity and emptiness and pray to a god who does not save." The *Aleinu* entered the liturgy as part of the afternoon prayers on Rosh Hashanah, the New Year. By the twelfth century, it had been appended to the end of all services. In the fourteenth century, several Jewish converts to Christianity testified that the Jews interpreted the words from Isaiah as referring to Jesus as the "god who does not save." They derived their understanding by using *gematria,* Hebrew numerology. The words "vain and empty" have the same numeric value as the Hebrew name of Jesus. A further addition of letters from the ten words yields the name Mohamed.[86]

In revealing this embarrassing secret, Margaritha's testimony substantiated the claims of previous converts. He further added that Jews spit three times when saying "vain and empty . . . a god who does not save." Scholars have been reluctant to accept the testimony of converts about such anti-Christian Jewish practices. They often prefer to adopt the rabbinic defense against converts' claims asserting that the prayer was introduced into the liturgy before Christianity and referred to pagans and their gods. Whatever the origin of the prayer, by the late twelfth century, the Hasidei Ashkenaz, as is illustrated in the work of Judah the Pious of Regensburg (d. 1217), had adopted the anti-Christian *gematria* with its attendant spitting.[87] Margaritha referred to Judah the Pious in *Der gantz Jüdisch glaub,* calling him a liar, but he also relied on him for information on prayer customs. Rabbi Judah was a major source for prayer with *kavanah,* proper intention and moral attitude.[88]

Margaritha correctly stated the custom, which certainly dated from the Hasidei Ashkenaz, of spitting three times when speaking the ten words. He gave a detailed explanation of how *gematria* functioned to equate the letters of *L'hevel va'la'rik* (vain and empty) with the numeric value of *Yeshu.*[89]

(Margaritha did not include a similar *gematria* for Muhamet.) The Hasidei Ashkenaz's *gematria* was used by Abraham ben Azriel in his thirteenth-century *Arugat ha Bosem,* where he noted that the numerical value of *L'hevel va rik* equaled that of *Yeshu* and *Muhammad.* The anti-Christian reading of the *Aleinu* seen in the prayer book of the Hasidei Ashkenaz is difficult to document in succeeding generations because it was primarily an oral tradition. The custom of spitting three times, however, was so common that it became part of a witticism. Because the *Aleinu* is the last prayer of a service, those who came late were said to "come for the spitting" (*er kummt tsum oysshpayen*).

Margaritha explained that in Germany the ten offending words were directed against Christians in particular.

> These words read [in Hebrew] *Shehem korim umistachevim loeheval vorik umispallelim le el lo joschia,* that is, they kneel and bow to a foolishness and vanity and pray to a god that cannot help. And when they pray these ten words, they spit three times against Christ and his believers.[90]

Margaritha agreed with the rabbis who defended the Jews in debate that the words themselves were from scripture and not on their face anti-Christian. Nonetheless, he argued from his own experience, the Jews interpreted scripture through the "Cabala" and its hermeneutics, such as *gematria.* By this means, within the Jewish community scripture was perverted against its plain meaning and directed against the Christian faith.

> The Jews have here a great secret and Cabala that I must somewhat expose. Since they now are under the Christians and live with them, they cannot speak aloud things that curse Jesus. However, they have placed a disgraceful name in place of the holy name. As follows, his name in Hebrew is *Jeschua,* ישוע Jesus, a savior who heals the people from their sins and helps [them]. . . . [When the Jews said A god who is not Jeshua or does not save—el-lo Yeshua—they denied Jesus] And so they speak under the ten words, they bow and turn to foolishness and vanity. So they mean with these words *foolishness and vanity* the precious name of Jesus. [Emphasis mine]
>
> They have . . . many great secrets in their writings, and prayers with the letters and with the numbers of letters. Also, here is the name worthy of holiness, in which we must be saved; it has the numerical value in Hebrew of 386. Now in place of this holy name they have taken two words, *Loehevel v'orik,* which in German mean a foolishness and

a vanity. Their total is 383 and [the Jews] have with diligence made it 3 less [than Jesus] because the Christians believe that in this salvific name ישוע *Jeschua* the trinity is to be understood.[91]

Margaritha argued further that for Jews disparaging Jesus and Christians went well beyond daily prayer. On the street and in other contacts with Christians, Jews were deceivers. They honored God and the Holy Spirit, but they would not speak the name "Jesus"; instead, they used a shameful abbreviated form that had a derogatory *gematria.*

When the Jews in all honesty and uprightly must mention Jesus, as they sometimes must do because of the Christians, they call him *Jeschu* ישו. And so they do when they speak with one another, they always hang thereafter ימח שמו *imach schmo,* his name be blotted out. And it is common that they in mentioning *Jeschu,* they say it barely aloud as if they give the correct name *Jeshua,* that means savior. They do not mention Him completely.[92]

Margaritha also pointed out that the false name *Jeschu* has a *gematria* of 316, the same as *v'orik,* in vain. This was the same *gematria* used by the Hasidei Ashkenaz. Margaritha revealed this kabbalistic tradition and passed it on to the Christians in order to defend Jesus. The Jews used the incorrect name *Jeschu* because "they want to give to understand that *Jeschu* will end only in vanity."

Margaritha, as a follower of the true Messiah, had his eyes opened to the vanity of rabbinism and wanted to curb Jewish disrespect. This he did in the hope that the Jews would be humbled, accept Jesus as the Messiah, and not continue to vainly wait for their imagined one. He suggested that the authorities in Germany follow those of Venice, who banned the ten words from printed prayer books.

I showed above how at a certain time the Venetians required their Jews to omit certain offensive and abusive words from their books which pertained to Christians and their beliefs. This place is one of the places where they had to omit ten words.[93]

The censorship rules in Venice, a center of printing, influenced other locales where Venetian books were sold. Naphtali Wieder discusses the censorship of prayer books in Venice in the 1520s.[94] Margaritha's knowledge of Venetian censorship was probably gained in two ways: by personal travel in Italy, noted in his discussion of Jewish physicians, and by his reading of prayer books printed in Italy.[95] He described the appearance of the censored page:

> So when they [Venetian Jews] write their prayer books they put them [the ten words] in again. [When they] print them they show a secret mark and they allow space ten words long. Then when he [the worshiper] comes to it everyone thinks to himself to pray these ten words. The Jews in Germany write them in and the Jews of Prague print them.[96]

In Venice, the censored portion of the *Aleinu* was transmitted as an oral tradition. In Germany and in Prague (home of Margaritha's uncle), there was no censorship, so the words could be written or printed in the space provided.

Jews were justifiably aghast when converts, such as Margaritha, revealed secrets, such as those concerning the *Aleinu.*[97] Persecution was easier to bear if one could at least silently mock the persecutors. Embarrassment and danger resulted from the publication of insider hostility and jokes. Margaritha's revelation was in defense of the Christian Messiah, but, as he knew, it also put German Jews at risk. Part of the debate between Rabbi Josel of Rosheim, imperial counselor, and Margaritha, which will be detailed in the following chapter, focused on the meaning of the *Aleinu.*[98] The point here is that Margaritha's shift from Jewish Messianism to the Christian Messiah led him to promulgate arguments that, while not new, put additional pressure on his former coreligionists. Indeed, Margaritha meant the Jewish community no good. His justification for advocating repressive measures against the Jewish community lay in his hope for the salvation of individual Jews. If Christians adopted certain anti-Jewish policies, unhappy Jews would be more likely to convert. Even if Christians did not adopt more stringent policies, his revelations would at least put them on guard in their discussions and dealings with Jews. Margaritha, however, was not one of those converts who sought to win favor by retelling false stories of host desecration and human sacrifice (blood libels). Regarding Jewish Messianism and hostility to Christians, he was an honest, albeit biased, reporter.[99]

Conclusion

In *Der gantz Jüdisch glaub* and his other works, Margaritha expressed doubts that the stiff-necked Jews, blinded by their rabbis, would convert en masse. Only a few might do so. Still, he deeply desired "that God would illuminate all Jews, his brothers after the flesh," as he had been. He wanted them to share his knowledge of the "Messiah who has been sent." The Jew Margaritha had longed for salvation. Belief in the Christian Messiah made it possible for him to see the falseness of rabbinism and the correct meaning of scripture. His salvation came with his rebirth in 1521. Freedom awaited other Jews who would embrace the truth. They also could share the new life and insight into scripture that he had found.

4

Anthonius Margaritha—Christian

"May the heretic have no hope!"

Prayer Book

Margaritha's conversion was by all measures sincere. He retreated from impure rabbinism to the faith of the Messiah who had come. He acknowledged his Jewish birth, but rejoiced in his new birth. Whether his fiancée/wife shared his conviction cannot be known; she is, for us, a silent player in his drama. Before his conversion, Margaritha had traveled to and studied in Prague, Crakow, and Italy. His father, uncles, and brothers held honored positions in Poland, Bohemia, and Italy. When he converted, all possibility of life and livelihood as a Jewish scholar ended. He continued to view himself as a learned person, although he had neither Latin nor university training. Apparently, with little aptitude for or ability in the language, he never became even minimally skillful in Latin, and his German continued to be far from perfect. Even had he considered a nonintellectual career, he had no entrée to guild or to trade. Had he been single, he might, like many converts, have entered a religious order, but as a married man, he was limited to what seemed a natural profession for him, the teaching of Hebrew and Jewish topics. For that line of work his qualifications, sufficient for ordinary if not outstanding work in the Jewish communities, were barely adequate and turned out to hold little hope for providing more than a subsistence living. At best he could aspire to lectureships as a Hebrew teacher, not as a professor.

I

It is difficult to trace Margaritha's the activities in his early years as a Christian.[1] His works and public records reveal stays in Altenzelle (c. 1522), Tübingen (unknown date), Augsburg (1530), Meissen (1530–31), Leipzig (1531–33), and Vienna (1533–42).[2] During the years 1522 to about 1525, Margaritha taught Hebrew to Bernhard Ziegler (1496–1556). Ziegler had studied at the University of Leipzig beginning in 1512. He became a Cistercian monk (brothers of St. Bernard) in the monastery at Altenzelle about 1521. In the mid-1520s he embraced Lutheranism.[3] By 1525/26, he was identified as a Hebraist in a plan to establish a Lutheran academy in Liegnitz for the purpose of opposing the more radical protestant Schwenckfelders.[4] Since Margaritha converted to Catholicism about the same time as Ziegler entered the monastery, and Ziegler was a recognized Lutheran Hebrew scholar in 1525/26, he probably studied with Margaritha during his time in the monastery and, perhaps, immediately thereafter. Although the Cistercians had a "collegium Bernhardium" at the University of Leipzig, where Ziegler studied and taught, it is reasonable to assume that Margaritha taught Hebrew to Ziegler and the other monks during the period of 1522 to 1525 at their house in Altenzelle. He may also have worked with them in Leipzig, where he later held a teaching position.

Margaritha, as a new Christian with Hebrew skills, would have been welcome among the monks as both a teacher and as a student of Christian doctrine. He must have taught the Cistercians for some time and with attention to his duties, for Ziegler became a competent Hebraist. In July 1529, Luther referred to Ziegler as "a true Hebraist" and teacher in Ansbach.[5] The connection between Ziegler and Luther may in part explain the great reformer's interest in *Der gantz Jüdisch glaub.*

Although Margaritha seems to have been comfortable in the society of Cistercians, his wife would have had no place there.[6] The pair may have occupied quarters separate from the clerics or perhaps she lived without him elsewhere in Altenzelle or even in Leipzig. Margaritha complained in his *Isaiah Commentary* that people in the Jewish communities in the cities where they lived treated his family and him poorly. He complained that they denied his family financial support.[7] His grievance indicates that he and his wife lived near Jewish neighborhoods and maintained some contact with Jews. As Jews by birth, they may have felt a right to Jewish charity, especially if his wife had not converted. By the early 1520s, only a few German towns officially allowed Jews to reside within them. Although Leipzig's Jews had declined in numbers subsequent to persecutions in 1442, they were probably not totally expelled until the general expulsion from Saxony in

1540.[8] Even after the expulsion, some Jews may have remained in Leipzig. In this earlier period, Margaritha's wife may have made Jewish contacts in the city while he taught the Cistercians.

After leaving Augsburg, Margaritha served as an instructor of Hebrew in Leipzig from 1531 to 1533. It was there from the press of Melchior Lotther that he issued a second edition of *Der gantz Jüdisch glaub* (see Appendix C) and his *Psalter*. It is certain that his wife and children then lived with him in Leipzig. At least one child was born in 1530 in his Augsburg period; the "churfürst zu Sachsen" (Elector of Saxony) was its godparent.[9] When Margaritha accepted a position at the University of Vienna in 1533, he went there without his wife and children. In 1534 he requested financial help from Leipzig for his family. The city "by grace" granted two gulden because "his wife is left impoverished in Leipzig with small children."[10] The wife's situation at that time seems close to what he described in the *Isaiah Commentary*, published in 1534, the year after his arrival in Vienna. The *Commentary*, given its length, was probably begun in Leipzig; it described his life there and earlier. He wrote of the financial consequences of his conversion:

> It is true that 13 years ago before I was baptized, I was like Paul, my father's teachings almost set aside. In all lands Moses and the Talmud truly protected [me] and at the same time I had no want of sustenance. I cannot hide that the Hebrews saw for some years [that] I, my wife and children wanted for physical sustenance. They would have gladly drawn me again to the synagogue with money and other kinds of support.[11]

Perhaps cultural affinities or even missionary motives kept the Margaritha family in touch with the Jewish communities where they lived. His account demonstrates that apostate Jews were encouraged to return, and it seems reasonable that the Leipzig Jewish community was one that tempted Margaritha with promises of support. Jews in other places the Margarithas visited may also have had an inclination to bring them back.

That Margaritha also had missionary motives in interacting with Jews is borne out by his account of an incident in Tübingen.[12] He argued the meaning of Isaiah 53 with Jews in that city. "With such an interpretation [that Jesus meets the criteria for Messiahship] the Jews cannot argue. I myself [proved this when I] tried to read it this way with them in Tübingen."[13]

The cultural and financial attraction of the Jewish world for Margaritha are seen in his mention of his family's offer to move him to Turkey, support him, and procure for him a teaching position, if he returned to Judaism.[14] In the second edition of *Der gantz Jüdisch glaub* (Leipzig, 1531), Margaritha reported that Christians who converted to Judaism or Jews returning to Judaism were usually sent to Turkey. As the son of a rabbi, he was both an object of interest for return and, as a Christian, a problem for Jews. The threatening aspect of his conversion is revealed at the end of *Der gantz Jüdisch glaub.* Margaritha was aware that the Jews would try to discredit him; "I also know full well that as soon as the Jews learn the contents of this book [they] will gather in Worms [to oppose it] because their chief rabbi Samuel [*sic*] is now there."[15]

Margaritha's reports of continuing contacts with Jews raise the question of what was the degree of contact that a convert maintained with the Jewish world. Margaritha's comments provide evidence that converts were not completely ostracized. Passing references concerning many converted Jews indicate continuing personal and economic contacts with family, friends, and community.[16] Given that some converts returned to Judaism, the hope of his family that the wayward Jew might leave the faith of heretics never died. Still, conversion created a significant and often irreparable breach. Margaritha argued that physical hardship could drive Jews into the arms of Christianity; Margaritha's constant poverty may have encouraged the Jews to think that disillusioned in his Christian life, he might return to Judaism. Conversely, Margaritha was aware of Christians who converted to Judaism. In *Der gantz Jüdisch glaub,* he mentions meeting three "*Gerim*" (converts) in Hungary.[17] In the translation of the prayer book, he described Jews making converts and sending them to Turkey and Russia. This, he thought, Christian leaders should not tolerate.[18]

In 1536, Margaritha begged the University of Vienna for money, stating that he needed it within two days or he, his four children, and his wife would perish or be reduced to working at the city cemetery.[19] He worried about his family's physical and spiritual welfare. In the *Isaiah Commentary,* he touchingly expressed this:

> [God] knows that all my wants and desires are nothing other than—pray it be God's will—that I, a poor great sinner wish to live here on earth until my unraised children come to understanding and study and learn something through which they may be of use to God and man. Amen.[20]

Margaritha had been a Christian for thirteen years when he wrote this plea. His wife had suffered as much or more than he had. She must have often felt alone. In 1535 their oldest child was nine or ten years old, the child baptized in Augsburg was four years old. We do not know the ages of the other two children. At his death in 1542, Margaritha's oldest child was about seventeen years old. Margaritha did not live to "raise" the others. There is no way of knowing his wife's age, but she was probably several years younger than he. As Jews of good ancestry and with distinguished living relatives, Margaritha's wife and children could have lived better had he not converted.

As Margaritha does not mention his wife's devotion to Christianity or lack thereof, it is impossible to know what she did after his death, if indeed she outlived him. She and the children are not mentioned in a postmortem inventory of his apartment made by the university, which states that children's beds remained in one room. The proceeds of the sale of the resources found in his apartment were used to bury him.[21] The entire family may have perished between 1534 and 1542. One might make too much of Margaritha's desire to live "until my unraised children come to understanding" by inferring that his wife had different goals than he. The financial security of the Jewish world, a world she knew and into which she could easily fit, may have been attractive. Did the family remain Christian after his death? Without documentation, the faith and disposition of his wife and children is mere speculation.

II

Margaritha lived during momentous events in the Protestant Reformation and the Catholic response, yet he makes no mention of the theological debates and the personalities involved in them. His silence is all the more astonishing considering that he taught Hebrew to priests who became Protestants and was in Augsburg during the imperial diet of 1530. *Der gantz Jüdisch glaub* was a best seller in the city at the same time that the Protestant princes presented what became known as the Augsburg Confession. The Confession was a matter of debate between the Catholic theologian Johannes Eck and Lutheran polemicists. Margaritha took no note of the conflict in his writings.

Margaritha's omission of the Reformation from his writings stands at odds with Eliezer Eilburg, who referred to Martin Luther as "the filthy monk," whose influence helped drive his family from their home.[22] Other Jews took note of the Reformation in terms of their own messianic expectations, or with the hope that God would punish Christians for their treatment of the Jews.[23] Indeed, Rabbi Josel of Rosheim, who debated with Margaritha at the Diet, as discussed below, was a witness to the Reformation and made many notes of what he saw. The fact that Margaritha lived in Catholic cities and taught at Catholic schools does not fully account for his seeming indifference to the theological upheaval going on around him.

Even his absolute fidelity to Catholicism is an insufficient explanation for his silence.

Even more puzzling than Margaritha's silence concerning the Reformation is his failure to mention the spectacular failed Messiah, Shlomo Molcho (Diego Pires) (c. 1500–1532). Molcho, born to Marrano parents, "returned" to Judaism. He and his "Elijah," David Reubeni, met with Pope Clement VII. They prophesied and preached Jewish redemption and sought to join together Christians and Jews in an alliance against Turkish advances into Europe. Molcho the Messiah was famous from 1529 until 1532, when Emperor Charles arrested him near Regensburg. Molcho refused to return to Christianity and was executed that year in Mantua.[24] Josel of Rosheim avoided meeting Molcho, but commented on his messianic mission. Why then did Margaritha not take advantage of a golden opportunity to prove once again that the Jews were deluded and that the Messiah had already come?

III

Margaritha's intellectual and polemical activities are much more open to study than are his opinions of the Reformation, Molcho, and the details of his family life. While he was teaching in Augsburg, the publication of *Der gantz Jüdisch glaub* gave him a measure of fame. The success of the first edition (March 1530) made an additional printing necessary within a month. But perhaps an unintended consequence of the book's success was the need for him to defend it in open debate. The book's depiction of Jewish hostility to Christianity created such a stir before the 1530 Diet of Augsburg that Emperor Charles V was impelled to investigate its charges. He ordered Margaritha and a representative of the Jewish community to debate whether it presented a true account of Jewish attitudes and actions. The confrontation took place in Augsburg on June 25, 1530, with Rabbi Josel of Rosheim, the emperor's Jewish advisor, defending the Jews.[25] On Josel's shoulders rested the responsibility to avert the anti-Jewish consequences of a shift in imperial policy should the emperor favor Margaritha's position.

The emperor appointed a commission of two, Dr. Mathias Helldt (Held) and Dr. Brandtners, to judge the proceeding. The three theses to be debated were drawn from *Der gantz Jüdisch glaub:* Was it true that Jews (1) cursed Christians, (2) slandered Jesus in the *Aleinu* prayer, and (3) circumcised (i.e., converted) non-Jews.[26] Given that Margaritha was reporting actual Jewish practices, Josel faced a daunting task. He used traditional rabbinic defenses, referring to the Hebrew Scriptures, accepted by both

Figure 4a. Woodcut from *Der gantz Jüdisch glaub* (Frankfurt am Main, 1544). Author's collection.

sides as authoritative, and the Talmud. Although the Talmud was much maligned by Christians, it was acknowledged as a crucial source for rabbinic opinions, especially about Christianity.

Josel's account of the exchange was brief. He argued from the Pentateuch that Moses forbade cursing the gods of others. The Jews were commanded to love others as themselves; therefore, they were obliged not to hate Christians. He did not report that he had defended the offensive words in the *Aleinu* as coming from Isaiah; they could not, therefore, refer to Christians, but it is likely that he did so. He did state that the Talmud teaches that all pious non-Jews have a place in the world to come equal to Jewish priests.[27] Josel wrote that despite his limitations, "through the grace of God," his presentation was successful, for the judges ruled in his favor.[28]

The defeated Margaritha was imprisoned but released through the efforts of Johann Faber (Fabri), who was Bishop of Vienna from 1530 to 1541.

Figure 4b. Woodcut from *Der gantz Jüdisch glaub* (Frankfurt am Main, 1544). Author's collection.

Margaritha's defeat was a major event in his life, and he made a point of protesting the decision in the second edition of *Der gantz Jüdisch glaub*. While in custody, he must have wondered how a rabbi citing scripture could triumph over the facts of Jewish practice. Upon his release from prison, he was banished from Augsburg. He traveled to Leipzig, perhaps with the help of friends made during his teaching of the Cistercians. He became a Hebrew lecturer there in 1531 and published the second edition of *Der gantz Jüdisch glaub*. On the title page he identified himself as "Hebrew reader of the praiseworthy University and Prince's City Leyptzig."[29] Smarting from the Augsburg debacle, he continued the debate in additions he made to *Der gantz Jüdisch glaub*. In the introduction, he claimed that the Jews cursed the emperor. He prayed that God would save him from the "crafty Jews." He also offered proof that Jews did convert Christians, recounting how a short time before finishing the second edition:

Figure 4c. Woodcut from *Der gantz Jüdisch glaub* (Frankfurt am Main, 1544). Author's collection.

> a born Christian, also not unlearned, testified with his highest oath before the honorable worthy man Master Johannes Stramburck, rector of the praiseworthy University of Leipzig, that through various stratagems, the Jews [tried to] convince him to undergo circumcision and become a Jew.[30]

This testimony confirmed Margaritha's charge.

Later, in his *Isaiah Commentary* (1534), Margaritha also digressed to explain his loss of the Augsburg debate. Josel of Rosheim was "a sly person" who "had made false money." (Is he charging that the judges were bribed?) The Jews defended themselves by the arguments Josel had used, but that defense was a kind of trickery. For such practices, "all Jews should be punished."[31]

For his part, Josel continued to attack Margaritha in deed and in his writings. Most noteworthy, he claimed that Margaritha had not only converted from Judaism to Catholicism but also had apostatized again and become a Lutheran. Margaritha was thus allied with Luther in becoming a thorn in the side of the Jews.[32] Luther did cite Margaritha in *The Jews and*

Their Lies in 1543, but Margaritha was dead by that date. In 1543, Josel managed to obtain a ban on the publication of *Der gantz Jüdisch glaub* and Luther's book in Strassburg.[33] Josel's accusation, if true, would have further discredited Margaritha with the emperor, as was probably intended. However, it is unlikely that Margaritha embraced Lutheranism. Leipzig was a Catholic city during most of the 1530s, and in his attempt to keep it so, Duke Georg expelled Protestants from the university and the city. Among those expelled was Margaritha's former student, Bernhard Ziegler. Lutheran affiliation would have cost Margaritha his position during his tenure at the University of Leipzig (1531–33). He was long gone by 1539, when after Duke Georg's death, his brother and successor Heinrich (the Pious) made the duchy of Saxony, the city, and the university officially Lutheran.[34] (Ziegler returned and was one of the leaders in bringing the Reformation to the university.)

Additional evidence for Margaritha's fidelity to the Catholic Church is his relationship with the Johann Faber, Bishop of Vienna. The bishop had arranged for his release from prison in Augsburg in 1530 and remained his patron. He helped him to obtain a position at the University of Vienna. Faber was a noted campaigner against Protestants and coauthor of the refutation of the Confession of Augsburg. Only Josel's statement, which may have been based on rumor or inference, supports the idea that Margaritha became a Lutheran. What is known about Margaritha's life does not support the idea that he was ever, from the time of his conversion to his death, anything other than a Catholic.

In Leipzig, Margaritha taught publicly at the university and gave private lessons. Maria Diemling discovered that he tutored a student named Huitter in biblical Hebrew.[35] In addition to preparing the second edition of *Der gantz Jüdisch glaub,* which included his printed response to Josel, he composed his *Psalter* and translation of Matthew for publication by the same Leipzigian printer. The *Psalter* marked a shift from the polemics of *Der gantz Jüdisch glaub,* and he appears to have produced it for the dual purpose of providing a Hebrew teaching aid and establishing an academic reputation. The Latin translation of the Hebrew introduction is an indication of his interaction with learned Christian colleagues. He could not personally supply a scholarly, that is, Latin, introduction to the Hebrew text of the Psalms. An anonymous colleague had to translate the words of "our friend Antonius Margarita." Other converted Jews who entered academe, such as Matthew Adrian, Paul Ricci, Immanuel Tremellius, and Johannes Isaak (father of Stephan Isaak), knew Latin beforehand, or were able to gain sufficient proficiency in it to write and lecture.[36] A lecturer who was unable to communicate in Latin and had to rely on others to translate his written words into Latin was at a distinct disadvantage. Lectures were usually held in Latin; scholarly writing required it. Margaritha had only his awkward German with which to communicate with his students and colleagues. Margaritha could not progress academically at a university knowing only Hebrew and German.

Unlike *Der gantz Jüdisch glaub*, the *Psalter* was apparently commercially unsuccessful—few copies exist today and scholars in the sixteenth century do not mention it. It may have had a small press run to begin with and little or no demand for additional copies.[37] Modern scholars have remained relatively unaware of its status as the first printing of Matthew in Hebrew. Margaritha's idiosyncratic Hebrew did not affect his edition of the Psalms, for he duplicated a vocalized text. The *Psalter*'s failure may have been in part related to its place of publication. Leipzig was a Catholic island in an increasingly Protestant area of Germany. Duke Georg banned the sale of Protestant books in the city. Luther's best-selling translation of the Christian scriptures fell under the ban. The Protestants reciprocated by avoiding Leipzig printings. Leipzig booksellers, unable to sell popular Protestant works and trying to operate in a city that Protestant book buyers avoided, complained to the duke about their economic distress.

By the time the *Psalter* appeared on May 4, 1533, Margaritha was probably readying himself to leave Leipzig and assume a position in Vienna. His friend, Bishop Faber, encouraged him to do so. Margaritha's departure was in part related to his state of financial distress in Leipzig. He seems to have lived in near poverty, a condition into which his wife and children had demonstrably sunk by 1534. Vienna offered the hope of making more money and of obtaining a higher academic status at the university. The *Psalter*'s failure, while not the cause of his move, depressed any hope he had of supporting his family with scholarly publications in Leipzig. Neither the *Psalter* nor *Der gantz Jüdisch glaub* could be considered the works of a serious, up-and-coming university lecturer. With his move to Vienna, Margaritha took a position as teacher of Hebrew in a small university; perhaps it would lead to better things. What opportunity he thought awaited him in Vienna that exceeded those in Leipzig is difficult to assess.[38]

IV

The University of Vienna was small and beset with financial, political, and social problems. In 1529 it had fewer than thirty students.[39] It, like the city and citizens, suffered under inflation caused in part by the military threat of the Turks. Vienna also suffered from the plague, which had become endemic in the city. The university, which had never been an important educational institute, had with the Reformation fallen further into decline.

Ferdinand I, Archduke of Austria, King of Hungary and Bohemia, and brother of Emperor Charles, desired to revive and reform the university. As part of his efforts, Hebrew was added to the curriculum.[40] Margaritha accepted the position of Hebrew lecturer at a promised salary of eighty gulden a year and was given a place in the archduke's "Collegium." The collegium was to pay thirty-two gulden of his salary and the university the remainder. Before Ferdinand's reform, the collegium had consisted of seven members. The reform added three new positions in addition to that of Hebraist.[41] The collegium provided only bachelor quarters, so Margaritha had to find a suitable apartment for his family in the city at his own expense.

Margaritha arrived in Vienna probably hopeful of achieving financial security, but certainly at that time impoverished. In his favor was Johann Faber's patronage and his status as the author of two works, one successful and one not.[42] His prospects as a former Jew hired to teach Christians were similar to those outlined years earlier in a letter of Johannes Reuchlin. Reuchlin stated that because of their lack of Latin and formal Christian education, many converts were of marginal use as Hebrew teachers.[43] University teaching also required knowledge of academic procedures and formal grammar. Jews such as Margaritha had learned Hebrew as children by reading and using texts. They had largely picked up grammar from context. They had also heard Hebrew, in the prayers of their fathers, from infancy. They were not grammarians.

Thus did Margaritha begin his career at the University of Vienna. His eighty gulden per annum salary would have ameliorated his financial needs, but the salary was not completely paid. Even had Margaritha been an excellent and desirable academic, the university was regularly unable to meet its financial obligations. Because of this failure, Margaritha was forced to beg the university for funds almost every year until 1539.[44] Just as in Leipzig, he faced continuing insolvency.

On the other hand, Margaritha may have benefited from the university's financial problems. Had the university been solvent it might have replaced him with a university-trained scholar. As it was, Margaritha was plagued by questions concerning his academic competence. In 1536 the university authorities informed the Austrian government that Margaritha was unqualified to teach in Latin.[45] This meant that he could not meet the needs of students, such as the "Hungarian, Bohemian and Italian," who did not speak German.[46] The university officials suggested replacing him with a Minorite (Franciscan) friar. They noted that the Minorite was not a good Hebraist, but that he would teach for free. Margaritha fought for his position and asserted his worth. The archduke did not immediately accede to the university's request to "hire" the unsalaried teacher. Instead, he required it to test both the Minorite and Margaritha.

During the controversy surrounding his competition with the Minorite, Margaritha stated unequivocally that he could not afford to stay in Vienna if he lost his lectureship. He was straightforward in his conferences with the officials investigating his qualifications and status.[47] He played down the relevance of Latin to his work. Latin had not been a condition of his initial employment, and he was a successful teacher whose students did learn Hebrew. The weaknesses of the Minorite served to substantiate Margaritha's claim to competence. The Minorite was found to be less able than Margaritha because he made Hebrew too difficult to learn. Margaritha was retained as lecturer and a member of the archduke's collegium. He was reappointed in 1539 and continued in his position until his death in 1542.[48]

Margaritha believed that he contributed to the university's educational mission; he even believed that he was a superior teacher of Hebrew. In his *Isaiah Commentary,* he discussed Hebrew education among the Jews. He argued that compared to him, other Jews knew little grammar. In fact, many could not correctly understand the technical aspects of his *Isaiah Commentary.* Jews had less grasp of grammar than did Christian students, especially his students. He boasted that the students who studied "one year with me" were superior to Jews in their knowledge of the language.[49] The *Isaiah Commentary* gives some insight into Margaritha's teaching methods and why he felt superior to many other Hebraists and most Jews.

The several sections of the *Isaiah Commentary* illustrate Margaritha's approach to Hebrew study. In the first section, he translated some verses of Isaiah 53 into German. In the second, he presented and attempted to refute three major Jewish commentaries, the Targum Jonathan, Rashi, and David Kimchi. In the third, he stated and refuted arguments from the Talmud. He compared the two Testaments, Old and New, in section four and again examined the Chaldean-Aramaic Targum Jonathan in the fifth section. The work ended with Margaritha's complaint about the outcome of the disputation with Josel at Augsburg.

In the classroom, Margaritha must have used a similar back and forth between scripture, rabbinic texts, and Christian doctrine. This would have mimicked the rabbinic study with which he was familiar from his youth. For example, he compared the Christian understanding of Isaiah with two works critical of Christianity, Rabbi Joseph Kimchi's *Sepher Ha Galui,* a grammatical text with philosophical polemical aspects, and *Sepher Ha Bris,* a critique of Christianity. He likened both books to the *Sepher Nizzahon.* He specifically charged that Kimchi misunderstood the nature of the Messiah and had misconstrued scriptural references to him.[50]

Margaritha was able to use many rabbinic texts and competently translate them, something he probably required of his students. He was versed in the Hebrew Scriptures. He must have used a technique common among the Jews of pitting the opinions of one authority against another and then harmonizing them. He certainly shared his insights about the points made by the authorities with his students. He transmitted (in German) a technical understanding of Hebrew grammar.[51] Margaritha did not necessarily value himself above Christian Hebraists, such as Reuchlin, but he did argue that he could teach at a university level. His *Isaiah Commentary* supported this contention. Margaritha's attack on the weakness in technical Hebrew of Jewish hermeneutics clearly referred to average Jews, not members of rabbinic families and serious scholars; Margaritha had learned grammar, as did other well-trained Jews. Both Jews and Christians studied Rabbi David Kimchi's grammatical text, the *Book of Roots.* Margaritha, as the son of a rabbi, looked down on less-educated Jews. This condescension probably extended to incompetent Hebrew-teaching Jewish converts. These ignorant Jews angered him; not only did they compete for students, but also their poor understanding of Hebrew damaged the reputation of all Jewish Hebraists.

V

While in Vienna, Margaritha composed at least two and perhaps as many as five works, as well as the *Isaiah Commentary. A Brief Account and Indication of Where the Christian Ceremony of the Ass of Comfort Is Found in the Two Testaments* was published in 1541. Margaritha's printed pamphlet, "Brief Interpretation of the Word Halleluia," is undated. Three lost, unpublished works of unknown content were mentioned in the eighteenth century.[52] In *Der gantz Jüdisch glaub,* Margaritha had referred to several proposed studies of Jews and usury, and, in his defense of his teaching position in 1539, he stated that he had a work on the Trinity ready for publication.[53] The three texts published in Vienna evince a continuing preoccupation with proving Christianity and refuting Judaism. The most scholarly, and the longest, was the *Isaiah Commentary.* Its linguistic analysis and textual criticism would have qualified it as an academic achievement had it been written in Latin rather than in German. Unfortunately for Margaritha's scholarly pretensions, it could be regarded as popular theology rather than as scholarship.

Margaritha's *Brief Account . . . of the Ass of Comfort* dealt with the prophecy that the Messiah would enter Jerusalem on such an animal. Zechariah 9:9 prophesied:

Rejoice greatly, O daughter of Zion,
Shout, O daughter of Jerusalem;
Behold, thy king cometh unto thee,
He is triumphant, and victorious,
Lowly, and riding upon an ass,
Even upon a colt the foal of an ass.

The Gospel of Matthew tells the story of Jesus's fulfillment of the prophecy. Before entering Jerusalem, Jesus dispatched two of his disciples to retrieve an ass and its colt. "All this was done, that it might be fulfilled which was spoken by the prophet: Tell ye the daughter of Sion, Behold, thy King cometh unto thee, meek, and sitting upon an ass, and a colt the foal of an ass" (Matthew 21:4–5). Jesus then entered Jerusalem to the shouts of the multitude.

Margaritha found this episode such a clear fulfillment of one of the signs of the Messiah that as a Hebraist at the "praiseworthy University of Vienna," he felt compelled to write against the blind and stiff-necked Jews, who did not acknowledge it. He desired that God give the Holy Ghost to the Jews and their scholars (his father, brothers, and uncles?), to inspire them, so that their eyes would open to the truth.

Another motivation for explicating the Ass of Comfort prophesies was to counter the way Jews and Turks used the scriptures. Unbelievers ridiculed Christian festivals, such as the celebration of Jesus's entry into Jerusalem (Margaritha called it the "Ass Celebration") and the way Christians made pictures of the ass. According to Margaritha, the Jews' ridicule presented only a minor theological problem, but the attitude of the Turks was both a theological and an existential threat.

Margaritha discussed how Rashi had taught that Jesus did not fulfill the conditions for the triumphant Messiah. Margaritha argued that, contra Rashi, the verses in Zechariah clearly referred to Jesus. The Christian ceremonies and the art commemorating Jesus's entrance into Jerusalem before his crucifixion were proper and based in scripture. Margaritha claimed he knew that to be the case, because the Holy Ghost had illuminated him. He had turned from Jewish errors and understood the significance of the ass. The Jews, enmeshed in their lies, joked that when the Messiah arrived in Jerusalem, he would ride on an ass and be accompanied by the Jews, but the Christians would sit on the ass's tail.[54] Such crude humor was a secret affront to Christians, which Margaritha exposed.

In the midst of his discussion of the ass, Margaritha returned to the Jewish idea of two Messiahs, which he had refuted in *Der gantz Jüdisch glaub.* Margaritha attacked as foolish the Jewish belief that there would be

Der gantz Jüdisch glaub
mit sampt eyner gründtlichenn
vnd warhafftigen anzeygunge/ aller satzungen/ Cere-
monien/ gebetten/ heymliche vnd öffentliche gebreüch/ deren sich die
Juden halten/ durch das gantz Jar/ mit schönen vnnd gegründten
Argumenten wider jren glauben/ durch Anthonium Margaritham Hebreyschen Leser/ der löblichen Vniuersitet vnd
Fürstlichen Stat Leyptzigk/ beschryben vnd
an tag gegeben.

Durch jn selbst/gemehrt vnd gebessert/M.D.XXXI.

Figure 5. Title page from *Der gantz Jüdisch glaub* (1530 and 1531). Courtesy of Klau Library, Hebrew Union College–Jewish Institute of Religion compared to 1544 printing, author's collection.

Der gantz Jüdisch
Glaub.
Mit sampt einer gründ
lichen vnd warhafftigen anzeigunge/
aller satzungen/Ceremonië/gebetten/heymliche vnd
öffentliche gebreüch/derë sich die Juden halte/durch
das gantz Jar/mit schönen vnnd gegründten Argu
menten wider jren glauben/durch Anthonium
Margaritham Hebreischen Leser/der
löblichen Vniuersitet vnnd Fürst
lichen Statt Leypzigk/be
schriben vnnd an tag
geben.
Getruckt zů Franckfurt am Mayn.
M. D. XLIIII.

Figure 5. Title page from *Der gantz Jüdisch glaub* (1530 and 1531). Courtesy of Klau Library, Hebrew Union College–Jewish Institute of Religion compared to 1544 printing, author's collection.

two Messiahs. The Messiah ben Joseph, the military leader and ultimate casualty, was imaginary, without basis in scripture. Jesus, however, as a descendant of Judah, qualified as the Messiah ben Judah.

More to the point of the theme was the fact that Rashi identified the ass of the Messiah with the ass used by Abraham on his journey to sacrifice

Isaac. Margaritha agreed that the ass of Isaac's binding was the animal that brought Jesus into the city for his sacrifice. The offering of Isaac foreshadowed the offering of Jesus Christ. Those who understood that truth did not mock ceremonies commemorating such a holy event.

Margaritha's exposition of the "Ass of Comfort" hardly furthered his reputation as a scholar. He merely repeated the scriptures and interpretations already well known to Christians. The Jewish knowledge that he imparted consisted of a bad joke and a smattering of Rashi's commentary. His reasons for choosing to publish on this topic are unclear, but undoubtedly he hoped to augment his finances. The pamphlet also shows his continuing desire to prove his Christian bona fides. Written a year before his death, it is a testimonial of his faith, his rejection of Judaism, and his hope for the conversion of Jews.

Margaritha's desire for security in the form of patronage was clearly behind his undated and very brief discourse on the word *Halleluia.* He dedicated it to Arnold von Bruck, the "capelmaister" of King Ferdinand, that is, Archduke Ferdinand of Austria, King of Hungary and Bohemia. This was appropriate, for "halleluia" is a musical or poetic word. Margaritha noted that the word is used in connection with musical instruments in Kings, Nehemiah, and the Psalms. King David used "halleluia" in many of his psalms. Margaritha pointed out that psalms beginning "myssmor Ladavid" (Song of David) were those written by the king. He also discussed similar songs found in the New Testament. In I Corinthians 14, Paul made the statement, "I will inform my brothers of your name and they will sing your praise in the midst of the congregation." Only after situating the word in its musical context did Margaritha translate "Alleluia (Halleluia)." The word is a compound of *Hallelu* "praise" and *jah* "God." He asserted that *Jah* specifically referred to God the Son. *Jah* was a two-letter part of the Tetragrammaton, the full four-letter name for God the Father, the Creator. Wanting all peoples to acknowledge God, David, who had been moved by the spirit of God, used the word *Halleluia*in his psalms. This use showed that David understood the Trinity. A correct understanding of the Tetragrammaton and its parts would lead the Jews to Christianity. Margaritha testified that the Jewish kabbalists were aware of the Trinitarian meaning of the Tetragrammaton, and that simple Jews unknowingly sing of the Trinity on the Sabbath and at weddings when they say *Halleluia.* They would be led to Christianity if they understood that *Halleluia* was a manifestation of the holy four-letter name, and its full meaning was that all souls praise Christ (*jah*).[55]

What, if any, patronage Margaritha received from Arnold von Bruck is unknown. The pamphlet, like the *Brief Account,* added nothing to his scholarly credentials. The meaning of *Halleluia* was well known. Margaritha's commentary is a further reflection of the author's preoccupation with

Christian Messianism. He believed that the Hebrew language itself testified to the truth of the Christian Messiah. Before Jesus, great Jewish leaders, including David, understood who the Messiah would be, that is, God. Ancient Jews had a clear understanding of the Tetragrammaton, and used its parts in prophecy. Only after Jesus did the rabbis obscure traditional texts. Margaritha thanked God, yet again, in print for his own recognition of the true Messiah and his conversion to Christianity.

Margaritha's Jewish birth and education largely defined his Christianity. He focused on the fact that Jesus was the Messiah. In his writings he used the tools of Hebrew, Jewish commentaries, and scriptures, learned from his father and other Jewish teachers. His Jewish training allowed him to prove the Christian case to his own satisfaction. With the possible exception of his defense of the ass pictures, Margaritha did not involve himself with the issues that separated Protestants from Catholics. Works or grace, tradition or the plain meaning of scripture, Luther versus Rome, transubstantiation or consubstantiation, none seemed to concern him. At least he did not write about them. He remained to a degree a Jewish stranger, focused on the great Jewish question of the coming of the Messiah, in an increasingly fractured Christian world.

Conclusion

If Margaritha were born in the 1490s, as seems most likely, he spent most of his life as a Jew. His conversion in 1521 and his death in 1542 meant that he spent about twenty-one years as a Christian. Given the longevity of his father and grandfather, his death was probably premature, caused by illness such as the plague outbreak of February 1542, which caused a short-term closure of the University of Vienna.[56] It was as a Christian convert that Margaritha made his mark on the German-speaking world. His efforts to follow his family's scholarly tradition determined his work as a Hebrew teacher and author of books interpreting the Jewish world for Christians. Preparation for rabbinic life did not qualify him to be a Christian scholar. Without the benefit of a formal Christian education, he was destined to be a peripheral figure in university and intellectual life. His earning potential was extremely limited.

The poverty in which he and his family lived brought the two parts of his life into focus. As a member of a prominent rabbinic family, he had lived well. That former economic status tempted him to return to Judaism. The Jews offered to support him if he returned. He was disappointed that they gave him and his family no help while he remained a Christian. Margaritha framed his situation in terms of the life of Paul. Like Paul, Margaritha chose to follow the path to spiritual certainty, rather than the road to worldly comfort. The themes of scholarship, family, and poverty that marked his life and writings are apparent in the final significant document concerning him, the inventory of his possessions at death.[57]

At his death, Margaritha lived in a house in the "back of Bächerstrasse in the alley that leads to the Holy Cross place." He and his family occupied two rooms, a living room and a bedroom. The living room was set up for cooking. There was a table where Margaritha worked. It was fitted with a drawer in which he kept correspondence. Next to a trunk was a place to sleep. The room also contained a bookcase. The second room, a bedroom, was fitted with beds and two cribs (probably sleeping places for the older children). There were sundry lamps, pots, pans, and clothing, all well used. The bedding was "poorly filled (*fünf Pöllster, aberübellgefüllt*)."

The most valuable listed items were twenty-three large books in Hebrew and Latin, bound in leather and vellum. He also left twelve small books in Hebrew, German, and Latin, also bound in leather and vellum. Such a collection was valuable, and Margaritha must have struggled to purchase them. No titles are given; Masters Hansen Sanndtler and Leonhardter Wirtinnger Sindicii, the university's agents, recorded only quantities. One can assume that copies of Margaritha's own works were among the books. Perhaps he had each edition (1530, 1531) of the *Der gantz Jüdisch glaub* as well as his non–best sellers. It seems reasonable that he also retained his old prayer book and the rabbinic commentaries, which he had cited in the *Isaiah Commentary.* He might well have owned a Vulgate Bible and some German translations. These conjectures are based upon references in his writings. The sale of such assets paid Margaritha's burial expenses.

The final accounting of the contents of the apartment was an obligation the university owed to its lecturer. It reveals the truth of Margaritha's statements about his Christian life. His possessions were few, worn, and with the exception perhaps of his books, of little value. He died in his forties or early fifties. The whereabouts of his wife and children, then and later, are unknown. Was he ill among his books and children's beds, dying without anyone to take care of him? His Jewish father, brothers, and uncles were in Prague, Cracow, and Italy. He bragged about their status in the Jewish community, yet his life's mission had been to expose rabbinism and its unnecessary burdens. Had his steadfastness in that mission finally totally alienated them?

Margaritha envisioned himself as someone who accepted the freedom of Christianity and its concomitant burden of financial want. He rejected the spiritual prison of Judaism with its attendant physical comforts. Whatever spiritual joy he experienced in accepting the "Messiah Who Has Been Sent" was attended with sacrifice in this world.

Margaritha had hoped to inspire his Jewish brothers and sisters of the flesh to embrace Christianity. He also hoped to see his children grown and serving God. Neither hope was fulfilled. His works, it seems, did not lead many, if any, Jews to convert. His early death frustrated his wish to see all his children grown. From the beginning of his Christian life to its end he was left only with hope. In his own words, his "hope [is] in the Messiah who has been sent." That Messiah would transcend this earthly world and make things right in the world to come.

The Christian Margaritha was assured of salvation, but what about his Jewish self? In *Der gantz Jüdisch glaub,* he described Moses Wolf as a traitor, a "mosser (מוסר)"[58] Josel of Rosheim and other Jews took a similar view of Margaritha. He was a traitor and a heretic who attacked God's people. His family maintained some contact and desired his return. Perhaps their attitude was similar to that of Rabbi Meir toward his apostate teacher Elisha ben Abuyah. The Talmudic story goes:

> After some time Elisha b. Abuyah was taken ill, and they came and told R. Meir, "Elisha your master is sick." He went to him [Elisha] and appealed to him, "Return in penitence." He [Elisha] said to him, "Will they accept me after all this?" He [Meir] responded, "Is it not written, *Thou turnest man to contrition* (Ps. xc, 3), even when one's life is crushed." At that, Elisha b. Abuyah burst into tears and died. And R. Meir rejoiced and said, "It appears that my master passed away in the midst of repentance." And when they buried him, fire came to consume his grave.[59]

The story was well known and may have encouraged Jews who had lost family members to conversion. Margaritha's family knew that repentance could save Anthonius, even at the moment of death. For his part, Margaritha could anticipate a better existence after death, as either a Christian or a Jew, than he had known in his difficult earthly life.

Appendix A

Margaritha's Refutation of the Jewish Faith

Margaritha appended his Refutation of Judaism to the end of *Der gantz Jüdisch glaub,* a placement that may indicate that it was composed somewhat later than the rest of the work. Certainly he considered the ethnography and prayer book translation that preceded it as preparation for its arguments and conclusions. He poured his knowledge, ability to argue, and deep religious emotions into the Refutation, an apologia for rejecting the faith of his fathers. Although his rambling style and organization might blunt Margaritha's points, these rhetorical characteristics reveal the essential Anthonius, with his stream of consciousness, almost Talmudic, approach to writing. The Refutation focuses on Messianism and rabbinic perfidy in obscuring the convergence of true Judaism with Christianity. This approach agreed with Margaritha's status as both a knowledgeable Jew and a Christian. It reveals that his intellectual, spiritual, and psychological situation was at a relatively early point of integration. The Refutation, therefore, is usefully understood in light of the long ongoing dispute between Christians and Jews on the issues of hermeneutics and the Messiah.

The analysis of Margaritha's arguments can be approached in several ways. *Der gantz Jüdisch glaub* and the Refutation are part of the tradition of anti-Jewish polemic by converts and specifically by German converts in the sixteenth century, as noted above. Carben and Pfefferkorn presented pictures of Judaism and argued in essentially similar ways, even using the same words. Comparing and contrasting the three converts was useful in the body of this biography of Margaritha, but for the purposes of this appendix, with its translation of the Refutation, another approach may serve better to clarify Margaritha's position. The Refutation deals with many of the same crucial issues as were debated in the disputations between rabbis and Christian theologians over the centuries. The accounts of the events in Tortosa, Spain, in 1413–14 seem especially relevant.[1] It is unknowable whether Margaritha knew about the Tortosa disputation. The questions debated there went to the essence of the Jewish and Christian doctrines of the Messiah. As a Jew, Margaritha was taught the Jewish position; as a Christian, he accepted the Catholic teaching and opposed it to the Jewish. Many of his arguments follow those made at Tortosa.

The central issue at Tortosa was whether the Messiah had come. The convert Joshua Halorki (Geronimo de Santa Fe) convinced Pope Benedict XIII that he could prove to the Jews that the Messiah had come. The pope said, "Maestre Geronimo said that he wished to prove that the Messiah had come, and this from your own Talmud . . . your Torah was once true but was abolished"[2] The arguments Geronimo made were taken from scripture, Midrash (the nonlegal discussions and stories in the Talmud and homiletic literature), and other traditional Jewish texts.

A major scriptural argument Christians often used was found in Genesis 49:10, "The scepter shall not depart from Judah nor the ruler's staff from between his feet until Shiloh comes." Obviously, the scepter and ruler's staff had departed from the Jews, for they lived without a king and were scattered throughout the world. "Shiloh," the Messiah, therefore, must have come.

Geronimo invoked a Talmudic passage, *Sanhedrin* 97a, to the effect that the world would last six thousand years; two thousand of chaos, two thousand of Torah, and two thousand of the Messiah. This view led to an analysis of Jewish and world history that confirmed that the Messiah would come at about the time Jesus had been born.

The defending rabbis noted that the Talmud gave no specific time as to when during the final two thousand years the Messiah would actually be present. They also argued that the Shiloh passage was ambiguous.

Geronimo claimed that the Jews not only misunderstood their scriptures but also had falsified the Talmud. He charged that the rabbis, in order to hide the fact that the Messiah had come, after the time of Jesus, edited the Talmud. This argument was reported in a Christian account of the dispute:

> [It] behooves you to know how this teaching, called the Talmud among the Jews, took root when that tribe or society of rabbis named the Pharisees, who were in the time of the Second Temple, as can be plainly shown, through their adverse fortune, or rather obstinacy, did not acknowledge the true Messiah who then came, but had groundless hate for him, despite the fact that they witnessed great miracles, which were done every day in his name.[3]

The concept of Messiah dominated all medieval Christian-Jewish debates, including that at Tortosa. It is fascinating to observe that often the challenged Jewish scholar defended the Jewish position by declaring that the concept of the Messiah was a nonessential doctrine of Judaism. Nachmanides (Rabbi Moses ben Nachman) stressed this in the debate at Barcelona in 1263, as is recorded in his account of the arguments, *Vikuah* (Disputation). He tells how he answered his interlocutor, the convert Fray Paul (Dominican Friar Pablo Christiani), and addressed King James of Aragon.

> However, I spoke myself: "My lord King, hear me. The Messiah is not fundamental to our religion. Why, you are worth more to me than the Messiah! You are a king, and he is a king. You are a Gentile king, and he is a Jewish king; for the Messiah is only a king of flesh and blood like you. When I serve my Creator in your territory in exile and in affliction and servitude and reproach of the peoples who 'reproach us continually,' my reward is great. For I am offering a sacrifice to God from my body, by which I shall be found more and more worthy of the life of the world to come. But when there will be a king of Israel of my religion ruling over all the peoples, and there will be no choice for me but to remain in the Jewish religion, my reward will not be so great."[4]

Nachmanides's understanding of the role of the Messiah in Judaism was explicitly shared by Rabbi Joseph Albo, who participated at Tortosa but left before the disputation ended. He wrote about the nonfundamental role of the Messiah to Judaism in his *Sefer Ikkarim* (Book of fundamentals). The *Sefer Ikkarim* was a popular work, in manuscript and print, that Soncino first printed in 1485. It deals with almost all of the issues broached at Tortosa as well as others touching on Christian-Jewish disagreements. Because it had been printed, *Sefer Ikkarim* was more easily available as a source for Jewish arguments than was Mühlhausen's *Sefer Nizzachon.*

With regard to the Messiah, Albo stated his role in the Jewish faith succinctly:

> Each who believes in the teachings of Moses is obliged to believe that the Messiah will come. . . . It is specifically commanded in the Pentateuch to believe the words of the prophets, "You should hear him (Deut. 18:15)" and the prophets foretell the coming of the Messiah. So it is clear that one who does not believe in the Messiah denies the words of the prophets and transgresses a commandment. All agree [however] the true belief in the Messiah is not a fundamental [belief of Judaism].[5]

Rabbinic families, such as the Margoleses, were certainly aware of the issues of conflict between Christianity and Judaism. Christian beliefs and Jewish refutations were simply a part of their world. The various disputations of Christians with great rabbis were at least part of folklore. Communal rabbis encountered Christian beliefs and hostilities often enough. The bread controversies in Regensburg had theological as well as social components. The Margoleses seem to have owned or had access to a manuscript of Mühlhausen's *Sefer Nizzachon.* It is likely that they also had a copy of Albo's *Sefer Ikkarim.* The result of the long tradition of Christian-Jewish "dialogue" was that Anthonius Margaritha would have known the Jewish arguments against Christianity. In becoming a Christian, he chose to embrace the Christian position, adopting its questions, theology, and scriptural-Talmudic-historical interpretations.

The Refutation in *Der gantz Jüdisch glaub* is a polemical work that reveals something of what Margaritha had been taught and believed as a Jew from the perspective of what he had become as a Christian. It provides a picture of Margaritha's psychology. Although primarily a Christian attack on Judaism, it is also valuable as a document containing a record of what Jews believed about their own beleaguered faith.

When read from the above perspective, the Refutation gains coherence and meaning. Margaritha's difficulties with German and his stream-of-consciousness style, however, still present problems. The unifying theme is Margaritha's faith in Jesus as the Messiah. He wrote the Refutation to disabuse the Jews from their hope in salvation "through their unknown Messiah" and their belief that the words of the prophets were yet to be fulfilled. Margaritha also seems to have addressed the status of Messianic belief in Judaism, challenging the position of Maimonides, Nachmanides, and Albo.

> Now, however, Moses, along with all other prophets, wrote about such a Messiah and redeemer. If you were shown that such a Messiah no longer will nor can come, you must then consider that there is no God who spoke with Moses and the prophets, rather that they made it all up and that the entire law is false. Heaven forefend. Or you must think

> that God himself spoke orally with Moses and the prophets; and that everything concerning a savior and Messiah was spoken and written from the mouth and spirit of God. If that same Messiah has not come nor will come is without a doubt because he has already come.[6]

Margaritha reasoned that the Jews, as did other peoples, must surely have known about Jesus and his miracles. "All peoples acknowledge and testify about many great miracles from the crucified Messiah. Indeed, our fathers themselves wrote much about his miraculous works." These historical facts were not passed on in Jewish texts. In part, there was a cover-up because, "Him our fathers crucified through the blindness of their sins, that the scriptures were fulfilled which announced such a crucifixion." Also, even though, "the Gospel became fashionable and many Jews accepted it, [the rabbis] recognized the need to interpret the scriptures so evilly that thereby the rest of the Jews would be retained."

He gave an example from the Talmudic tractate *Succoth* of the early rabbinic misinterpretation of the scriptures:

> They turn to the last chapter in the book [concerned with] a Messiah who will be a son of Joseph, who will be slain in the battle of Gog-megog. There one sees blindness compounding blindness. They write a great deal in this passage about their imagined Messiah and the destruction of the evil spirit, which they call the *gezer hora* יצר הרע . . . . [W]hen the Messiah will see that the Messiah son of Joseph is smitten and dies, the Messiah son of David will speak before the presence of God רובנה של עולם [*sic*] *Rabono schel olam*, "O Master of the World, I desire from you but life."

Margaritha rejected the nonbiblical concept of two Messiahs, seeing it as a rabbinic reshaping of Judaism made after the composition and promulgation of the Christian Gospels.

> Ask the Jews how they came to [the idea] of the Messiah, son of Joseph—none can answer. I say, as I have shown before, that these [ideas] were written after Christ's birth, and they stole and adapted them from the Gospel, hoping to blind the Jews and to draw them away from the Christian faith.

Margaritha gave another example of the rabbinical distortion of the truth, the creation of the *Toldoth Jesu*,[7] a work clearly formulated to counter the Gospels. Its narrative presented a pseudohistory of Jesus.

> They say that Mary, the eternally pure, chaste virgin, through dishonor and adultery became pregnant, and also that she foolishly received this Christ from a carpenter or smith, and that Christ was born of such an adultery.

In another way, Margaritha also challenged the teaching that the Messiah was not an essential doctrine of Judaism. Before the rabbis, Margaritha wrote in adopting a Christian position, the Hebrew Scriptures had been pure, but the rabbinic lies had distorted their message. The rabbinic position concerning the nonessential nature of the Messiah denied the message of Isaiah and could be easily refuted by the Christians.

> One should understand, therefore, that when the time of redemption comes, [God] will not restrain, but rather hasten it. It follows, therefore, that the time for such redemption is determined and that no sin can stand in its way. The Jews answer this argument, saying, "What does it matter if I were already told that no Messiah is coming? I would nevertheless not apostatize from my one true God and take up the Christian belief." Answer: "It is all well and good that you, Jew, believe in the One God. You do this through the law God gave and spoke orally to Moses, which was established with many marvelous signs, as many peoples testified. Now, however, Moses, along with all other prophets, wrote about such a Messiah and redeemer."

Margaritha ignored the distinction between an essential doctrine of faith and a belief required by the prophets. He equated rabbinic doctrinal minimalism with a denial of the Messiah. By his argument, this rabbinic attitude was tantamount to rejecting Moses and the prophets. The scriptures testify to the existence of the Messiah, and the Jews must accept that truth rather than rely on rabbinic dissembling.

> If you were shown that such a Messiah no longer will nor can come, you must then consider that there is no God who spoke with Moses and the prophets, rather that they made it all up and that the entire law is false.

The medieval debates between Christians and Jews had dealt with the question of whether or not the promised Messiah had already come. Margaritha, in the tradition of the convert-disputants, invoked Jewish texts to prove that the time for the Messiah's coming had passed. If the time had passed and the prophets did not lie, the Messiah must have come. On the question of whether or not the time for the Messiah's coming had passed, the prophet Daniel provided irrefutable evidence of when the Messiah would arrive.

> The third witness is Daniel in the 9th chapter [v. 24] of his book: "Seventy weeks will be enough to complete, fulfill, and remove the misdeeds and sins from upon your people and the holy city and to bring eternal righteousness and seal and fulfill the oracles of the prophets." Therefore, it is certain that Christ our Savior has come and established the kingdom. This was decreed by prophecy, and no prophet is any more found among the Jews. Understand that the 70 weeks means 70 times 7 years or 490. "70 weeks" mentioned in the text means 70 free years, because after 6 years there was a free year [*shmitah*], such as after 6 work days there is a Sabbath, then the week is over. After the free year, a week of years is over, as the learned well know. No Jew can deny this.

Margaritha argued that prophecy and history revealed that at the time of the destruction of the second temple, because the Jews had rejected the Messiah, God had cast them off. Their want of secular or spiritual power, priests or prophets, was proof of their fallen state. Margaritha does not cite Genesis 49, the scepter prophecy, in his Refutation, but in the ethnographic part of *Der gantz Jüdisch glaub,* he argued that the Jewish loss of political autonomy proved that the Messiah had already come:

> Also, during the Babylonian captivity, they had the law, priests, and prophets with them, such as Daniel, Nehemiah, Ezra, Haggai, Zechariah, [and] Malachi. So one cannot point to an end to the second captivity, and will never know one. They still have no law, priests, nor prophets, also no sovereignty, for more than 1500 years. The Jewish commentators themselves acknowledge and write that the aforementioned passage and scripture refers to the destruction of the second temple.

Margaritha's knowledge of Jewish and Christian proof texts, beliefs, and the continuing arguments about the Messiah allowed him to construct a polemic designed to prove not only that the Messiah had come but also that the early rabbis had hidden that truth from the Jews. The Refutation is, in spite of its shortcomings, a revealing document, corresponding to a report of a Christian-Jewish disputation. The venue of the debate, however, was within Margaritha's life and mind. He was genuinely moved by the fact that "God has cast off the Jews in manifold ways." As a true descendant of Abraham, he had found the Messiah in Jesus, another true descendant of the patriarch. He wished that other Jews of Abraham's seed would read *Der gantz Jüdisch glaub.* If they were to do so, they would understand that

> God wants that all Jews think about these and similar things and read the Talmud [correctly]. So will God, without a doubt, open the eyes of many and pull them out of the grave curse in Deut 28. Those who do not must remain eternally stuck therein.

Deuteronomy 28:15–68 promises that Israel will be cursed if it does not obey God, and verses 63–64 specifically predict that the sinful people will be expelled from the land and dispersed throughout the world.

In translating the Refutation, I have tried to retain something of Margaritha's infelicitous style, even at the expense of English style. Some of his thoughts required that I make an interpretation of the awkward German. I hope the translation conveys a feeling of Margaritha's prose. He admitted that he missed the art of German rhetoric. I have taken the liberty of inserting punctuation marks and breaking the text into paragraphs where I thought it would be helpful for a reader attempting to follow Margaritha's argument. For those who wish to consult the Refutation in its original German, I have provided a reproduction of the pages from my copy of the Frankfurt printing of 1544. It is one of the most pristine copies I have seen, allowing clear reproductions to be made. It also contains the material added to the Refutation in the second edition. The spelling is somewhat improved over the 1530 and 1531 texts, where forms such as "prauch" were used instead of "brauch."

The Refutation (Wider den gantzenglauben der Juden)

At the end and close of this little book, I will set forth certain natural and scriptural reasons against the entire belief of the Jews. Their entire belief and hope is that God will still redeem them through their unknown Messiah and that he will be a fortunate and warlike man. [The Jews] themselves don't know how and in what personage the Messiah will rule. For if ten of their writers write of such a Messiah, none writes [the same] as another. I will show here a little about how the poor, simple Jews are so confused by Talmudists and turned from Christ, and how they have many comforting scriptures that lead to their two imaginary Messiahs. It happened that when the Gospel became fashionable and many Jews accepted it, [the rabbis] recognized the need to interpret the scriptures so evilly that thereby the rest of the Jews would be retained.

To begin, [the Jews] have the salutary words of Zachar. 12[:12] where he says, "Look to me whom you pierced." Similarly, "and the Earth will mourn, each and every family individually." These scriptures were indeed certainly perfectly fulfilled in Christ. They turn to the last chapter in the book of *Laub* [Talmud *Sukkah* 52a] [*Lauberhüte* in later printings], which concerns a Messiah who will be a son of Joseph, who will be slain in the battle of Gogmegog. There one sees blindness compounding blindness. They write a great deal in this passage about their imaginary Messiah and the destruction of the evil spirit, which they call the *gezer hora* יצר הרע. They also write there among other things about the advent of the Messiah, son of David, how God will speak to him, "Ask me, I shall give you" and all the things in the noble scripture Psalm 2: "Ask me, I shall give you the heathens as an inheritance." And meanwhile, when the Messiah will see that the Messiah son of Joseph is smitten and dies, the Messiah son of David will speak before the presence of God רובנה של עולם [*sic*] *Rabono schel olam,* "O Master of the World, I desire from you but life." God will say to him, "I will give you eternal life which you have not desired," for David your father prophesied already about you as [is] written in Psalm 21[:4]: "He desired life from you and you gave him long and endless days." Now see, everyone, how they have deliberately bent and twisted the Holy Scriptures so that the verses are turned forcefully from Christ to their imagery Messiah! Ask the Jews how they came to [the idea] of the Messiah, son of Joseph—none can answer. I say, as I have shown before, that these [ideas] were written after Christ's birth, and they stole and adapted them from the Gospel, hoping to blind the Jews and to draw them away from the Christian faith.

In sum, Isaiah 59 must be fulfilled, where, among other things, he says, "They will be as the blind groping at the wall." There are many similar passages, the purpose of which is to note well that all the prophets write of the true and correct Messiah, that he will be poor, humble, and insignificant. And, above all, his strength will be spiritual, and he will remove all men's sins by his suffering and death. Meanwhile, such a one has come who completely fulfilled his office, whom their fathers, through the blindness of their sins, rejected, disdained, and, indeed, crucified. Therefore, they can write nothing fundamental or genuine about their imaginary, warrior Messiah.

Now I will show present-day Jews briefly about the advent of the true, correct Messiah, that he has already come. First, I will prove on the basis of reason and nature that all peoples and nations that sustain wisdom believe and acknowledge that God spoke to Moses and other prophets. And also that through them, were done many miraculous signs. In like manner, the same peoples and nations, indeed the Jews themselves, know, believe and acknowledge the miraculous deeds that Christ and his apostles did.

Why shouldn't I also believe and keep the Gospel of Christ as well as the Law of Moses, considering that Moses himself and all the prophets testified and gave signs of such a Christ. And therefore, all nations acknowledge that such signs occurred through Christ as the prophets previously had written about him. After all this, all nations, including many Jews, came and accepted his Gospel and glory, which has now lasted longer than the law and sovereignty of the Jews. If the Gospel of Christ were an idolatrous and fictitious thing [constructed by] the apostles, as the blind Jews believe, say, and write in the above-mentioned booklet *Toldoth Jesu* (The history of Jesus), how could it remain and stand? Rather should it not have collapsed long since, like all other imaginary idolatries? That this has not occurred is clear. Because of all these things, the blind Jews should open their hearts and eyes. Instead, the Jews write and say that their sins hinder the advent of their Messiah and sustain the spurious belief of the Christians. This cannot be for many reasons. First, how can God be a righteous judge and allow a vain religion to remain so long in the whole world on account of the sins of a handful of Jews? Second, the Jews comment on the last verse of Isaiah 60, where he says, "I am God, I will hasten you in your time." One should understand, therefore, that when the time of redemption comes, [God] will not restrain, but rather hasten it. It follows, therefore, that the time for such redemption is determined and that no sin can stand in its way. The Jews answer this argument, saying, "What does it matter if I were already told that no Messiah is coming? I would nevertheless not apostatize from my one true God and take up the Christian belief." Answer: "It is all well and good that you, Jew, believe in the One God. You do this through the law God gave and spoke orally to Moses, which was established with many marvelous signs, as many peoples testified. Now, however, Moses, along with all other prophets, wrote about such a Messiah and redeemer. If you were shown that such a Messiah no longer will nor can come, you must then consider that there is no God who spoke with Moses and the prophets, rather that they made it all up and that the entire law is false, heaven forefend. Or you must think that God himself spoke orally with Moses and the prophets, and that everything concerning a savior and Messiah was spoken and written from the mouth and spirit of God. If that same Messiah has not come nor will come, it is without a doubt because he has already come. [It is] he whom our fathers crucified through the blindness of their sins, so that the scriptures were fulfilled which announced such a crucifixion. All peoples acknowledge and testify to many great miracles by the crucified Messiah. Indeed, our fathers themselves write much about his miraculous works. Therefore, I will accept such a Messiah with thankful praise and not say that there is no God and that all scripture is false and made up." If a Jew would rather say that it is better that the Messiah has yet to come, as they now believe and hope, to this I say, "God is a truly righteous judge and our fathers openly transgressed the entire law in first temple times. They did all the sins and blasphemies of which man can think—overflowing abominations. Indeed, they slew the pious prophets. For all of this, God punished them with no more than seventy years in Babylon; they were left with prophets and priests. After seventy years, he placed them in their land again with their goods and possessions, and the temple was rebuilt.

"Your fathers of the second temple [period], in whom one cannot find so many sins as those who slew the prophets, were not as idolatrous; yet God punished them so severely that they have had neither priests nor prophets, or sovereignty for more than 1,500 years. They are also abominable, offensive, and an example to all peoples (Deut. 28.) Now, you, Jew, must either acknowledge that God is an unrighteous judge, heaven forefend, or you must confess that your fathers of the second temple committed a sin greater than all these other sins, namely the great, grave, insufferable sin. Your fathers stumbled so hard on this cornerstone and they have scorned and mocked it."

About this, David said in Psalm 118[:22], "The stone the builders rejected has become the chief cornerstone." This stone has become a cause of your stumbling, as Isaiah said in c. 8[:14], "And he will be a holiness and a stumbling block and a rock of stumbling to the two houses of Israel." As Hosea said at 14[:9], "The way of God is righteous and the just shall walk it and the transgressors will stumble." As is also said in Daniel 11[35], "And among the understanding some will fall." And from these [passages], it is apparent that these Jews stumbled so hard on the cornerstone, that they have been punished for more than 1,500 years. And still they will not accept [him] about whom all prophets have testified—rather they crucified, despised, and mocked him.

They do the same thing today, again and again. For example, they say that Mary, the eternally pure, chaste virgin, through dishonor and adultery became pregnant, and also that she foolishly received this Christ from a carpenter or smith, and that Christ was born of such an adultery. They write this and many similar things in the booklet called *Toldoth Jesu.* They wholly believe this book and because of it continue to stumble on this cornerstone, upon which they must stumble. And that is the cause of God's unending anger toward them. Now enough has been shown that the Jews must admit either that no Messiah is coming or rather that he has come, or they must say that there is no God and the entire Old Testament is fictitious, heaven forefend.

[I] shall now prove and draw out from the scripture that Jeschua ישוע, Jesus, who was crucified by the Jews under Pontius Pilate, is the true Messiah. Everyone can see this in Isa. 53 and in all the prophets. And it is clear that for more than 1,500 years the Jews have had no prophets, visions, not a single comfort from God. [I] shall establish this with three witnesses, as the scripture Deut. 19[:15] teaches us: Upon two or three witnesses all things should be established.

Note that these following witnesses agree completely and do not contradict one another. [The first:] David says in the spirit, Psalm 74[:8–9], that after the destruction of the second temple, there will be no more prophets—with these words, "They have burned your holiness with fire." He said further, "We will see our signs no more and there will be no prophet with us who knows how long this will be." The second witness: Jeremiah, ch. 2[:9] in his Lamentations says, "Your king and lords are captive among the peoples, and your prophets can find no more vision from God." These two witnesses cannot have spoken about the destruction of the first temple, for they themselves knew beforehand through Jer. 25 that their captivity would be only 70 years, and there are more such passages. Therefore, they must speak only of this [present] captivity. Also, during the Babylonian captivity, they had the law, priests, and prophets with them, such as Daniel, Nehemiah, Ezra, Haggai, Zechariah, [and] Malachi. So one cannot point to an end to the second captivity, and will never know one. They still have no law, priests, nor prophets, also no sovereignty, for more than 1,500 years. The Jewish commentators themselves acknowledge and write that the aforementioned passage and scripture refers to the destruction of the second temple.

The third witness is Daniel in the 9th chapter [v. 24] of his book: "Seventy weeks will be enough to complete, fulfill, and remove the misdeeds and sins from upon your people and the holy city and to bring eternal righteousness and seal and fulfill the oracles of the prophets." Therefore, it is certain that Christ our Savior has come and established the kingdom. This was decreed by prophecy, and no prophet is any more found among the Jews. Understand that the 70 weeks means 70 times 7 years or 490. "70 weeks" mentioned in the text means 70 free years, because after 6 years there was a free year [*shmitah*], such as after 6 work days there is a Sabbath, then the week is over. After the free year, a week of years is over, as the learned well know. No Jew can deny this. Compute one [year] after another, from when Titus Vespasian destroyed the temple [back] to the time the angel Gabriel spoke the above prophecy to Daniel and made it known, in the first year of Darius's son Aehosverosch—[you will] find that it is 490 years, following the meaning of the seventieth free year in Hebrew, *schmitos* שמטות.

If the Jews had no other scripture against them than these three witnesses (and they could think of others), why do they wait for another Messiah? They can see decisively that their condition is as the witnesses have prophesied and testified—they have no prophets and no sovereignty, but rather are still in harsh captivity.

If God will, I will compose a booklet containing a dialogue with the Jews in which I shall bring together all the sayings of the Old Testament that refer to Christ and the Apostles, the repudiation of the Jews, and the acceptance of the heathen, and I will show and explore that these sayings are fulfilled in Christ and his apostles. All this [I shall do] for the glory of my savior Jesus Christ and for the Jews, that they consider it and that many may be illuminated, Amen. Indeed, such an illumination cannot occur unless one removes from them the accursed usury, as I mentioned above. But I fear it will not happen so easily; the reason being that where there is a Jewish house in a village, it taints and uses the leaders—judges, notaries, and all officers. The same is true where there are more houses, and likewise with another twenty. The same happens also when they are many. Because of such use, [the leaders] treasure and tolerate them. Such as take money from the Jews strengthen them vastly in their blindness. The reason is a passage in Hosea 8:[10], "Even so they will give money to the people. I will gather them and they will have a little hope because of the gift they give the kings and lords." From this the Jews falsely draw comfort and say, "The prophet has predicted it," and they are comforted that the king and lords will take money from them and leave them alone until the arrival of their fictitious Messiahs. So they greatly congratulate one another and say, "See we arrange our affairs and all things with our money," according to the content of the above-mentioned scripture. [They also say], "If God were not so powerful and shielded us, as this passage says, and made the promise to our fathers, the Christians [would] break all of us in three days, if they knew that we crucified their God and daily curse and mock all those who believe in him. Still God ordained that they take money from us and leave us to sojourn and do business among them."

It is indeed true that no group is more litigious than the Jews. And they arrange all things, crooked or straight, because of their great wealth. The first thing a Jew does before he litigates is to determine which judge, servant, or counselor is a בעל שוחד *Baal schocked,* a person who takes a bribe and a gift. How do they get them to take bribes? Woe to them that take bribes from them. Even those who do not take bribes from them nevertheless take gifts and presents at New Year, Martin's night, Fast Night (Shrove

Tuesday), and Channukah (Kirchweyhe[8]). The Jews also bring a pretty little thing to his wife and children. The Jews bring him something beautifully smithed, giving him half cash with these words, "Your wisdom can indeed bring in [convert?] us poor Jews."

Therefore he has subverted the good man, for he has sneaked in evil gifts. Therefore the Jews have much evil for which to answer. There are, God be praised, many judges here and there for whom such things do not work. These the Jews call טפשים רשעים *roschaim* or *typsim,* that is, godless or evil people. In sum, Christian leadership is obligated before God to bring and drive the Jews to work and to reject their *hellküchlein,* as indeed some are now doing.

There are those who say and teach, one should not bar the earthly path of Jews, but rather should hold their hand, sit in filth and stain [with them], not scorn them, not fear them, rather one should be friendly, loving, brotherly toward them in order that they will so much the sooner be moved to the Christian faith. To this I say, the more a Christian acts friendly, brotherly, and well intended toward Jews, the more the Jew curses, ridicules, and scorns him, with Christ and his faith, and thinks to himself, "This Christian knows that I am an enemy to him, including his God and belief. [I] curse and ridicule. Still, God sees to it that he must love me. And that is the correct sign of our salvation and the arrival of our Messiah. For God also put our fathers in Egypt. There they served the Egyptians 400 years and as the time of redemption neared, God made the Egyptians have a love for our fathers. And there through all Egypt was emptied, as you find in Ex. 12. Therefore it will soon come and occur that God will redeem us and will deliver to us the Christians' goods and punish them much harder than the Egyptians." They so pray as shown above. Many scriptures allege [in their opinion] that when their Messiah comes, they will take all the goods of the Christians. Now see each one [of you] what good follows when one shows himself friendly to the Jews.

Now follows in brief the comforts with which Jews comfort themselves in their long captivity.

1. The first and almost the foremost is [the practice of] usury and idleness shown above—for which use they [cite] a passage of Prov. 22, "He who borrows must be a servant to him who loans." It follows, therefore, that the Christians are their servants.

2. The second, they comfort themselves with their money and with it they hush up all their crooked and evil transactions, according to the passage [in] Hosea 8 noted above.

3. Third, they comfort themselves now so much that certain Christians for a while have become friendlier and more sociable with them. So much

so that now they may deal openly and travel more freely in certain places, where in the past they would not have dared to go. Similarly they give them nowadays much good will which in previous times seldom happened. In consequence, they curse and scorn Christ and all his followers more, as shown above.

[I] will also still examine the Jewish art; whoever does them good or wants to do good is their enemy and hateful, and they do him evil when they can and may. As you find with the three pious, holy men, who in all things prefigured Christ; the first, Joseph who did much good and wanted to do [good], they did [him] evil to the point where he himself said, Gen. 44, "Why have you rewarded good with evil?" Similarly, David who is entirely a type of Christ, speaks and says, Psalm 35, "He has repaid me evil instead of good." Likewise, the holy pious prophet, Jeremiah 18[:20] said, "Shall evil be repaid instead of good, for you dug a grave for my body."

They have done evil instead of good to all the prophets, also to Moses himself, and indeed to Christ, whom all these foreshadowed, and they did the same over and over. I say, therefore, for mercy's sake, one should allow the Jews to live among us as an example, and we should force [them] to do work, because God once cursed them you cannot be kind to them. In sum, what God has discarded and scorned, no one should lift up and make great, because a vexation of our faith follows. Now God has cast off the Jews in manifold ways in scripture, notably Deut. 28 at the end.

4. Now follows their fourth comfort, namely they congratulate and comfort themselves greatly on account of the things God did for their fathers Abraham, Isaac, and Jacob. And through such a promise [to the patriarchs], he will now redeem them, as he has often done. Answer: There is now no Jew who can say exactly that he is from the seed and lineage of Abraham. This can be tested from the scriptures and from their commentaries, namely, one clearly finds in Second Chronicles at the end of the second chapter, that at the time of Solomon, one hundred fifty-three thousand three hundred foreigners were to be found in Israel. Now if one computes how many foreigners were there before and after—who can say for certain whether he is from the seed of Abraham or from these foreigners. Also they write in their commentary on Ex. 5, that as the Egyptians had power of life and death over the men, so they also had power over the women and slept with them; thereafter, no one knew for sure whether he was descended from Abraham or an Egyptian. From this it can also be concluded that in Babylon and in this long captivity, similar things occurred, and so it is that most all Jews are of doubtful ancestry. In brief, the Jews must agree that all those who do Abraham's work are his children, [and] those who do not do it are not his children. As it stands today, no nation does less of Abraham's

work than the Jews. Indeed, they themselves write that piety and merit are the Patriarchs' [not their own], in Hebrew:

זכות אבות תמו *sochus ovos tamu.* And they write in [reference to] Hosea 2[:10], where the text says, "And a man will not protect you from my hand," and also in many other places, they acknowledge such. [So the merit of men, the Patriarchs, cannot help them.]

[After the first edition, the section on Abraham's children was lengthened by the following, which I have put in italics.]

It is true that no one can say with certainty that he is a descendant of Abraham. [The Jews] doubt themselves, so they have three rules and signs to determine who is or is not from Abraham. Namely, who does Abraham's work, but they leave out the best part of Abraham's work (namely belief). They also write and speak about those descended from Abraham that they have three attributes exactly like Abraham, namely: mercy, modesty, and charity. Who is rewarded for mercy? One who is merciful in a place where he can expect no wage or reward. These three virtues are called in Hebrew rachmonim, bayschonim, gemek chosodim רחמוניםביישונים גימלי חסודים. *[The practice of] these virtues rests on the entire community. However, it is clearly known that no people (volk) on the earth is [as] immodest and merciless [as] the present supposed Jews. So it follows that they are not from Abraham's family because they do not honor the primary aspect [of] Abraham's belief.*

If one [of them] were to ask in a friendly [manner] and say, "It is true that we Jews truly cannot say who is from the seed and family of Abraham. Neither can Christians prove that Christ was from the family of Abraham and David." "On the contrary," I answer, "as to the reason which turns on the foreigners. It is indeed known that at the time the Jews lived in their land, one could distinguish foreigners from genuine Israelites. The reason was that the foreigners had no state of their own. Now the Israelites have as much a state as the Ger גת[*sic*]. *So no one can say with truth whether he is descended from an Israelite or a foreigner." The answer to the second argument concerning the Egyptians is that whether or not the Egyptians had power over their women (as they themselves write), God preserved the [line] from which Christ should come. He continually kept it from all blemishes, as he kept the seven thousand who did not bow before Baal. Therefore, the supposed Jews may well be bastards and foreigners and Christ indeed from the family of Abraham, along with all the Jews who accepted the Christian belief in apostolic times and thereafter.*

5. Now follows the fifth comfort, namely that they have in the scriptures, here and there, many precious passages about their redemption and the coming of the Messiah. However, with their own commentaries and writings, I shall convince them that the greater part of the same passages

occurred and were fulfilled in the Babylonian affliction and that the lesser part must have been fulfilled in the coming of Christ, and now, some few are still to be fulfilled in the second coming of Christ. Who can account for their blindness? They must indeed remain blind to the end, which will follow in the conclusions.

6. Sixthly, they comfort themselves greatly with [the legend of] the 10 tribes that the king of Assyria drove out and led back to Assyria and placed in the city Chalo/Chouor by the stream Goson and in the city Modai, as you find in 4 Kings 17[:6]. It is a great wonder to me why they hope these 10 tribes, called the Red Jews, will come and redeem them. They also have little Hebrew and German booklets in which they write many lies and fairy tales about these 10 tribes. They also write about a stream named Sabbathion, which stream is so wild and wave-tossed during the week that no one can cross it—only on the Sabbath is the water calm. And these Red Jews dwell in the midst of these waters, and pepper comes from the same area. And on Friday, the Red Jews place many sacks of pepper on the port of these waters. So the heathen come on the Sabbath and exchange in its place a like amount of grain. And when God wants to redeem the Jews here, in this land, he will make the stream still and at rest.

Oh dear God, how can they be so foolish. I have researched many experienced merchants and others. They know nothing about it. How is it possible that for 2,200 years no one has found out anything about such a large people and wondrous stream? In sum, it is apparent from the scriptures that the ten tribes were driven out, they mixed with the heathen, and they worshipped all manner of idols. How much better it would have been if they had prophets among them. Even worse, they mixed with the heathen and accepted foreign beliefs. Because they were dispersed and had no more prophets, their names and tribes were completely destroyed and extinguished.

The Jews, however, say, "How can it be that the ten tribes were so completely destroyed, because the prophets say in many places that God will redeem Judah and Israel and restore them to their homeland." Answer: "The King of Assyria did not completely remove the ten tribes—according to the custom, [if] one removed only the best, leading, and greater part of the people, one could say that the entire people was taken away. Also, one finds information that the remainder of the ten tribes moved to the kingdom of Judah because of war and such. Namely, you will find it in 2 Chronicles Ch. 15[:9], that then there were many Israelites from Ephraim/Manasseh and Simeon that came to Judah; similarly, in the above mentioned book, Ch. 31[:6], 'And the children of Israel and Judah, who dwelt in the cities of Judah.' And there are many similar passages. And when the prophets spoke of the future comforting of Israel, they meant the people who dwelt in the land of Judah and those who remained here and there in their land [Samaria]. Without a doubt, many of the ten tribes came to the Christian faith with other heathens. Also, all scriptures show that the Redeemer will come from the tribe of Judah and not from the ten lost tribes. Therefore, this comfort of the Jews is false in many ways."

Now at the end and conclusion follows the foremost comfort of all, which they call the golden *affenn* [golden *also* or *even though*],[9] and they mean that no scripture can be shown to contradict it. And in spite of the evils and trials that occur, they comfort themselves with this *affen*. And so [when] they read in the Church [synagogue] the passage about this *affen*, they sing and read happily, loudly, and with bright. One finds it in Levit. at the end of Ch. 26[:44–45]: "And even though they will be in the land of their enemies, I will not cast them off nor destroy them, rather I will remember the first covenant, how I brought them out of Egypt." Understand that this passage and comfort begins in the Hebrew language with the word *Aff* אף. *Aff* means "and also" [even though]. Therefore, because of this prophecy and comfort, they say that God cannot and may not forsake them. The Jews have with this passage, word, and false comfort convinced the pious Christian Emperor Frederick, of blessed memory, so that he said that the Jews have an *Affen* in their scriptures, which they should write in golden letters.

Now I will, with God's help, answer this Golden *Affe* and imaginary comfort and demonstrate their lack of understanding and blindness. First, one should know why there are two curses [given to the Jews], the first in Levit. 26 and the second in Deut. 28. Now one cannot say that in the five books of Moses that one [passage] contradicts another, so it cannot be that the two curses are the same thing, for one is entirely different than the other. Namely [in] Levit. stands this Golden *Affe* and comfort; also in the same curse, there is no pronouncement that the seed and children will also be cursed. Also in many other ways they are different. But the second curse, Deut. 28, says not a thing of any comfort. [It] says specifically that this curse should apply for an endless eternity to them and all their progeny. That this is an endless curse [is established because] the text specifically places a consignification, the word מלה *m milo,* before the word *Olam* עולם which means eternal. It is known by those knowledgeable in this language [Hebrew] that when a consignification stands before or after the word *Olam* then it means "at all times" incontrovertibly "endless time." Further, the curse in Deuteronomy refers not to peace in the land, as in Lev. Therefore, it is certain that the curse in Deut. refers to the second destruction and dispersion, which occurred through Titus Vespasian, which dispersion will be for an endless eternity, as is now apparent from the 1,500 years [of exile] which agrees with this curse, and also [with] the passages in the New Testament which say that the Generation will not pass away forever, and such things. Then [these scriptures] must be about a diminished people, who are eternally cursed as an example to all nations, according to this curse. But the curse of Levit. 26 refers to the first destruction and dispersion into Babylon. And after 70 years of the Babylonian captivity, the Golden *Aff* and comfort were completely fulfilled; for God brought them home again after seventy years and established them in their fatherland, and thus fulfilled the curse. Levit. 26 does not mention the offspring and children, that they should suffer, because the same children were redeemed.

Also, your own commentators write that the curse of Leviticus [26:34–35] is limited to a specific time. Namely, the text says, "Then will the festivals occur in the land, as long as it lies desolate and you are in the land of your enemies. Yes, then the land will celebrate and its celebrations be pleasing, as long as it lies desolate. But it could not celebrate in your festivals when you lived therein." Understand that you were commanded in Exodus 23[:11] that the earth's fields should be fallow every seven years, and so also says the text of Levit. 26; the land can rest because you are driven from it. Because you lived in it [and did not keep this commandment], it could not rest. And so write your commentators, that they transgressed this commandment seventy times, therefore the land celebrated seventy years and was at peace the seventy years that they were in Babylon. From this it can be fundamentally and incontrovertibly asserted that the curse in Levit. 26 was completely fulfilled, including the Golden *Affe* and comfort. And the curse in Deut. 28 is fulfilled daily to the end. Therefore, the Jewish comfort and Golden *Aff* are answered with the truth. God wants that all Jews think about these and similar things and read the Talmud [correctly]. So will God, without a doubt, open the eyes of many and pull them out of the grave curse in Deut 28. Those who do not must remain eternally stuck therein.

I ask each and every good-hearted Christian reader not to think ill of my overlong writings. If I mentioned a thing twice, or that this or that sentence is not correct, or that it misses the art of German rhetoric, rather think and know that I am not so well schooled in the German language. Therefore, I have decided absolutely to write no more in German except two brief tractates. If God is gracious and grants me strength and health, I will publish a few useful and important things in the holy Hebrew language.

der todten / vnd in seinem gewalt seind die leibe eines
jeden der da lebet / auch der athem oder geist aller me-
nigklichē creatur ist in deiner hand / in deine hand vñ
gewalt befelhe ich meinen geist / erlöse mich Got / der
du ein warhafftiger Gott bist / vnser Gott der du bist
im himel / verschaff daß dein name allein sei / vnd dein
künigreich bestect allwege / der Herr soll immer vnd
ewig vber vns regieren.

[illegible] Jiru Enenu / vnser augen werden es sehen.

VNser augen werden es sehen / vnd wirt sich vnser
hertz erfrewen / vnd vnsere seele auch wirt in deiner hülffe mit warheit frolocken / wenn man zů
Zion sagen wirt / dein Herr hat geregieret / got ist künig / gott hat regiert / vnnd wirt in ewigkeit regieren /
deñ das künigreich ist dein / vnd immer vnd ewig wirst
du in den ceren regieren / denn es ist kein König denn
nur du allein.

Gelobet seiestu Got der da König ist in seiner Ee-
re alle zeit / steets wirt er vber vns / vnd vber alle seine
werck immer vnd ewig regieren.

Darnach singet der vorsinger das Kadesch gar
auß / sampt allen Ceremonien wie oben angezeiget /
Nemlich dz er iii. tritt hinder sich thůt ⁊c. Darnach
beten sie das gebet / dz fast wider Christum / alle Christen vnd Christliche oberkeit ist / Nemlich da die zehē
wort innen begriffen seind / die sie nicht im den text
schreibē / wie obstehet / darnach kompt der waise / der
seinen vatter das jar verloren hat / vnd betet dz klein
Kadesch wie deñ obsteet / darnach sagt wol etwañ einer / der ander nicht / etliche lobsprechungen / vnd mit
dem

dem selben geen sie auß der kirchen / vnd sprechen vn-
der der thür dē verß / Gott füre mich ⁊c. wie obē steht.

End dises Betbüchleins.

Damit das ich aber anzeige / wo vnnd wenn sie die
hundert Lobsprechung vollendt erfüllendt / nemlich
inn dem Benedicite / das sie des tags sprechen / so sie
gessen haben / wie zum teyl angezeiget.

Ich laß hie am ende dises Betbüchleins ein jeden
leser wissen / Das ich allhie innen die zal der psalmen
nach Hebreischer zall gesetzt hab. Auch so inn disem
Büchlein etwann ein text in der Biblien angezogen
worden ist / habe ich nicht eben auff mein teutsch wie
ich pflege zů vertcütsch en acht gehabt / deñ es gar vn-
uerstendtlich wer / wort zů wort also zů verdolmetschē
aber wol das teütsch genommen / das jetzt im meisten
brauch ist / vnd jederman gewonet hat.

Zůmend vnd beschluß dises Büchleins / will ich etlich grund vnd natürlich vnd schrifftlich / wider den
gantzen glauben der Juden setzen / denn all jr glaub
vnd hoffnung ist / das sie Gott noch erlösen werde /
durch jren vnbekanten Moschiach / Der selb werde
ein glückhafftiger streitbarer man sein / wissen doch
selbs nicht / wie vnd was gestalt der Moschiach regieren werde / denn wo x. jrer scribentē / von solchē Moschiach schreiben / schreibet keiner wie der ander. Ich
will hie ein wenig anzeigen / wie die armen einseltigē
Juden / so hart von den Thalmudischen verfürt / vñ
von Christo abgewendet werden / vnd haben vil heil-
sa mer spruch auff jre ertichte zwen Moschiachim ge-
füret / vnd solches ist geschehen / da das Euangelium
erstlich im schwange gangen / vnd vil Juden da selbige angenommen / seind / y zů ge faren / die schrifft so

f

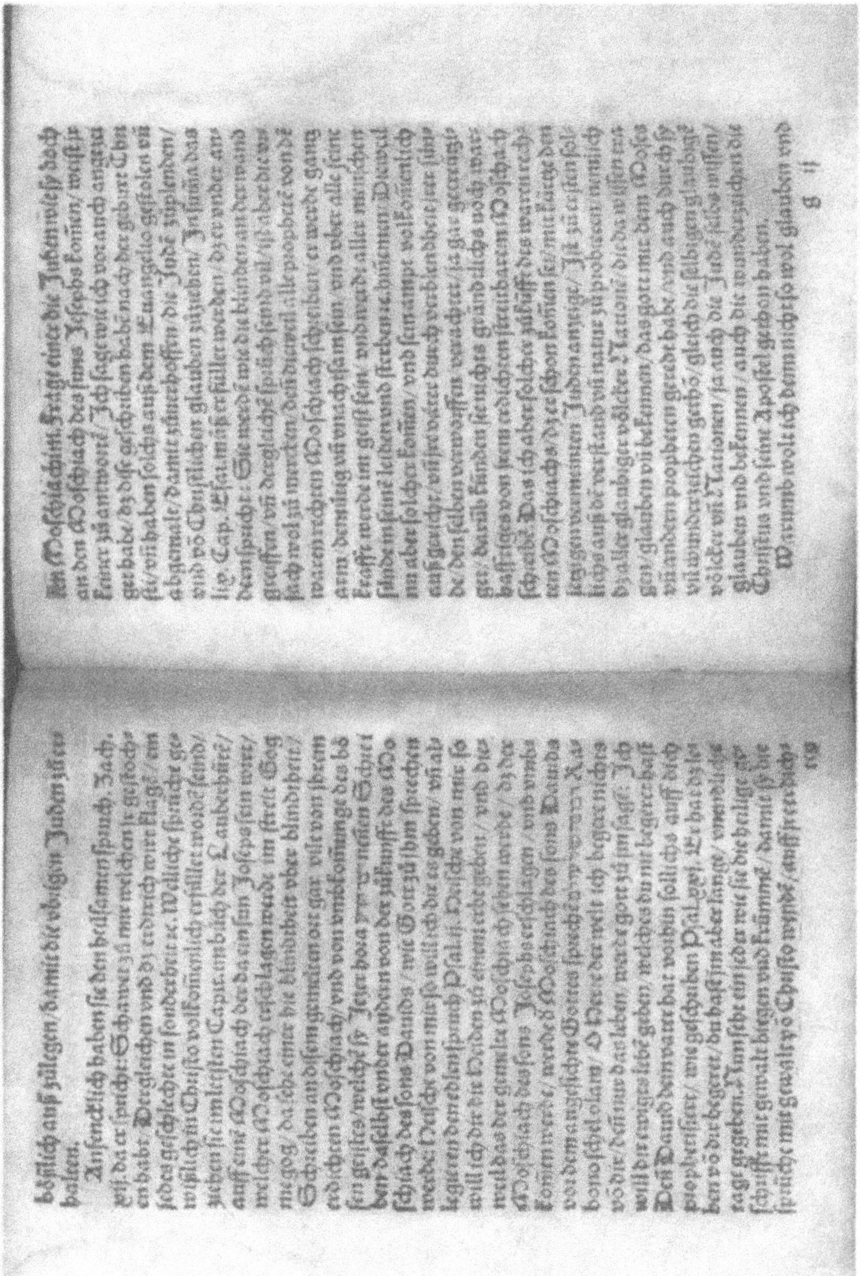

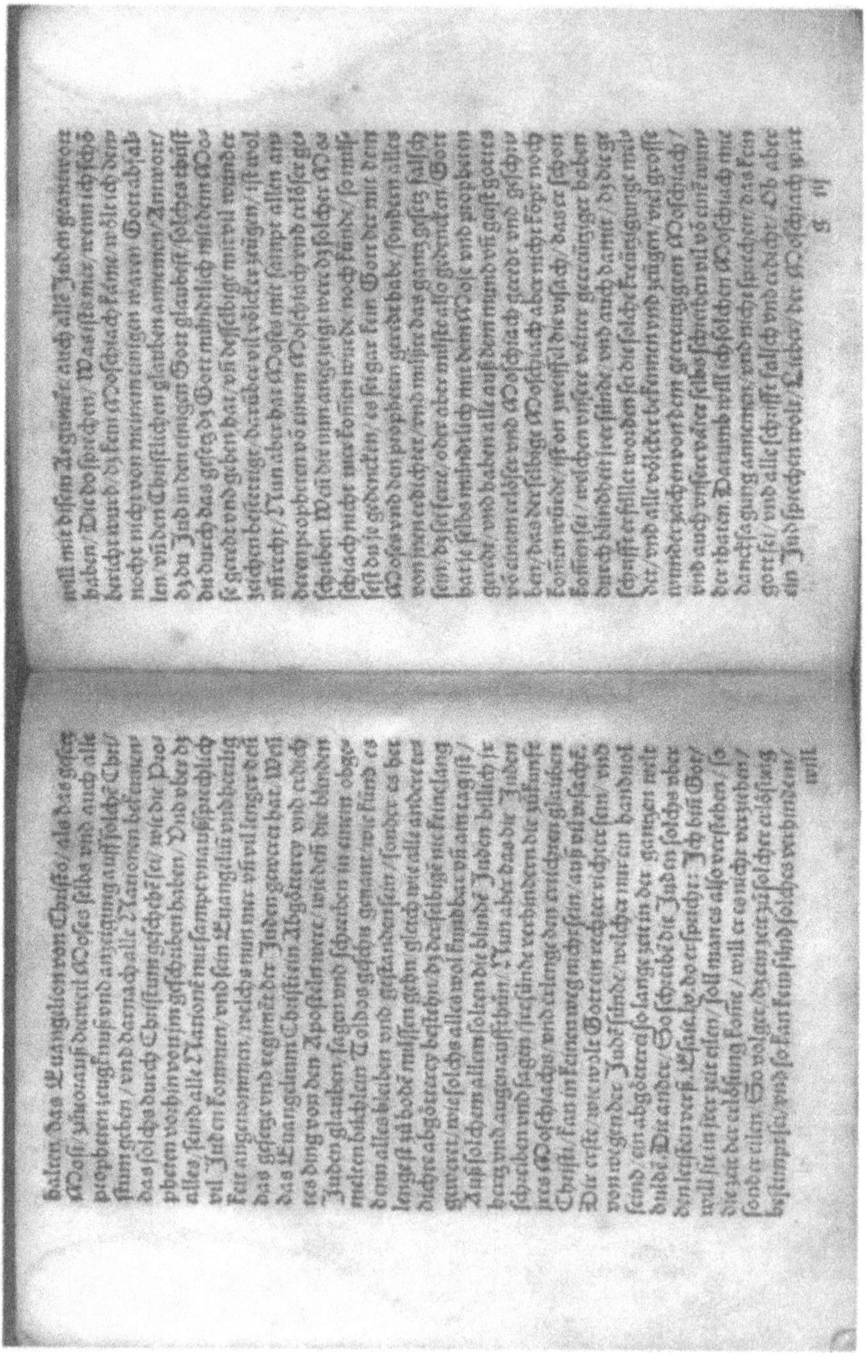

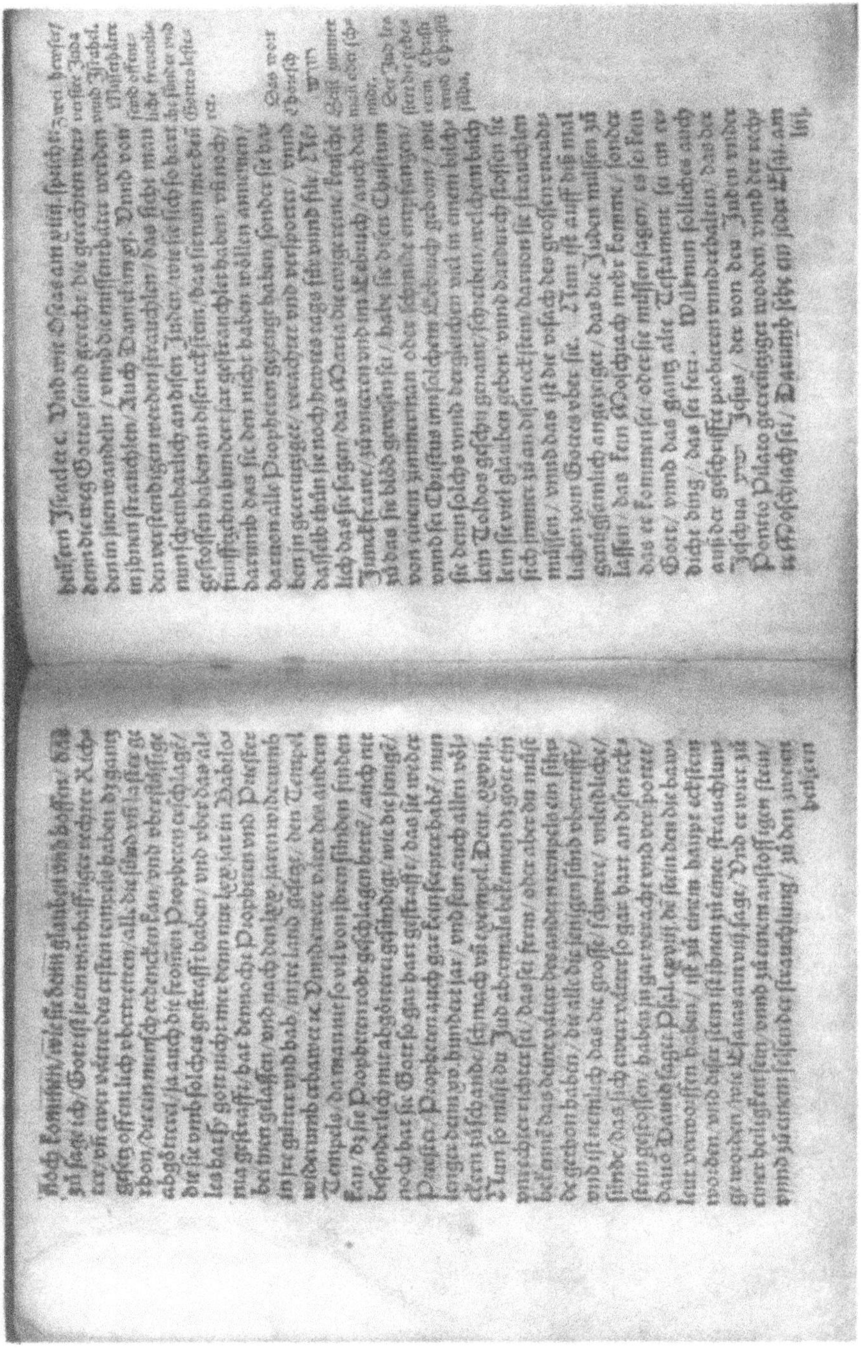

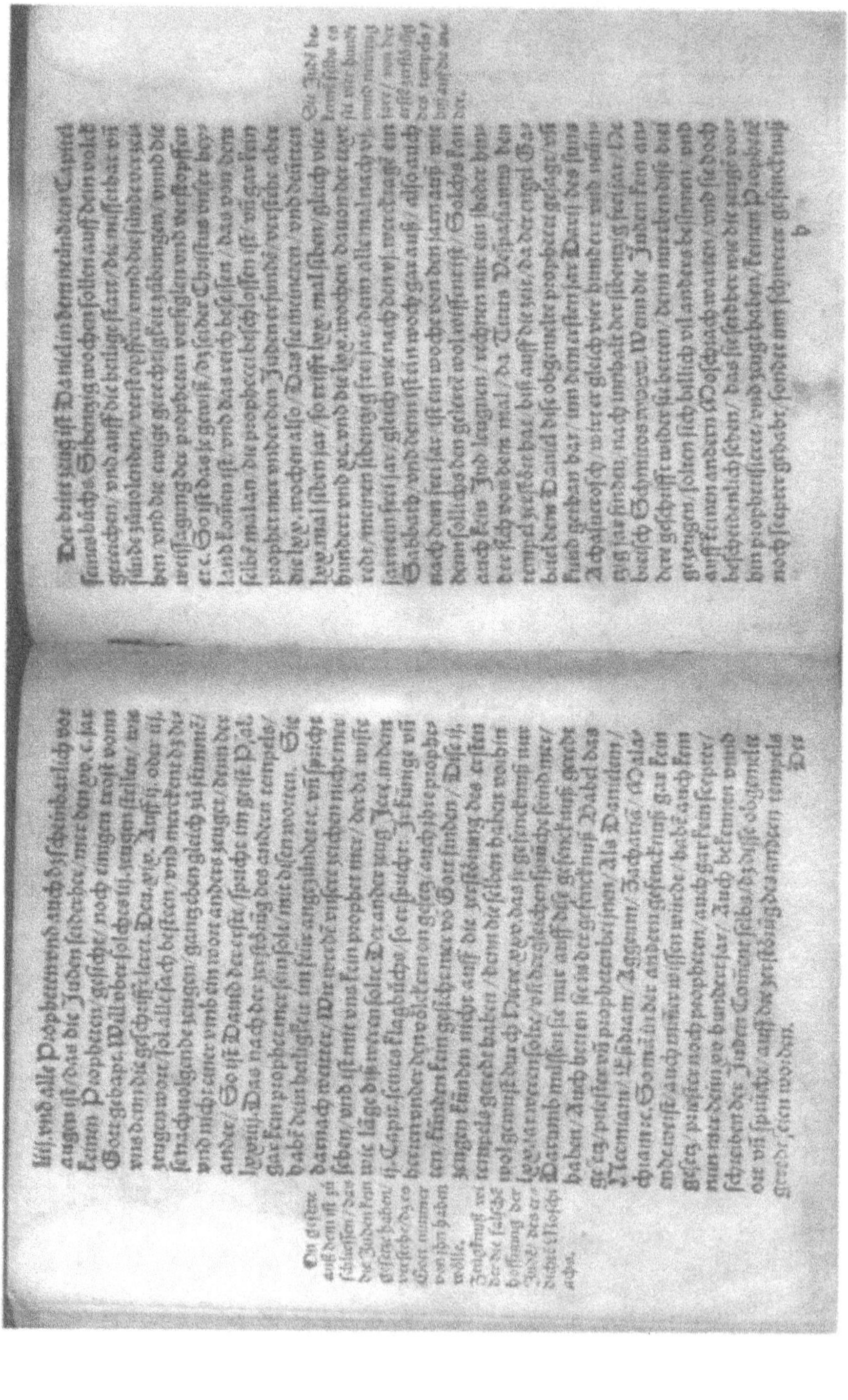

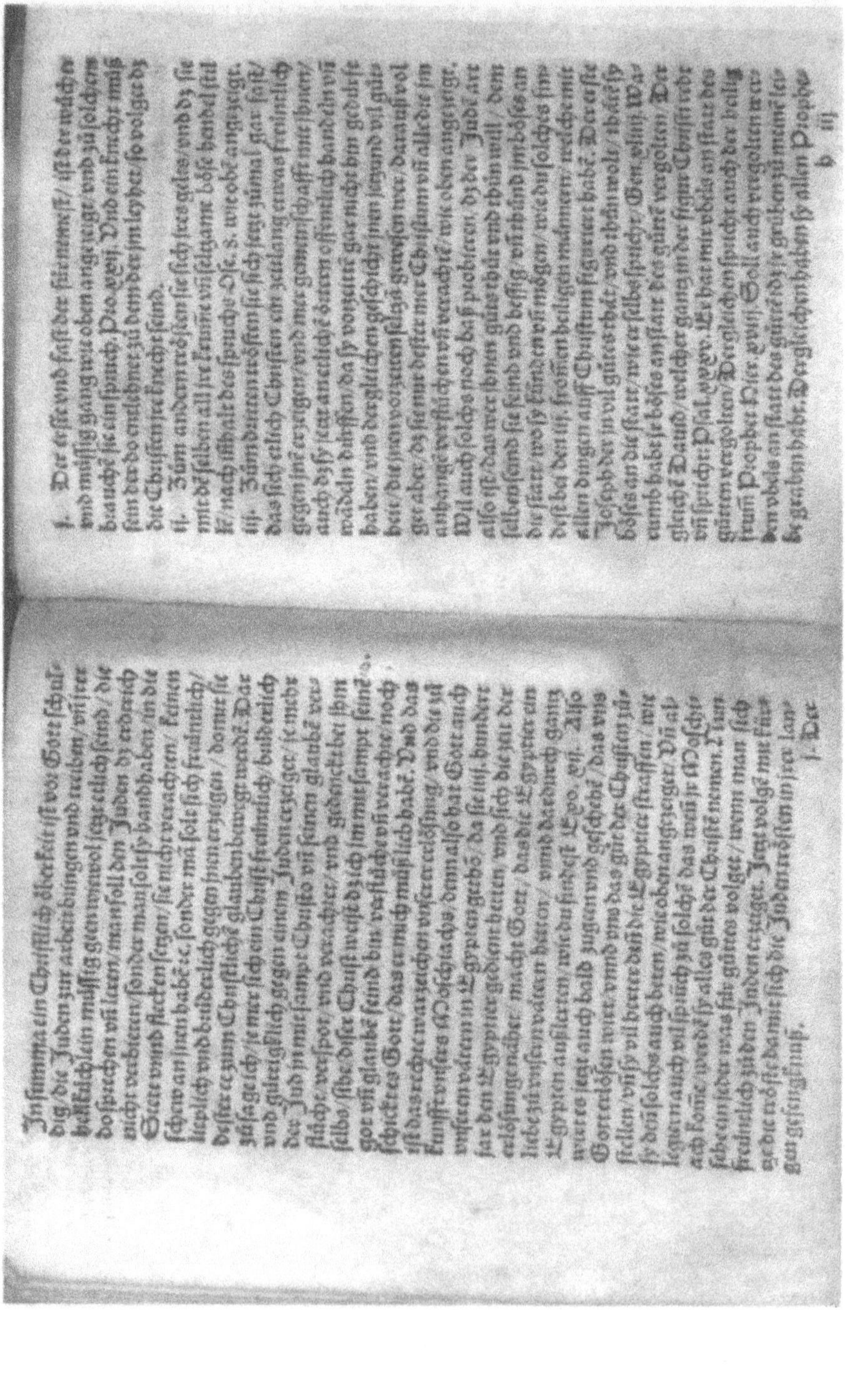

Jnsumma ein Christlich öberkeit ist vor Gott schul-
dig/ die Juden zur arbeit bringen vnd treiben/ vñ jrer
heilkichlein müssig geen wiewol jetzt etlich seind/ die
do sprechen vñ leren/ man soll den Juden dz erdtrich
nicht verbieten/ sonder man solt sy handhaben/ in die
Stett vnnd flecken setzen/ sie nicht verachten/ keinen
schew an jnen habē ꝛc. sonder mā solt sich freüntlich/
lieplich vnd brüderlich gegen jnen erzeigen/ domit sie
dester ee zum Christlichē glauben bewegt werdē. Dar
zů sage ich/ je mer sich ein Christ freüntlich/ brüderlich
vnd gütigklich gegen einem Juden erzeiget/ je mehr
der Jud jn mit sampt Christo vñ seinen glaubē ver-
flücht/ verspot/ vnd verachtet/ vnd gedenckt bei jhm
selbs/ sihe diser Christ weiſt dz ich jm mit sampt seinē
got vñ glaubē feind bin/ verflůche vñ veracht/ noch
schickt es Gott/ das er mich müß lieb habē. Vnd das
ist das recht warzeichen vnserer erlösung/ vnd die zů
kunfft vnsers Moschiachs/ denn also hat Gott auch
vnseren vätern in Egypten gethō/ da sie iiij. hundert
jar den Egyptier gedient hetten/ vnd sich die zeit der
erlösunge näher macht Gott/ das die Egyptier ein
liebe zů vnsern vätern hetten/ vnnd dardurch gantz
Egypten außlerten/ wie du findest Exo. xij. Also
wirt es jetzt auch bald zugeen vnd geschehē/ das vns
Gott erlösen wirt/ vnnd vns das gůt der Christen zů-
stellen/ vñ sy vil herter dañ die Egyptier straffen/ wie
sy deñ solchs auch beten/ wie oben angezeiget. Vñ al-
legiern auch vil sprüch zů solchē das weñ jr Moschiach kome/ werdē sy alles gůt der Christē nemen. Nun
sihe ein jeder was für güttes volget/ wenn man sich
freüntlich zů den Juden erzeiget. Jetzt volgē mit kür-
ge die tröste damit sich die Juden trösten in jrer langen gefengknuß.

j. Der

j. Der erste vnd fast der fürnemest/ ist der wůcher
vnd müssig gang wie oben angezeigt/ vnd zů solchem
brauchē sie ein spruch. Pro. xxij. Vnd ein knecht můß
sein der do entlehnet zů dem der jm leyhet/ so volget dz
die Christen jre knecht seind.

ij. Zům andern trösten sie sich jres gelts/ vnd dz sie
mit dē selben all jre kreüme vñ seltzame böse hendel stil
lē/ nach jnhalt des spruchs Ose. 8. wie obē angezeigt.

iij. Zům dritten trösten sie sich jetzt zůmal gar fast/
das sich etlich Christen ein zeitlang etwas freüntlich
gegen jnē erzeigen/ vnd mer gemeinschafft mit jhnen/
auch dz sy jetz an etlichē örtern offentlich handeln vñ
wädeln dürffen/ da sy vorzeittē gar nicht hin gedürfft
haben/ vnd dergleichen geschicht jnen jetzund vil gůts
heit/ die jnen vorzeiten seltzā gewesen wer/ darauß vol
get aber/ dz sie nur dester mer Christum vñ alle die jm
anhangē verflüchen vñ verachtē/ wie oben angezeigt.
Wil auch solchs noch baß probieren/ dz der Judē art
also ist/ das wer jhnen gůts thůt vnd thůn will/ dem
selben seind sie feind vnd hessig/ vñ thůnd jm böses an
die statt/ wo sy kündē vñ mögen/ wie du solches findest bei den iij. frommen heiligen männern/ welche mit
allen dingen auff Christum figuriert habē. Der erste
Joseph der jn vil gůtes thät/ vnd thůn wolt/ thätē sy
böses an die statt/ wie er selbs spricht/ Gen. xliiij. Wa-
rumb habt jr böses an statt des gůttē vergolten/ Der
gleichē Dauid/ welcher gantz in der figur Christi redt
vñ spricht: Psal. xxxv. Er hat mir vbels an statt des
gůtten vergolten/ Dergleichen spricht auch der heilig
frum̃ Prophet Hier. xviij. Soll auch vergolten werden vbels an statt des güttē/ dz jr gruben zů meinē leibe graben habt. Dergleichen haben sy allen Prophe-

b iij

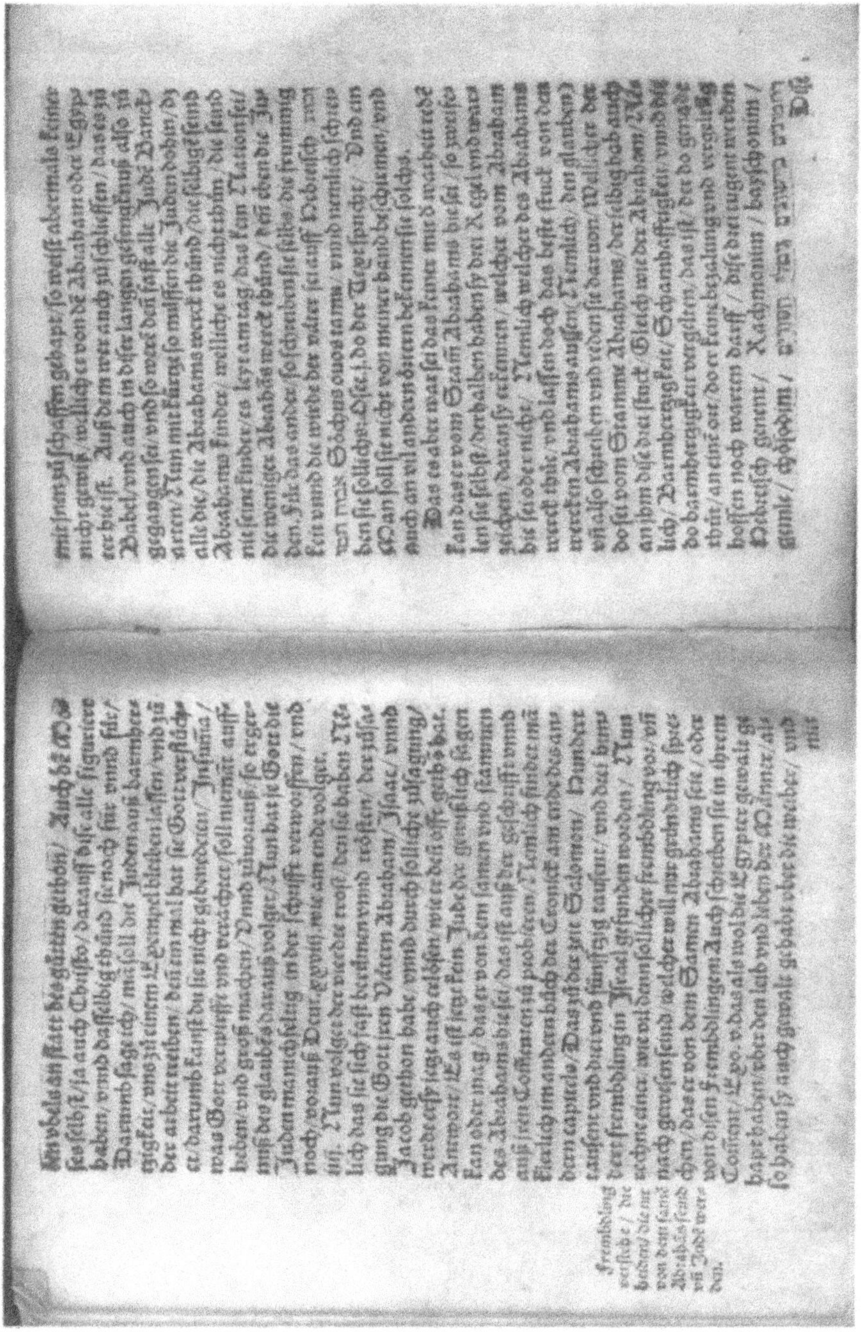

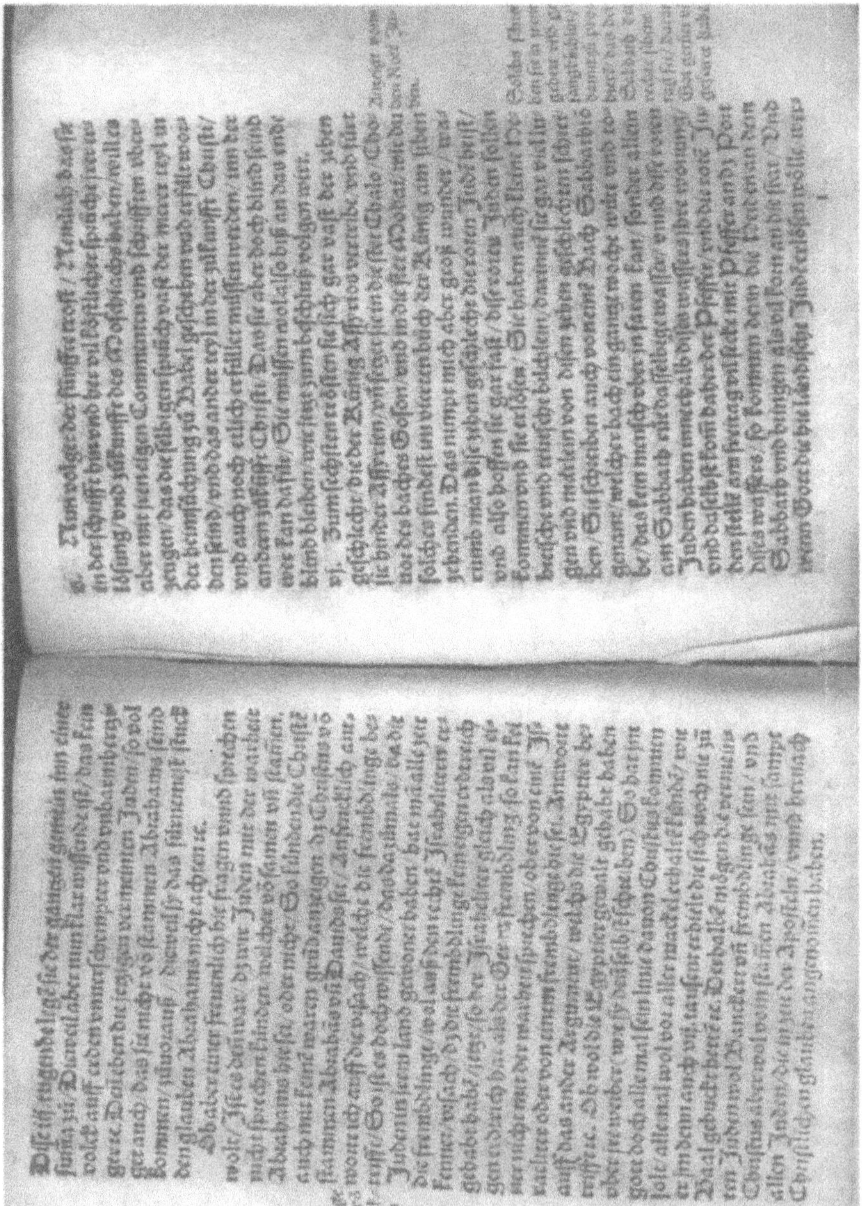

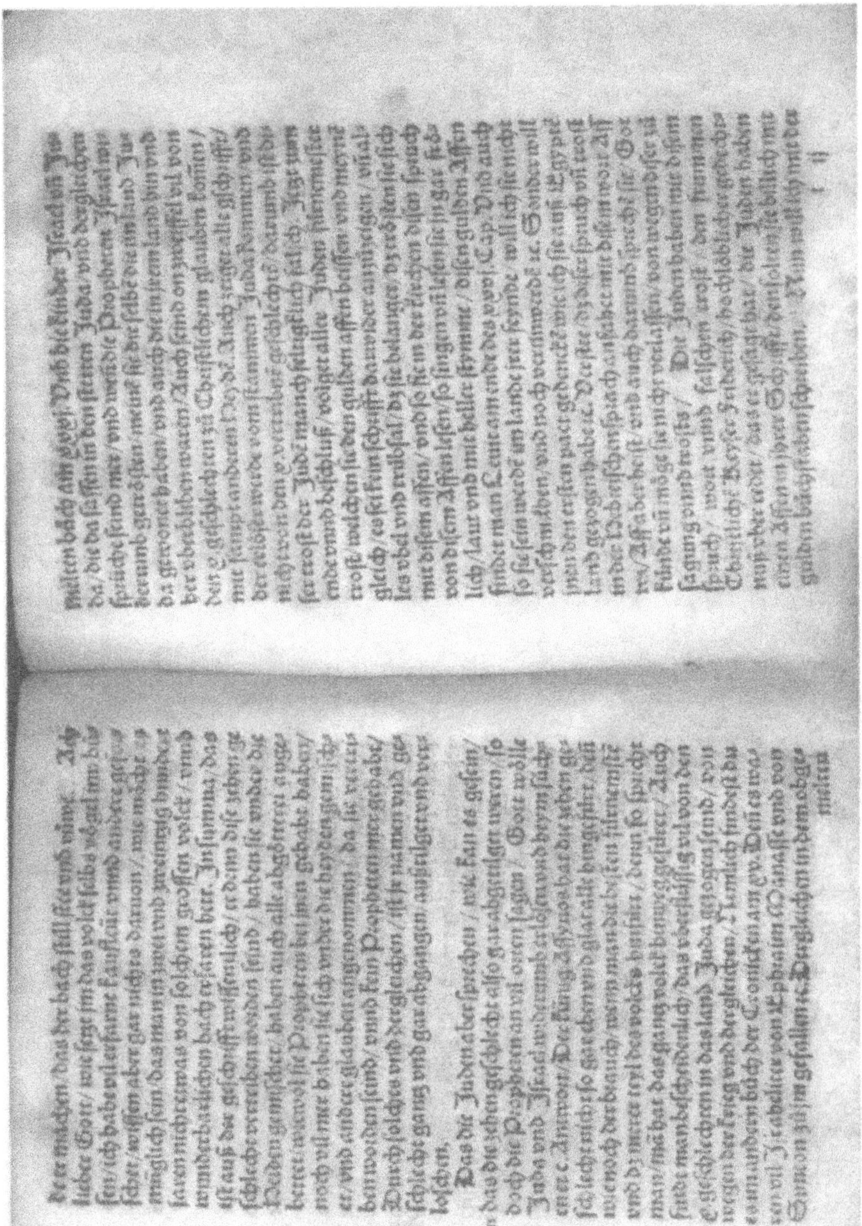

Appendix B

Margaritha's Kabbalah

In the biography above, Margaritha's prayer kabbalah was briefly situated in the context of kabbalah in sixteenth-century Germany. The complexities of the phenomenon of which Margaritha was a part were left to this appendix with its full translation of the passages from *Der gantz Jüdisch glaub,* drawn from the 1530, 1531, and 1544 printings. Margaritha's discussion of the powers of divine names reflected the mainstream of kabbalah, from its earliest written expression in the *Sefer Yetzirah* (Book of formation), through the appearance of *Zohar,* the masterpiece of the kabbalistic circle of Moses de Leon in thirteenth-century Spain.[1] The roots of belief in the power of words, especially divine names, predate the kabbalah. The Talmudic tractate *Pirke Avoth,* 5:1 declares, "with ten utterances the world was created."[2] The mystery or "doing" of the creation (*ma'ase Bereshit*) was the kabbalistic designation for doctrines dealing with the physical world. This term derived, as did the *Avoth* passage, from Genesis 1, where God creates by words: "God said."

The Hebrew Scriptures, in particular Genesis, were a source for both Jewish and Christian kabbalah. In the late fifteenth century, Pico della Mirandola had the convert Flavius Mithridates, whose Jewish name may have been Samuel ben Nissim al-Faraj, translate several works by the noted kabbalist Menachem Recanati.[3] Pico was attracted to kabbalah because he saw in it a tradition handed down from Sinai that confirmed the convergence of Judaism, Neoplatonism, and Christianity. He educated himself through the works of Recanati concerning the powers of the divine emanations, or *sephiroth*—power (*gevurah*), glory (*tiferet*), majesty (*hod*), and so forth.[4] Pico also immersed himself in the lore of divine names, using Recanati and others. Flavius's translation of Recanati's *Commentary on the Daily Prayers* revealed that prayer was to be focused on the specific names that ruled certain powers. "If a man does not know how to address the name appointed . . . [this] is the cause of his incapability to fulfill his wish."[5] The divine, in his name *El,* the property of compassion, spoke with the prophets.[6] As *Elohim,* he called (drew, invited) day and night into existence.[7]

Flavius also translated Joseph Gikatilla's *Sha'arey Tzedek* (Gates of righteousness).[8] Gikatilla discussed the Tetragrammaton, its letters, and its powers. In their writings, both Recanati and Gikatilla represented a type of Jewish kabbalah that was known to most educated Jews. The members of Margaritha's family, at least the adult male members of it, had access to the kabbalistic knowledge found in such texts, even if they did not possess the actual works, for adepts taught kabbalah orally to their students. Whatever Pico knew of kabbalah, he had received through Flavius and other teachers, such as Johannes (Yohanan) Alemanno, just as they had learned from their fellow Jews before their conversions.

The convergence of Jewish kabbalah with Christian scholarship is seen in Johannes Reuchlin's *De Verbo Mirifico* (1494), as noted above. Reuchlin had unsuccessfully attempted to obtain kabbalistic texts from Anthonius's grandfather, Jacob Margoles. Even without those manuscripts, Reuchlin studied texts about the kabbalah of divine names, which formed the basis of *De Verbo Mirifico.* Having derived the significance of the various divine names from Jewish concepts, Reuchlin proceeded to conflate those Jewish kabbalistic ideas with Neoplatonism and Orphic mysteries. Reuchlin's work still remains an excellent source for Jewish ideas about the kabbalah, which the rabbis believed were teachings God gave to Adam, and transmitted to and through the patriarchs, Moses, and the prophets.

Reuchlin provided a more detailed elucidation of the kabbalah in *De Arte Cabalistica* (Hagenau, 1517). Much of Book III of that work deals with diverse names, many of which are derived from Exodus 14 and the miracles Moses performed. His exposition is very similar to that of Margaritha.

Although Margaritha could not have learned his prayer kabbalah from Reuchlin's or Paul Ricci's work, *Portae Lucis,* because he did not read Latin, he had been taught similar doctrines from Jewish sources, presumably some of the same works Reuchlin used. Margaritha's mention of Pico and

Reuchlin in his discussion of kabbalah was probably a rhetorical flourish, an appeal to the reader to appreciate the value of his own work, for were not great scholars associated with the kabbalah of divine names?

De Verbo Mirifico is a primer in the magic of divine names and reflects what Margaritha may have learned of the Jewish kabbalah. It is a highly focused text, which systematized the kind of Jewish data found in Pico's "Cabalistic Theses." Reuchlin demonstrated how the several Hebrew names for God not only reveal the secrets of creation and the nature of God but also enabled the adept to exercise power (magic) through them. The word *Ehieh* (Exodus 13:4), I will be, is the essence of divinity. *Hochma,* wisdom, made all things, as King David proved when he cried, "You made all in wisdom."[9] *Elohim* represented the divine plurality, which is to be understood as Unity.[10] The divine emanations, such as Wisdom (*Hochma*), Understanding (*Binah*), and Glory (*Tipheret*), were aspects of Unity and denoted the influence of divine Unity in the world. The Christian or Jewish kabbalist, by use of the appropriate divine name, had the power to control nature.

The foremost and most powerful name of God was the ineffable four-letter Tetragrammaton.[11] In the kabbalah, no higher power existed. The Tetragrammaton created the world and was the light of the world.[12] The four aspects of the human soul—sense, imagination, fantasy, and intelligence—correspond to its letters. The name had the power to heal and even to alter the nature and fate of human beings.[13] The addition of the Tetragrammaton's letter *hey* to his name changed the patriarch Abram into Abraham. He became an adept with great powers.[14] Nor was the ineffable name's power limited to the physical world, but, properly used, it could control the angels.[15]

The four-letter personal name of God is more concentrated in power than the seventy-two letter *Semhamaphoras* (Reuchlin's transliteration). Reuchlin structured *De Verbo Mirifico* to reveal this kabbalistic secret, which he also treated in *De Arte Cabalistica.* It was, in fact, one of the most widely known secrets of kabbalah. As noted above, Victor von Carben discussed the doctrine of the Tetragrammaton and clamed that the Talmud attributed Jesus's ability to work miracles to his theft of the word from the temple.[16] Margaritha ended his prayer kabbalah with the "great" four-letter name of God and a discussion of its relation to *Eheye* (Margaritha's transliteration of the word Reuchlin transliterates as *Ehieh*). He closed his prayer book translation with the seventy-two-letter name of God and declared that Jesus was the *Schem hamphorasch,* his transliteration of the Ashkenazic pronunciation of the wonder-working name.[17] Years later in his Christian life, Margaritha would still write of the four letters of "Adonai or Jehova, which fearful [name] is called the Tetragrammaton . . . to whose four letters no creature or creation in heaven or earth may add."[18]

The similarity of language and content in the work of Reuchlin and those of the converted Jews betrays common Jewish kabbalistic sources. Both Reuchlin and the converts testify to the power of divine names and the special virtues of the wonder-working word. The kabbalists distinguished the use of holy names from the profane practices of common magic. The effects of using the names of God arose from the knowledge of righteous adepts, such as Abraham and Moses. Celestial potency required study, understanding, and holiness. Practitioners and transmitters of the kabbalah were scholars of Jewish law who cultivated the skills and quality of character necessary to understand and employ the properties of divine names.[19]

The practices of kabbalistic magicians can be glimpsed in certain passages from their writings. Johannes Alemanno believed that the successful adept was following the example of Moses:

> The kabbalists believe that Moses . . . had precise knowledge of the spiritual world, which is called the world of the Sefiroth and the world of divine names, or the world of letters.[20]

The spiritual world was connected to the material world through "channels." Moses, as the archetypical kabbalist, manipulated the divine movement between the higher and lower worlds through "thoughts and prayers."[21]

Kabbalistic actions were neither purely spiritual nor completely intellectual, but they produced material effects in the world. Like Moses, the true kabbalist could work wonders in the world of matter. Moses performed his magic, which put to shame the Egyptian magicians, by means of prayer and by speaking divine names.[22] Although Moses was the greatest of the prophets, his accomplishments could be emulated to a degree by a knowledgeable, practical, and holy kabbalist.

Divine names were keys to the creative spiritual powers that had connected the spiritual world with the material world since the first moment of Genesis. Certainly no other human could usurp or even aspire to the extraordinary spiritual level and deeds of Moses. Still, an adept could gain a degree of spiritual insight and power. It is that lower level of magic that Pico and Reuchlin sought. They, however, had learned from Jews, who lived with daily meditations in prayer and in study. Among many rabbis and their families, the kabbalah of divine names, as it related to prayer, was intensively studied. Nonrabbinic members of congregations experienced esoteric knowledge at a lower level. Margaritha came from no ordinary family and he was well educated in the kabbalah of prayer.

As was discussed in chapter 3, Margaritha revealed kabbalistic secrets that were based in *gematria* in his discussion of the *Aleinu* prayer. The *Aleinu* was not merely a rejection of the Christian god Jesus, it was also a study of the Tetragrammaton, the letters of which were associated with Joshua and Jesus. Margaritha believed that the Jews missed the true point of the *Aleinu's gematria* in their hatred of Christianity. This approach to the *Aleinu* revealed an attitude toward the prayer book formed during Margaritha's Jewish education. The prayer book contained many prayers and meditations, but these were fully intelligible only in light of kabbalistic knowledge.

Margaritha's discussion of kabbalah is placed toward the end of the prayer book and concentrates on the divine names. These names were related to scriptural events and the powers of God manifested in those events. Many knowledgeable Jews surely engaged in meditations on the names and events in order to influence the world around them. Margaritha's kabbalistic understanding of the names of God had theurgic applications. These names held out hope of controlling nature and animals. Although Margaritha expressed skepticism of kabbalistic techniques, which theoretically could even invert God and the devil, he does not seem to have wholly rejected a practical use of kabbalah. In this, he may have been influenced by his Jewish training as well as by the beliefs of the Christian kabbalists whom he respected.

Moshe Idel, as noted above, has come to see that prayer books can be sources for the scholarly study of kabbalah. He illustrated the connection between formal prayers, commentaries on the prayers, and theurgic kabbalah with a quotation from R. Naftali Hirtz Treves's prayer book commentary:

> When [the people of] Israel bless God, then the glory becomes greater and ascends higher and higher, . . . as [it is written]: "Cause the Lord to ascend." Who can cause [the Lord] to ascend? The glory, that ascends according to the blessing and the praise.[23]

Hirtz Treves's commentary appears not only to support Idel's contention but also is evidence for the authenticity of Margaritha's prayer kabbalah. The quotation comes from a long discussion and was based, in part, on the interpretive tradition of Judah ha-Hasid and the Hasidei Ashkenaz. This is a good starting point for understanding how sixteenth-century German Jews, such as the Margoleses and Hirtz Treves, approached prayer and its power to affect the upper and lower worlds. For example, "the glory [of God] is by the merit of Jacob and by this [*al zeh*] He said, Israel is that [by which] I will be glorified and give you all the nations."[24] Such was the kabbalah of prayer, when Israel concentrated properly. In this perception, Margaritha and Hirtz Treves converge. Like so much of *Der gantz Jüdisch glaub,* the discussion of kabbalah adds to an understanding of Judaism in the sixteenth century. Margaritha is shown to be a source for the Jewish application of kabbalah to prayer.

The kabbalistic passages of *Der gantz Jüdisch glaub* translated below present the same problems of translation as does the Refutation (Appendix A); however, the briefer text is less convoluted, easing the translator's burden in rendering it in more idiomatic English. I retain Margaritha's phrase "in German," even though I then use an English word. As in Appendix A, the relevant pages from the Frankfurt edition of 1544 are reproduced for those who wish to read the original.

Translation

[After the prayerbook's listing of seventy-two verses of praise, which equate to the seventy-two-letter name of God, Margaritha began his section on kabbalah.]

Thereafter they pray a verse that is not from the 72 verses nor is it from the Psalter but rather from Dt. 6. "Hear O Israel, God our Lord is one God." Thereafter they add, "Praised be the true name of your Kingdom forever and ever." [Much of the kabbalah is based on Exodus 14, which recounts the redemption from Egypt.]

The primary reason I have noted this long prayer so carefully is that [in it] one sees what the Jewish Cabala is: namely the 72 angel names. From the 3 verses above, they count 216 letters. They write that these 216 letters have the same numerical value as the word *Arie* אריה, which means Lion. The word "lion" often refers to God, as in Amos 3. In sum, they say that every creature or created thing that hears it must do the will of whoever prays this prayer.

The 72 verses noted include the 72 names of the angels, which the Jews call the *schem hamphorasch,* the full (*aussgelegten*) name of God. It now may be the holiest thing that the Jews have. So I will briefly show how they derive parts of God's name from each angel name and what they hold about them.

About the First Angel

They write about the first angel, called והו *Vehu,* that he has the numerical value of 17, and this indicates אב זהב *Af Sohov,* which is also 17. In German, *affsohoff* means father of gold. God is called by this name because he gave the Israelites the gold and silver of the Egyptians by the sea. What such a holy thing means to the Jews and what is to be thought of such a cabala, each can decide for himself. If it suited me, I could easily use cabala to make from God a devil or from the devil a god. [I] will not, however, on that account throw out the entire cabala, because one can find much good therein. The third name is סיט *Sit.*[25] They write that its numerical value is 79, the same as the word *gomel* גומל that is, a redeemer. They apply *Sit* to God, who is a redeemer. God rewarded the Egyptians with evil and redeemed the Israelites with good. The word *Sit* also has the same value as אל הגדול *El hagodol,* which means "Great God." In a like manner, they attribute all 72 names to God. I will only describe certain things here because to write everything would require its own book.

The Ninth Angel is הזי *asi*

The interpretation of the ninth name, *Hasi* הזי is based on its numerical value, 22. This is the same as that of ואב אחד *Veav ached,* "one father." Understand that when the sea divided, all the [permutations] of this angel's name drew the Jews through the divided sea. This is the reason these angel names are derived from the three verses of Exodus 14, which deal with the dividing of the sea. They write further about this name that it also has the same sum as חביב *Choviv,* which means "Beloved," that is, God is loved by all and before all.

The Jews create many other names than these for God the Almighty in the Cabala, as their scholars well know. Others scholars, such as the pious Christian, the very learned doctor Reychlin, who have read the Cabala, also know more names. Among the most important writers on the Cabala are the noble, highborn, and well-learned Count Picus Mirandula, and, in our time, the Christian and most learned doctor Paulus Ricius, whose like in knowledge of Cabala has not lived among Christians and Jews.

What Is Cabala

Cabala means "tradition," that is a teaching of no specific teacher or master. One cannot say that this one or that one taught or began it. Some trace the Cabala to Adam, some to Noah, some to Moses. Finally, the Cabala is a teaching that one receives from another orally. The Jews, however, when they saw that they would spend many years of hardship in captivity, compiled the Cabala in books and therefore some attribute [this compiling] to Ezra.

The Tenth Name Is אלד

Ailed has the same numerical value as the word יהוד [*sic*] Jehudi. The great name of God יהוה *Jehovo* can be written with the letters of *Jehudi.* Come and follow [the idea] that God himself has a commonality [*gemanschafft*] with Judah and Judah with him. Such a commonality in Hebrew is שטופת *Schitophes,* meaning such a sameness that things are alike in all aspects and each has as much power as the other. Now I will ask a question: Does God have such a commonality with all Jews or only with the Patriarch Judah? The Jews will say with the Patriarch. Then I say further: How can it be that God could have such a commonality with a sinful, mortal man? So the Jew must [conclude that the commonality refers] to the Messiah, who is without sin and immortal. Will he or will he not be born of the patriarch Judah after the flesh, as all scriptures testify? So, it must follow that God the Father must have such commonality with the Messiah, his only begotten son from eternity. So he [the Jew] must conclude now that God the Father and the Son are two persons and one essence [*wesen*] and one commonality. If a Jew clearly grasped this, he would not be so opposed to the Trinity of the Christian faith. Seeing that the Jews grant a commonality to the Patriarch Judah with God and believe it, why should we not more easily believe that the Messiah, who is born after the flesh from Judah, has a commonality and unity with God. God himself spoke of the Messiah in Isaiah 7, "And you shall call his name Emanuel, that is, God is with us." And thereafter in [Is.] 9, "His name is called wonderful, counselor, and mighty God, an eternal father, a prince of peace."[26] Also in Jeremiah 23, the great name of God יהוה *Jehovo* is applied to the Messiah, it says

> "וזי אשר יקרא לו יהוה צדקנו *Vese oscher ikro la edonei Zidkenu,*" in German, "And that is his name by which man will call him, God our righteousness." From this, all should conclude that God has such a commonality with the Messiah and the Messiah with God both are one essence, as it is said.

This I will demonstrate from the Messiah's name. In Num. 13, Moses altered Joshua's name from הושע *Hoschua* to יהושע *Jehoschua.* Now Joshua is a type of the Messiah, who led the people to the Promised Land. Therefore, Moses lengthened his name with one letter י, *Jus,* from the great name of God. Therefore the true savior Christ, the true Messiah, is also named יהושע *Jehoschua* in Hebrew, as the Jews themselves acknowledge by cheekily calling [Jesus] ישו *Jeschu,* leaving out the two best letters of his name. As I show in the prayer book discussion, *Jeschu* is a made-up name which one can find written nowhere.

So now, the entire great name of God יהוה is in this name יהושע *Jehoschua,* which we call Jesus, as in the name יהודי *Jehudi.* So the above-mentioned commonality of God and the Messiah follows irrefutably. And they must call the Messiah *Jehoschua,* because *Jehoschua* means in German "God and Savior." That the Messiah is named *Jehoschua* is mentioned in the scriptures, especially in Isaiah chap. 62: "אמרו לבת ציון הנה ישעך בא *Imru levass Zion hine gischech bo,* Say to the daughter of Zion, Your savior comes." All argument about the Messiah is settled with Zach. 9 [*sic*]: "הנה מכלך יבוא לך צדיק ונושע הוא *Hine malckuch jovo loch zadik venoscho hu,* Behold, your king comes to you a righteous one and a savior is he."

About the Great Name of God יהוה Jehovo

I cannot stop here without saying a little about the correct name of God, as it is mentioned so often. I will show something of its origin. Moses asked God what his name was in Ex. 3. God answered him, "אהיה אשר אהיה *Eheye asher Eheye,* I will be what I will be." What more did Moses know than before from such an answer? These words in Hebrew contain three tenses, past, present, and future. So God answered Moses and showed him with these words that He is the Eternal—He was from the beginning, is now, and will be in the future. One can ascribe such a title neither to heavenly nor to earthly things—only to the eternal, one, and heavenly father who was the beginning of all things, and is now, and will be after all things. This word אהיה *Eheye* is applied to no created thing in the entirety of scripture. Only in Prov. 8 is this word applied to Wisdom. Indeed, that same Wisdom is Christ, from eternity our Messiah, whom God Himself often in scripture and in the Cabala calls "Wisdom" and "God's Wisdom." There is much more that could be said about this tenth name אלד *elad,* but for brevity's sake, I will stop and continue with the prayer book.

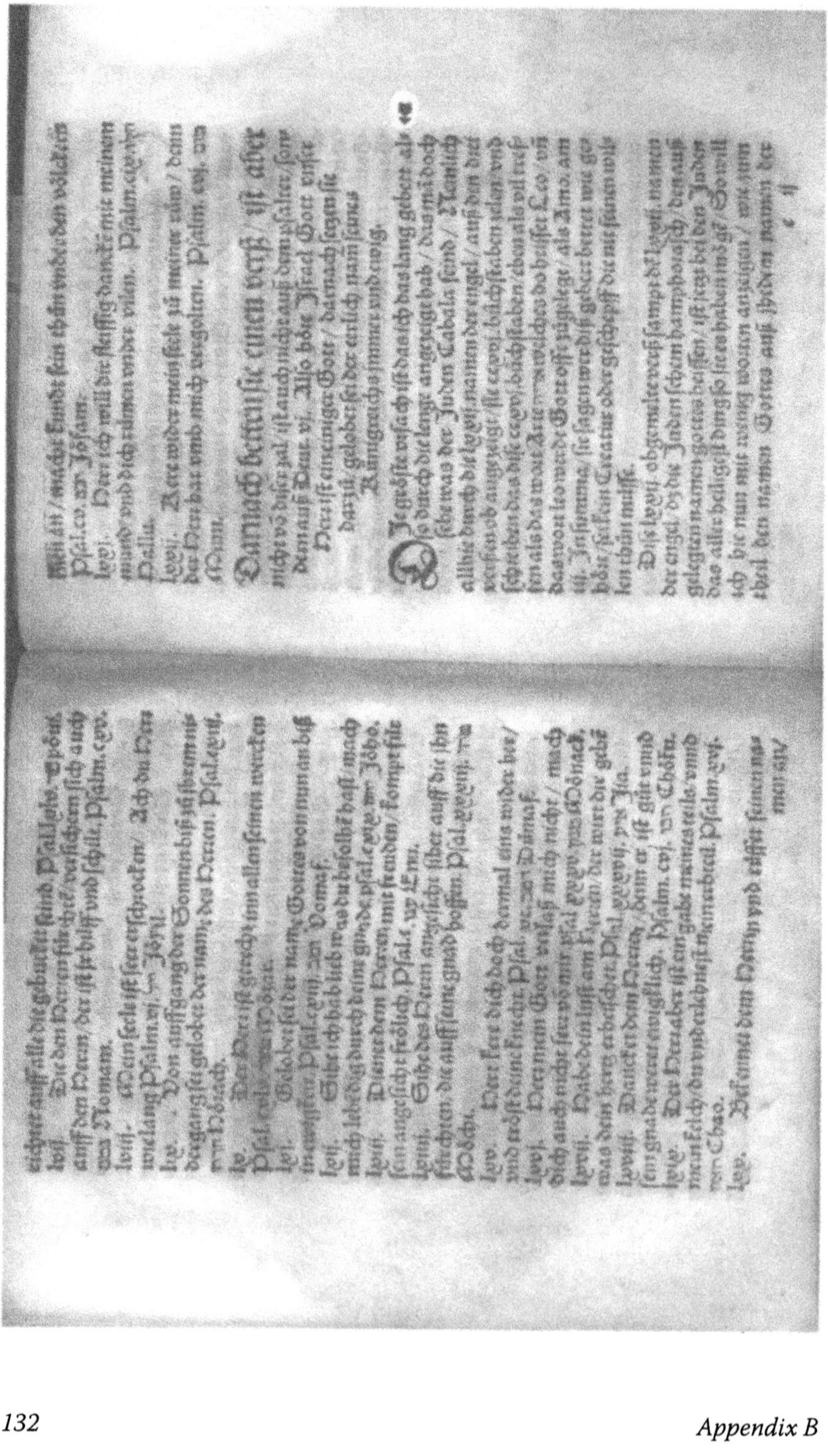

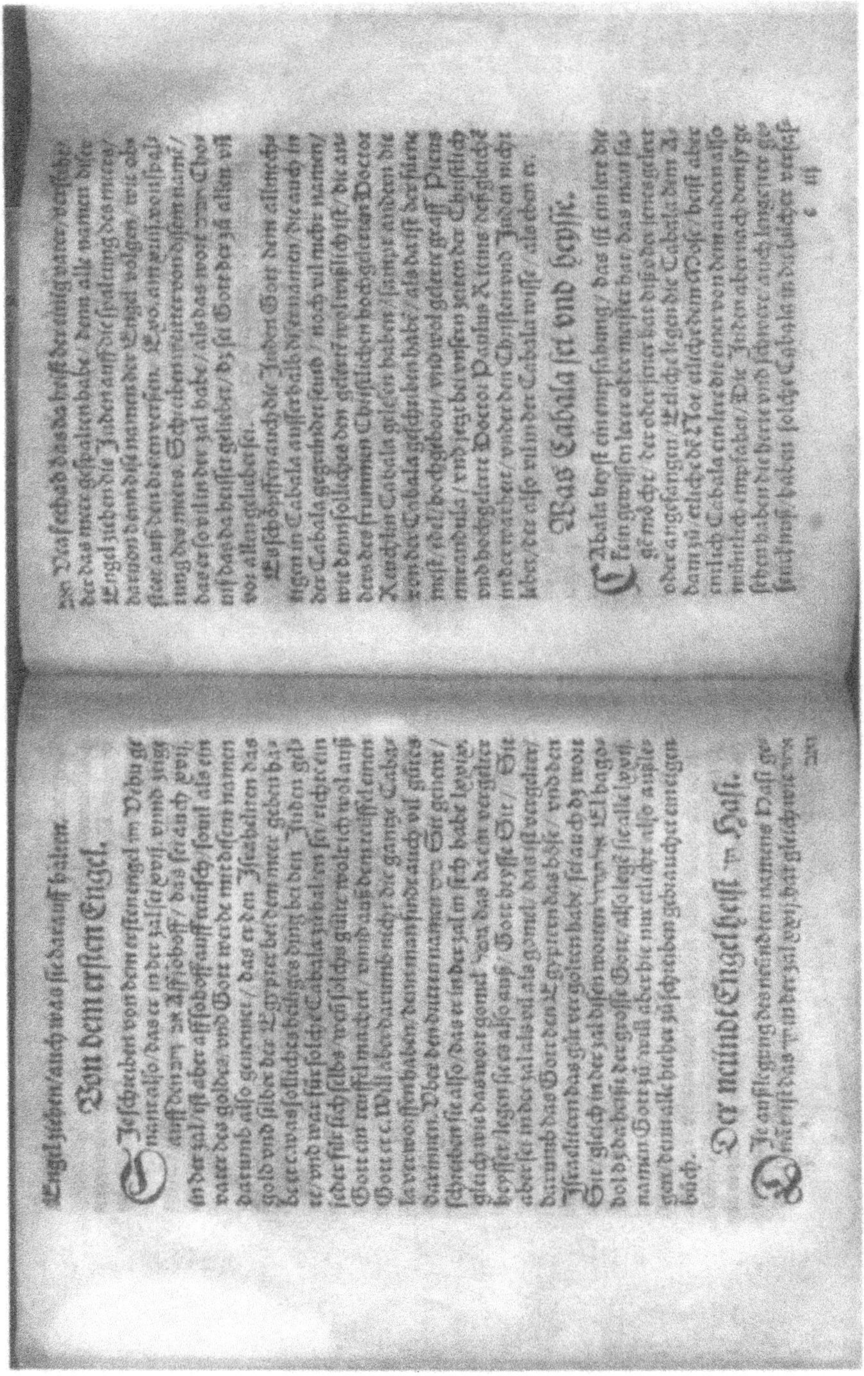
Von dem ersten Engel.

Der neündt Engel heißt Hasi.

Was Cabala sei und heisse.

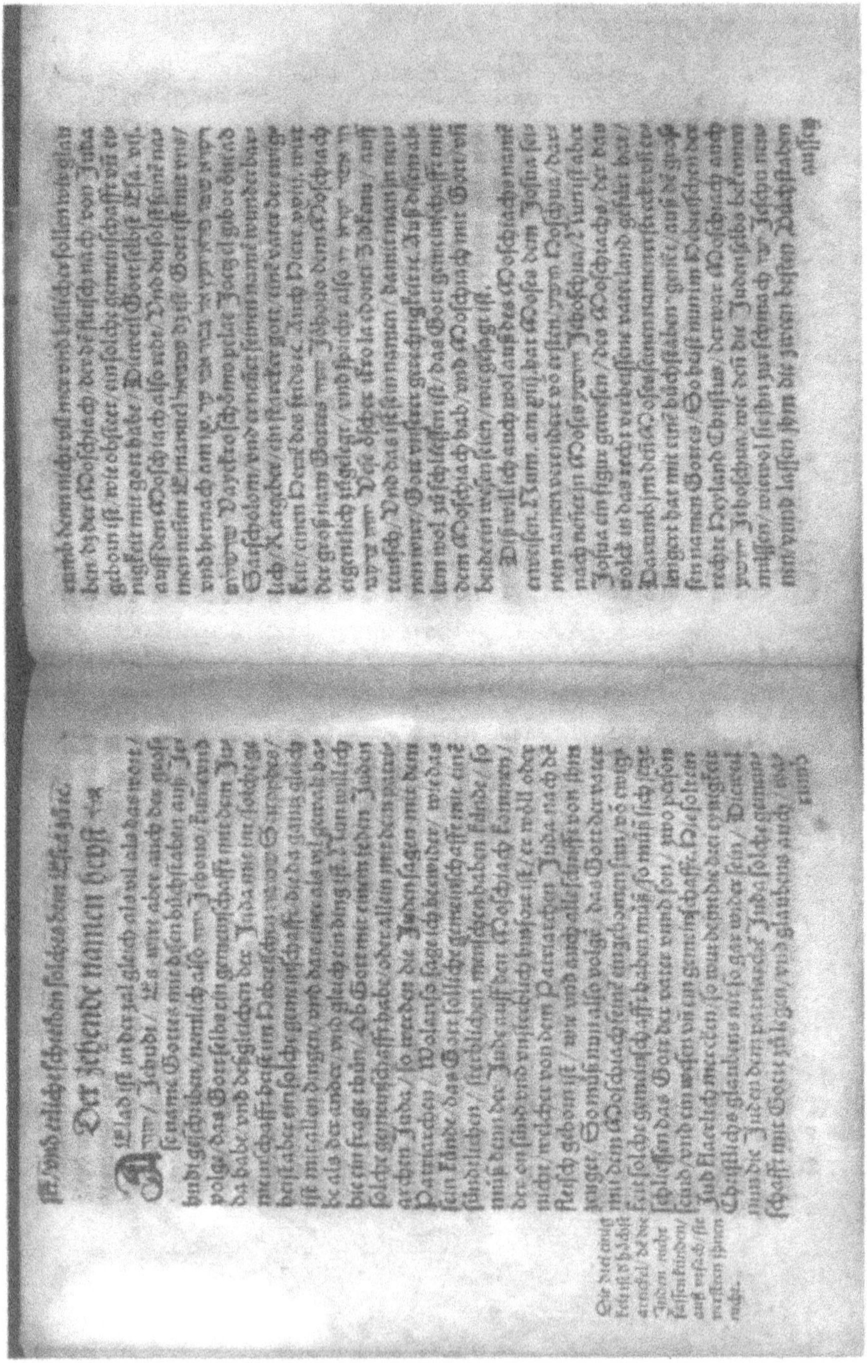

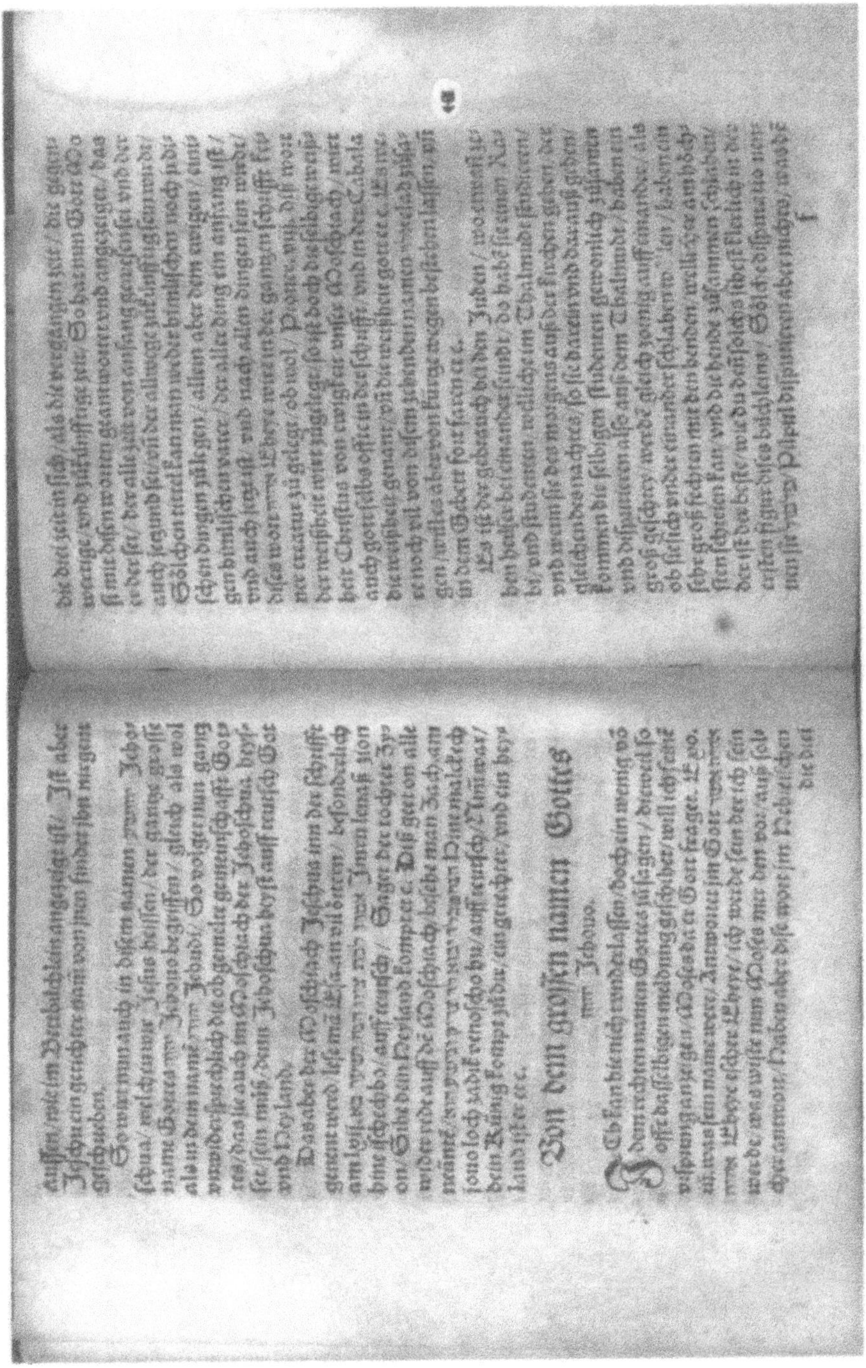

außen/ wie im Betbüchlein angezeigt ist/ Ist aber Jeschu ein gerichter nam von jnen findet jhn niergent geschrieben.

So wirt nun auch in disem namen [illegible] Jehoschua/ welchen wir Jesus heissen/ der gantze grosse name Gottes [illegible] Jehovo begriffen/ gleich als wol als in dem namē [illegible] Jehudi/ So volget nun gantz unwidersprechlich die obgemelte gemeinschafft Gottes/ das sie auch im Moschiach der Jehoschua heyssen sein muß/ denn Jehoschua heyst auff teutsch Gott und Heyland.

Das aber der Moschiach Jeschua inn der schrifft genent werd/ lese mā Esa. an vil örtern/ besonderlich am lxij. [illegible] Jmru lenaß zion hine jschechbo/ auff teutsch/ Saget der tochter Zyon/ Sihe dein Heyland kompt etc. Diß geet on alle widerrede auff dē Moschiach/ besehe man Zach. am neūntē/ [illegible] Hine malkech jovo loch zadik venoscho hu/ auff teutsch/ Nim war/ dein Künig kompt zů dir/ ein gerechter/ und ein heyland ist er etc.

Von dem grossen namen Gottes [illegible] Jehovo.

Ich kan hie nicht underlassen/ doch ein wenig vō dem rechten namen Gottes zů sagen/ dieweil so offt dasselbigen meldung geschihet/ will ich seine ursprung anzeigen/ Moses da er Gott fraget. Exo. iij. was sein name were/ Antwortet jm Gott [illegible] Ehye ascher Ehye/ ich werde sein der ich sein werde/ was wiste nun Moses mit den wor/ auß solcher antwort/ Haben aber dise wort im Hebreischen die drei

die drei zeit in sich/ als die vergangen zeit/ die gegenwertige/ und zůkünfftige zeit/ So hat nun Gott Mosi mit disen worten geantwortet und angezeiget/ das er der sei/ der alle zeit von anfang gewesen sei und der auch jetzund sei/ vñ der allwege zůkünfftig sein wirdt/ Sölchen tittel kan man weder himlischen noch jrdischen dingen zůlegen/ allein aber dem ewigen/ einigen himlischen vater/ der aller ding ein anfang ist/ und auch jetzt ist/ und nach allen dingen sein wirdt/ dises wort [illegible] Ehye wirt in der gantzen schrifft keiner creatur zů gelegt/ ob wol/ Prover. viij. diß wort der weißheit wirt zůgelegt/ so ist doch dieselbige weißheit Christus von ewigkeit unser Moschiach/ wirt auch gott selbs offt in der schrifft/ und in der Cabala die weißheit genant/ vñ die weißheit gott etc. Es were noch vil von disem zehenden namen [illegible] zůsagen/ will es aber von kürtze wegen bestehen lassen/ vñ in dem Gebett fort faren etc.

Es ist der gebrauch bei den Juden/ wo etwañ zehen heuser beieinander seindt/ do habē sie einen Rabi/ und studenten/ welliche im Thalmudt studieren/ und wenn sie des morgens auß der kirchen gehen/ der gleichen des nachts/ so sie darein und darauß gehen/ kommen die selbigen studenten gewonlich zůsamen und disputieren also auß dem Thalmudt/ haben ein groß geschrey/ werdē gleich zornig auff einander/ als ob sie sich under einander schlahen w[illegible]len/ haben ein sehr groß fechten mit den henden/ welliches am höchsten schreien kan/ und die hende zůsammen schlahen/ der ist der beste/ wie du deñ solchs sihest klerlich in der ersten figur dises büchleins/ Sölche disputatio nennen sie [illegible] Pilpul disputieren aber nichts/ was dē

f

Appendix C

Der gantz Jüdisch glaub *in the Sixteenth Century*

Der gantz Jüdisch glaub was Margaritha's most influential and enduring composition. Its history in the sixteenth century indicates how it might have shaped attitudes toward Jews and Judaism. Margaritha composed two editions, the first in 1530 and the second in 1531. The second edition contains changes made in response to his debate with Josel of Rosheim and subsequent imprisonment. Smarting from his treatment by the imperial authorities, he expanded the introduction with a section revealing that the Jews, while praising the emperor in public, cursed him and his empire in private. "They curse and ridicule Christianity . . . notably they refer to [his] imperial majesty with careful words and then curse and damn his imperial majesty and empire."[1] He also added a section to the "Refutation of the Jewish Faith" in which he argued that, unlike most Jews, Jesus was a true descendant of Abraham. Other true descendants were those Jews who had converted to Christianity in the past or who would convert in the future. "Christ [is] indeed from the family of Abraham with all the Jews who accepted the Christian belief in apostolic times and thereafter."[2] He then supplemented material in his commentary on the prayer book (see Appendix D). Finally, he altered the last page to read that the book was being issued in the tenth year of his rebirth, rather than the ninth, as he had written in the first edition.

I

The various printings of the two editions and their illustrations are instructive as to the availability of *Der gantz Jüdisch glaub* and its ethnographical import. The first edition was printed twice, in March and April 1530, in Augsburg by Heinrich Steyner. The second edition also had two printings in 1531. Steyner issued it in Augsburg without his name in a colophon, and Melchior Lotther printed it in Leipzig, with his name in a colophon. Each edition and printing used the same illustrations, which were taken from earlier works by Pfefferkorn[3] (see figs. 2). Lotther became Margaritha's publisher during his three-year residence in Leipzig.

Only one additional printing appeared before Margaritha's death in 1542. It was assembled from the first edition in 1540 by Jasper von Gennep, a Catholic printer and playwright in Cologne noted for his polemical work. This printing is not a complete copy of the book; it does not contain the translation of the prayer book, and no illustrations accompany the text. Further, it is poorly edited. For example, the "Christian reader" is told that the prayer book translation is part of the text, but it is not. This printing has only seventy-nine pages of text, a title page, and a colophon emblem. It is much shorter than the 183 pages of the first edition and the 215 pages of the second.

Von Gennep was the only printer to alter the text, aside from spelling and punctuation. He changed the title from *Der gantz Jüdisch glaub mit sampt ainer Warhaffligen enzeigunge aller Satgungen, Ceremonien*... to *Der Jüdisch glaub*... *mit allen Ceremonien, satzungen.* He also added a subtitle, which was explicitly anti-Jewish, unlike Margaritha's more "ethnographic" title in the earlier printings. It read "a counsel against the Jews that they oppress the poor, needy Christians with their usury . . . very dear to read [*eyn raitschlag widder die Juden / das sy die arme noittuerfftige Christē / mit jrē bedruechliehen wuecher nit so gar beswerlich und faelslich in sich Syndenmoegen*... *Gar lieblich zu lesen*]." It appears that Von Gennep's title page was not original to Margaritha's book, but was a woodcut designed for another work. It pictured the Virgin Mary at the top with the Latin motto, "Hail Full of Grace," and the Jewish notables Jacob, Ezekiel, Levi, Nathan, Obed, Aaron, Josiah, Solomon, and David on the sides. The bottom reads, in a Latin translation of Isaiah 11:1, "a shoot will come forth from the root of Jesse and a twig shall grow from his roots."

All other sixteenth-century issues (1544, 1556, and 1561) of *Der gantz Jüdisch glaub* originated in Frankfurt am Main and were based on the second edition of 1531. The Frankfurt printings of *Der gantz Jüdisch glaub* did not identify their printer. As they all use the same title page and illustrations, which were not copied from Pfefferkorn's work, it is reasonable to assume that they originated in the same publishing house (figs. 4). Maria Diemling suggested, with a question mark, that they were produced by the noted Frankfurt printer Christian Egenolff, and R. Po-chia Hsia stated that Egenolff was the printer.[4] The Egenolff attribution seems unlikely for two reasons. First, as far as is known, Egenolff placed his name and printer's device proudly on his publications. Second, two 1544 Frankfurt copies of *Der gantz Jüdisch glaub* are attributed in German library catalogs to the printer Cyriacus Jacob (Berlin, Staats bibliotheckzu Berlin Preussischer Kulturbesitz, VD16M977 and Bayerische Staats Bibliotheck, QLLC #220811048). It seems probable that Jacob and his printing house issued all of the Frankfurt editions.[5]

The printings after his death show the continuing relevance of Margaritha's work. If one assumes that a printing comprised not less than five hundred copies, which seems to have been a bare minimum in the sixteenth century, then there were at least 1,500 copies of the first edition and 1,000 of the second available during Margaritha's lifetime.[6] This comports with the fact that copies of the 1530 and 1531 printings are commonly found in European and American libraries. The Cologne printing is scarce. The Frankfurt printings may have contributed another 1,500 plus copies. The 1544 and 1561 Frankfurt issues are more common than the 1556, but not so plentiful in published library catalogs as those of 1530–31. Viewed by date of issue, *Der gantz Jüdisch glaub* was offered for purchase regularly over a thirty-year period. Demand must have driven its printing, but we cannot identify its specific readers. A reasonably common book in Germany, it was without doubt a preeminent source for information on Jewish life and practices in the sixteenth century. Like many such books, its survival rate was limited, making it ultimately scarce in the collections of individuals and libraries.

II

Although the woodcuts that Margaritha and his publishers chose for *Der gantz Jüdisch glaub* were copied from Pfefferkorn's published work, they were not mere decorations. They were illustrative of crucial points in the text. Each portrayed one or more common Jewish rituals, *kapporoth*, female immersion in the *mikveh*, the priestly blessing, penitential whipping before the Day of Atonement, and casting sins to the fish (*tashlich*). These illustrations may have appeared exotic and superstitious to German readers. They also depicted a Jewish ritual meal and the altar in the temple. Artistically crude, the woodcuts provided ethnographic information. The woodcuts make an obvious theological point; they show many of the Jewish figures as blindfolded with a kind of gauze veil. This comports with the popular understanding of Jews as blind. The synagogue was depicted with a blindfold in sculptures, paintings, and plays.[7]

A

The first illustration (fig. 2a) is of a synagogue sanctuary on New Year (Rosh Hashanah). The curtain (*parochat*) of the Holy Ark, which contained the scrolls of the Pentateuch (Torah), is open. A reader (cantor?) stands at a lectern, which holds a prayer book. Candles are lit on each side. All other figures are also standing, honoring the visible Torah when the ark is open. Two men hold ram's horns (*shofars*). They stand on either side of the table where the scroll of the Torah would be placed when it was read aloud. One man seems to be directing the other in the order of the *shofar* blowing. It is more likely that the reader or cantor would actually have called out the commands to blow.

The women and children are behind a frame (*mehitzah*), which separates them from the men. The position of the women and children shows the partition of the holy community (*kehillah*) during religious services, with men playing an active role and women sitting separately from them (see Appendix D below). In part, this reflects the fact that the synagogue was largely a male space. A further distinction between men and women is seen in their clothing. Although both are dressed in long garments that cover the arms and reach to the floor, only the men wear prayer shawls (*tallit*) with fringes (*tzizit*). All except one of the women are shown with covered hair, a sign of married status.

What seem strange in the picture are the two figures in the space between the women's gallery and the men. One appears to be a woman, the other a man holding a chicken. Both are kneeling. Such a posture would not comport with the open ark and the *shofar* blowing. This incongruous addition to the scene probably does not represent part of the service, but is included as a visual reference to the pre–Yom Kippur *kapporoth* ritual. The totality of this first woodcut presents the Jewish enactment of the well-known biblical practice of observing the beginning of the New Year. Although exotic to Christian eyes, with the exception of the chicken rite, it seems a benign representation of Jewish religion, neither unexpected nor superstitious.

The second woodcut (fig. 2b), unlike the New Year's illustration, depicts an extrabiblical act, the symbolic casting away of one's sins before Yom Kippur. The women are standing above the men near water. The women have bread in their aprons, and the men hold the bread in their robes. They are performing *tashlich,* throwing their sins, represented by breadcrumbs, into the water, on the first non-Sabbath day of the New Year.

Both Ashkenazic and Sephardic Jews practiced *tashlich,* although it is not mentioned in the Bible or in the Talmud or by the early rabbis. Before the middle of the sixteenth century, it was well established, although Josef Karo barely mentioned the ceremony in the *Shulchan Aruch* (1542). Moses Isserles commented on it in his *Mapah* to *Orach Chaim* 583:2. The textual basis, or rationalization, for the ceremony is Micah 7:19, "He will again be merciful to us, he will subdue our iniquities and cast into the depths all their sins."

What makes the picture appear unusual are the many fish heads peering out of the water. These are connected to a rabbinic belief that as God always watches humans, so do the fish, because their eyes never close. Given that *tashlich* is not a biblical practice and purports to remove sin without a savior, Margaritha's description of it must have seemed to Christians to be a proof of the fallen, superstitious nature of Jews. The men and women appear foolish and benighted. The text and the woodcut combine to form a very powerful polemic against rabbinic error.

The third woodcut (fig. 2c) actually contains four scenes. The top half illustrates the *kapporoth* ceremony. Margaritha criticized *kapporoth* at length, as discussed above, but his ridicule would not have carried the same weight without the picture. Men, women, and children kneel to have a rooster or hen waved above their heads and the propitiatory words recited. The fowls are clearly cocks for men and hens for women. *Kapporoth* does not take place in the sanctuary, but in a large room.

The lower left corner consists of two quite incompatible scenes. One is a festive dinner, either the meal before the Day of Atonement fast or the breaking of the fast. Below the diners are two women in a ritual bath (*mikveh*). One woman has her hair covered while the other's is unbound. Because Jewish law requires complete nudity when immersing in a *mikveh,* it can be concluded that the flowing-haired woman is purifying herself and that the other is a witness. The chaste nudity of the *mikveh* is certainly incongruous in front of the dining table.

The lower right corner of the woodcut shows a kitchen, which is a room apart from the dining room in the adjoining panel. It is impossible to determine what is being cooked, but it is almost certain that it is not the chickens from *kapporoth.* They were given to the poor.

The structure of woodcut 2c highlights the superstitious practice of *kapporoth* as explained by Margaritha. The juxtaposition of dining hall and *mikveh* may have led the reader to see Jews as sensual and unchaste, especially as neither woman covers her breasts. This was, of course, not necessarily the message Margaritha had in mind, as the woodcut was originally from Pfefferkorn's work. There is nothing in Margaritha's text that supports the idea that Jews were especially sensual.

The fourth woodcut (fig. 2d) depicts a synagogue interior on Yom Kippur, which occurs ten days after Rosh Hashanah. It completes the Days of Awe (*Yomim Norayim*), the holiest period of the Jewish year. The scene is a composite. Two men using special paddles are whipping the two kneeling figures on their exposed bottoms. This represents the custom under Jewish law of receiving blows, *makoth,* as punishment before Yom Kippur. Although the action is pictured as taking place in a synagogue, it would have been entirely inappropriate to expose a nether part of the body in a sanctuary.

Before the open Holy Ark, three barefoot figures cover their eyes. They are priests, *cohanim,* who are about to bless the congregation. Their feet would have been washed by the Levites of the congregation before they ascended the platform (*bimah*). The congregants face away from the priest while hearing the awesome words, "May the Lord bless you and protect you; may the Lord shine his countenance upon you and be gracious to you; may the Lord favor you and grant you peace" (Numbers 6:24–26). To the side, a reader stands with a prayer book. He would recite the words and the priests would repeat after him. The priestly blessing, which made up a significant portion of the service, recalled the atonement ceremony in the temple before its destruction. Indeed, much of the service was taken from scripture and followed the Talmudic passages that described the temple service. Again, the women and children observe the action from behind a *mehitzah.*

In days when physical punishment was common and the pious Christian humiliated his own flesh, the picture of paddling may have evoked some humor, but would not have been considered bizarre. A Christian would also have recognized the priestly blessing as appropriate in a religious ceremony. The significance of the scene, of course, was not self-explanatory, and the Christian reader needed an explanation of the biblical temple ceremony connection to the synagogue service. A Christian is included in the scene as the "Shabbos goy," the non-Jew who lit the candles in the synagogue, a task Jews could not do on a holy day. While the Jews avert their eyes, the Christian looks directly at the priests during the enactment of the blessing.

Of the illustrations chosen for *Der gantz Jüdisch glaub,* the woodcut of the altar, the holy fire, and the cherubs on the Ark of the Covenant (fig. 2e) is the most enigmatic. It is placed at the beginning of the prayer book translation and hence is not part of the ethnography illustrated by the other woodcuts. But if Margaritha himself chose this illustration from several available, it may be because he felt that the temple and its altar was the perfect icon for the prayer book, especially for the early section, which recounted the various offerings or sacrifices (*korbanoth*).

The daily prayers, and especially the recitation and study of the temple offerings, became the focus of Jewish worship after the destruction of the temple. The temple service was known technically as the *avodah,* or work. Daily worship was the *avodath lev,* the work/service of the heart. This transformation was explained on the basis of Hosea 14:2, "So we will offer for bullocks the sacrifices of our lips." Prayer was a true sacrifice from the heart, equivalent to the sacrifices brought to the temple (see Appendix D below for details).

On the sides of the woodcut are the directions of the compass in both Hebrew and German, corresponding to the sides of the altar. East is morning, west sunset, south midday, and north midnight. The directions around the altar were connected to both the temple and prayer. First, the daily offerings mentioned in the prayer book were often keyed to where they were located near the altar. For example, *Mishnah Zevahim* 5, the part of the Talmud that deals with offerings in the temple, specified that the holiest offerings were to be slaughtered on the north side of the altar and the blood was poured, sprinkled, toward the Holy of Holies, the rest of the blood was poured on the south side, and so on. Further, the three daily prayer services corresponded to the morning offerings and the afternoon sacrifices, which could be burned in the evening until midnight.

In Margaritha's view, the altar scene was a shorthand explanation of the prayer book on one hand and a critique of it on the other. The temple and its altar looked not to the service of the heart, but rather to the sacrifices that prefigured Jesus, who by his sacrifice and grace ended the need for temple sacrifice. Whatever sincerity the Jews evinced in prayer, and Margaritha did not doubt the genuineness of their devotion, they would have been better off to see the true meaning of the temple and understand why it had been destroyed. The prayer book, although based in scripture, was a singular example of the rabbinic constructions that kept the Jews from accepting the true Messiah. Margaritha's various anti-Jewish asides in his translation of the prayer book, such as those noted above and in Appendix D below, indicate that the choice of the altar woodcut alluded to the failure of the Jews to understand the purpose of their own temple. Jesus as the resurrected savior was the temple and its sacrificial cult personified. Jewish prayer was therefore based on a false premise and helped keep the Jews from accepting the Messiah.

B

The first Frankfurt printing of *Der gantz Jüdisch glaub* came out two years after Margaritha's death, and it is unlikely that he had anything to do with its publication. The woodcuts appear to have been specifically made for the work, unlike those in the editions of 1530 and 1531.[8] They do, however, have their own significance for sixteenth-century Jewish ethnography. As with the Pfefferkorn originals, the Frankfurt illustrations are composites showing several rituals in one panel, but display a superior artistic quality. They are more refined and realistic. The figures are no longer blindfolded, and some faces are individualistic and expressive. The number of woodcuts for the ethnography section was reduced from four to two. The New Year and *tashlich* scenes were omitted. The written text of *Der gantz Jüdisch glaub* remained the same as that of the 1531 second edition.

The ethnographic value of the Frankfurt woodcuts lies not only in their function as illustrations for Margaritha's text, a function they perform admirably as had the earlier ones. The unknown Frankfurt artist also provided a different view of the synagogue, Jews, and Jewish rituals than did the anti-Jewish creator of Pfefferkorn's woodcuts. The first Frankfurt illustration (fig. 4a) contains three scenes: a dinner, *kapporoth,* and women in a *mikveh.* There is no interior view of a synagogue, but the themes agree with the New Year's meal and the *kapporoth* before Yom Kippur.

The dinner scene seems genuinely joyous. The host, the *baal bayit* or master of the house, is a large man with the facial expression of someone engaged in pleasant talk. No women sit at the table. Those eating and one servant wear the round Jew-badge that was required by law after 1530 (see below). The meal consists of meat, and the diners sit on plush cushions. The meal scene in the Pfefferkorn illustrations takes place just behind the *mikveh.* In this one, the meal occurs above the other scenes in the frame.

To the left, men perform the *kapporoth* ritual. Two kneel with roosters and one, having completed the blessing, walks away. The right quarter pictures a *mikveh.* One woman covers her eyes, a traditional pose of concentration during the recitation of a blessing. Two fully dressed women observers, one of whom holds a towel, flank her. The head covering of the woman who is about to immerse herself lies in the foreground. The *mikveh* scene shows sensitivity to the ritual and does not depict the naked breasts with nipples. The representation of the immersing woman covering her eyes betrays some knowledge of the ritual on the part of the artist or designer. It is unlikely that the depiction of the *mikveh* in an anti-Jewish book was softened in deference to the Jewish community of Frankfurt.[9] One can tentatively hypothesize that the artist researched his subject.

The second woodcut is also a composite (fig. 4b). It shows the priestly blessing of the Day of Atonement and the whipping done the evening before. There are no non-Jews in the scene and the Jews wear prayer shawls that cover their Jew-badges. There are no women and no *mehitzah.* In the foreground, one man whips another with a paddle. To the side, four men engage in prayers of the type represented in the Pfefferkorn scene. The penitent being whipped does not bare his buttocks. This is a less defamatory illustration of the ritual than in the earlier woodcut.

The barefoot priests on the elevated platform add no information to that shown in the earlier illustration. The Holy Ark, however, is very different from that pictured in the woodcuts chosen by Margaritha. The synagogues pictured in the 1530–31 and Frankfurt printings may have been drawn with actual buildings in mind. However, it is unlikely that Margaritha can be shown to have visited either. The ark in the printings overseen by Margaritha is a large one with a full-length curtain (*parochet*) hanging before it. Such arks are well known in fourteenth- and fifteenth-century illustrations.[10] Most were Gothic in style, but some were large cabinets, such as the one depicted in *Der gantz Jüdisch glaub.*[11] The synagogue in Regensburg at the time Margaritha lived there probably housed a more elaborate ark than the one pictured in the 1530 woodcut.

The ark in the illustration in the Frankfurt *Der gantz Jüdisch glaub* is a niche ark, set into a wall. This type of ark is also known from illustrations in other texts.[12] This particular niche ark has a lock and no *parochet.* It is also to the side of the blessing priest, although across from the three seated men who may represent synagogue leaders. It was counter to Jewish practice not to have a curtain. It is, however, correct that candles would flank the reader who stood before the ark. This appears to be a synagogue scene drawn with the aid of memory or incomplete information, but not totally from imagination.

The altar woodcut (fig. 4c) in the Frankfurt printing adds nothing to the text of *Der gantz Jüdisch glaub* not found in the earlier cruder depiction. It differs mainly in presenting the altar, the utensils, and the other elements of the temple in a respectful, balanced, and artistic manner. The candelabrum (*menorah*) is pictured creatively, for an actual menorah's candles would be in a line, not at varying heights. The Ark of the Covenant does not have the cherubs attached; rather, they hover above it with earnest facial expressions. The stack of shew bread sits on its tray next to the gold vessels.

The ark and other illustrations of the Frankfurt printing do not convey the strident anti-Jewishness of the 1530–31 woodcuts. They perform the task of making Margaritha's words and criticism visual in a more neutral manner. Their artistry and deviation from the earlier pictures refine the message and add to an ethnographic view of Jews in a way that seems subtler than the accompanying critical text.

C

It is worth noting the differences between the title pages of the 1530 and 1531 printings and those of the Frankfurt (fig. 5). The earlier editions picture a group of twelve Jews, the later only two. The badge affixed to their coats identifies them as Jews. Jews had been required to wear a badge, here a (yellow) ring, in some jurisdictions since the thirteenth century. Augsburg required men to wear a yellow ring and women a yellow veil in 1434. In 1530, all German Jews were compelled by imperial edict to affix the badge to their clothing. By the third Frankfurt printing in 1561, the woodcut had become so worn down that in some copies the left figure lacks a badge, and only the right figure appears to wear one. Only one Jew was left to visually identify the subject of *Der gantz Jüdisch glaub,* an erring and persecuted people.[13]

Appendix D

Margaritha's Prayer Book

Margaritha's coupling of his ethnography with a translation of the prayer book was a logical outgrowth of his goal of explaining Judaism and its private and secret aspects to Christians. The prayer book was and is an essential element in Jewish religious life. In the sixteenth century, there was no secular Jewishness. Every Jew, even transients and the less observant, fell under the purview of the local *kehillah.* Each man participated to a lesser or greater degree in a daily life that stressed the requirement of praying three times. Prayer was not conceived of as a personal obligation only, but also as a communal duty, a necessary element of the service of God, which fell upon all males thirteen years old or older. Female members of the community were exempt from time-bound commandments, such as praying a specified number of times at certain times of the day; men were expected to attend synagogue prayer services each morning and each afternoon-evening. A quorum of ten qualified males was necessary to perform *all* the prayers. This number was derived from Abraham's negotiation with God over the fate of Sodom and Gomorrah; ten righteous men would have saved the cities. The number ten was reinforced in many texts, such as the Talmudic tractate *Pirke Avoth* 3:7, where Rabbi Chalafta states, "When ten sit together and occupy themselves with the Torah, the Shechinah [Divine Presence] abides among them."

I

The prayer book and the synagogue were the essence of the portable religion and culture of a people landless for nearly 1,500 years at the time of Margaritha's conversion. The synagogue dated from at least the Babylonian captivity, and its nascent prayers and rituals formed the basis of a liturgy that developed throughout the second temple period. The psalms, biblical passages, temple practices, and blessings developed for daily life were the materials from which the protorabbis, the scribes and Pharisees, created an order of prayer. The outlines of the prayer book existed when the *Mishnah* was written down under the direction of Rabbi Judah the Prince in the second century of the Common Era.[1] In its final form the prayerbook consisted of:

1. Introductory blessings and meditations;
2. Chapters of psalms and scriptural passages;
3. The "Service" proper with the call to worship and the *Shema* and its blessings;
4. The Standing Prayer (*amidah*) with its nineteen blessings;
5. Final materials, including the prayer for mercy, the *Aleinu,* and psalms.

In most cases, the end of the sections was marked by a doxology, the *kaddish.*

The development of the prayer book's specific blessings and meditations, which came to form the sections, can be traced in the Talmud.[2] The sages of the Talmud formulated and discussed the meanings and contexts of blessings in a variety of passages in several tractates that dealt with varied aspects of Jewish law. Such diffuse analyses of liturgical requirements presuppose that the elements of the liturgy were known and accepted as normative. The Talmud presents a worship structure consisting of morning blessings, acknowledgments of the creator, the *Shema* (the credal statement of God's unity), the *amidah* with its initial eighteen (and then nineteen) benedictions, and scripture study. The exact order of a service is not explicitly set forth, but extra-Talmudic tradition indicates that the order listed above has been used for centuries.

The blessings that were said upon rising were first associated, understandably, with morning activities in the home. Later, they became part of a communal recitation. They included general thanks to God for life and specific statements concerning his powers and mercies. As the Talmud says:

> When he wakes he says: "My God, the soul which thou hast placed in me is pure. Thou hast fashioned it in me. Thou didst breathe it into me, and Thou preservest it within me and Thou wilt one day take it from me and restore it to me in the time to come. So long as the soul is within me I give thanks unto Thee, O Lord, my God, and the God of my fathers, Sovereign of all worlds, Lord of all souls. Blessed art Thou, O Lord, who restorest souls to dead corpses." When he hears the cock crowing he should say: "Blessed is He who has given to the cock understanding to distinguish between day and night." When he opens his eyes he should say: "Blessed is He who opens the eyes of the blind." When he stretches himself and sits up, he should say: "Blessed is He who looseneth the bound." When he dresses he should say: "Blessed is He who clothes the naked." When he draws himself up he should say, "Blessed is He who raises the bowed." When he steps on the ground he should say, "Blessed is he who spread the earth on the waters."[3]

Rabbi Judah the Prince (second century CE), compiler of the *Mishnah,* taught that a man was obligated to say three additional blessings daily: Blessed art thou our God who has made me an Israelite (some manuscripts read: who has not made me a heathen), who has not made me a woman, and who has not made me a crude person.[4] Rabbi Aha ben Jacob (c. 300 CE) challenged saying "crude person" and reformulated the blessing to read, "did not make me a slave."[5] These blessings were predicated on the pride Jews felt in possessing God's commandments, which distinguished them from other nations. Men also felt gratitude that unlike women and slaves, they were obligated to keep the time-bound commandments.

The second component of the liturgy was the *Shema* and its blessings. The *Shema* was spoken at rising and at bedtime, as commanded in Deuteronomy 5:7: "when you lie down and when you rise up." The recitation became part of the synagogue service. "R. Joshua ben Levi says, even if a person read (*karah*) the *shema* in the synagogue, it is a commandment to read it on his bed."[6] The word *karah* means to call aloud. It seems that the custom of reciting the prayers aloud in the synagogue was established by this time (early third century CE). The requirement of saying the *shema* at home raised the question of the necessity of synagogue worship. The essential prayers could be done at home, but there was a strong social imperative to attend group worship, so strong that Abba Benjamin said, "The prayer of a man is heard only in the synagogue."[7]

The *amidah* or *tefillah* prayer consisted originally of eighteen benedictions. These became obligatory.

> R. Gamaliel says, every day a man should pray the 18. R. Joshua says the short form. R. Akiva says if his prayer is fluent in his mouth, he prays the 18, if not the short form.[8]

When Christianity became an issue in the form of Christian Jews who attended synagogue, a blessing (actually a curse) was added to the eighteen. The nineteenth benediction was composed at the court of Rabbi Gamliel in Javneh, where the eighteen benedictions were established as part of the liturgy.

> Our Rabbis taught: Simeon ha-Pakuli arranged the 18 benedictions in order before Rabban Gamaliel in Jabneh. Said Rabban Gamaliel to the Sages: Can any one among you frame a benediction relating to the *Minim* (heretics)? Samuel the Lesser arose and composed it.[9]

After the recitation of the *amidah* on Saturday, Monday, and Thursday, a section of the Torah (Pentateuch) was read. On Saturdays, festivals, and fast days, a lesson from the prophets followed the Torah reading. This was and remained the basic structure of the liturgy. Appropriate materials were added for special days, including a second *amidah* (*musaf*) to commemorate the additional sacrifices offered in the temple on Sabbaths and festivals. Of great importance to communal worship were two items of prayer clothing, the *tallit* and the *tefillin.* Each male was commanded to put on a four-corned garment with fringes (*tzitzit*), reciting the blessing, "Blessed is he who has made us holy with his commandments and commanded us to wrap ourselves with *tzitzit.*"[10] He also put on *tefillin,* two leather boxes containing the *Shema* and blessings from the Pentateuch (Deuteronomy 6:49; Exodus 13:10 and 11–16) and attached to straps.[11] One box was strapped to the head and the other to the upper left arm (or right arm if the worshipper was left-handed). He recited, "Blessed is he who has made us holy with his commandments and commanded us to affix (lay) *tefillin.*"[12] Absent such ritual items, the rabbis taught that the blessings, *amidah,* and scripture study were futile. The Jew thus surrounded himself with the precepts of the Torah by wearing fringes and *tefillin.* Without them, he was almost naked before God.[13]

II

The liturgy assembled in the last century BCE and the first centuries of the Common Era was the platform to which Jews of the next eleven centuries attached elements that expressed their needs and ameliorated their pain in wandering and persecution. It became more and more a portable replacement for the temple service, functioning to bind the people together wherever they lived and traveled. The psalms that the scholars selected and the poems that they composed invited the Divine Presence into their synagogues, communities, and homes. The prayer book of the immediate post-Talmudic period contained only a fraction of the material that was later used. The Talmudic sages had chosen to set the scriptural passages into a Hebrew context, although they conducted their daily affairs and legal discussions in Aramaic. The primary language of prayer could only be the Holy Tongue. Only a few passages were written in Aramaic, chiefly the doxology, or *kaddish,* which separated the major liturgical divisions. The wandering people thus retained a national language, which they used three times a day in their continuing conversation with God.

The basic prayer book was common to Jews wherever they resided. Very early on, the order of prayer of the communities in Palestine and Babylon diverged somewhat. Later, different congregations adapted the received basics to local customs, forming their own *nusach,* the text and order of prayer, but all *nusacoth* derive from either the Babylonian or Palestinian rite. Neither of these can be completely reconstructed from extant materials, but they can be seen to underlie the European and oriental orders of prayer. Because Babylon was the dominant center of Jewish study in the posttemple period, even the Palestinian tradition was influenced by it.

The Babylonian *nusach* is associated with Rabbi Amran Gaon (fl. 875 CE) and, because it was used in Spain (*Sephard*), came to be called the *Sephard nusach.* The Jews of Spain, Portugal, the Mediterranean, the orient, and Yemen used this *nusach* as the basis for their prayer services.

The Palestinian *nusach* is associated with Rabbi Saadia Gaon (882–942 CE). Ashkenazic prayer books, those of Germany, Poland, Bohemia, and Russia, developed from this *nusach.* Italian, Romanian, and a few areas of Turkey and the Balkans also followed the Palestinian *nusach.*[14] The Ashkenazic prayer book was the first to be published (1490). The Sephardic was first printed in 1524.[15] Margaritha, as will be discussed below, knew both liturgies and several variants. He was also aware of the hybrid liturgy of France, which had declined in use after the expulsion of the Jews from most of France in the fourteenth century. He indicated that French émigrés had introduced French terms into synagogue life in Regensburg and the Rheinland.

The fluid nature of the blessings and the *amidah* account for most of the differences in the various liturgies. Although the Talmud set the order of basic blessings and their obligatory nature, it did not prescribe the exact verbiage.[16] Variations in the liturgies could be simply a reordering of the blessings or a more complicated choosing of different Psalms and meditations.[17] In the *kaddish* all Sephardic, but not Ashkenazic, congregations added a messianic hope, "may he bring forth his redemption and hasten the coming of the Messiah."[18] (The Ashkenazic Hasidic Jews adopted this addendum in the eighteenth century.)

The technicalities of the Sephardic liturgy are generally of little consequence for a study of Margaritha's translation of the Ashkenazic prayer book. One difference between the Sephardic and Ashkenazic blessings highlights Margaritha's heightened sensitivity to the issue of Jewish condemnation of converts to Christianity. The benediction (curse) against the heretics was a Talmudic mandate. It was designed to ferret out heretics within the congregation. The basic idea, which exposed sectarian members of the community, was part of the service long before Christianity became a state religion and centuries before the rise of Islam. Although the blessing vilified and excluded sectarians, its actual wording was not prescribed. Later Jews, living as they did in Christian and Moslem states, were sensitive to the problems the blessing created for them. It was hardly politic to have a blessing that apparently cursed the people in control. Probably how the German Jews read the nineteenth benediction (which comes twelfth in the order of prayer) is impossible to determine.[19] The most common early modern Ashkenazic version reads, "For the *malshinim* let there be no hope." *Malshinim* means informers or traitors. Pfefferkorn and Reuchlin claimed that the cursed were called *m'shumdim,* and that is the word used in a 1580 printing of the prayer book from Salonika,[20] and in the Yemeni Sephardic prayer book. *M'shumdim* means apostates, that is, Jews who have converted to other religions. What became the normative Sephardic reading is "for the *malshinim* and for the *minim,*" for the traitors and for the Christians (heretics).[21] *Minim* were traditionally understood to be Christians, so the term would not have offended the Moslems with whom most Sephardim lived. On the other hand, it is understandable that the prayer books used in German cities, which are the bases of Margaritha's and Hirtz Treves's works, do not refer to *minim;* neither does Margaritha's translation. A prayerbook printed in Prague in 1519 uses *minim* in the blessing, but not *m'shumdim.* (It also contains the words "arrogant kingdom," *malchuth zadon.*)[22]

On historical and chronological grounds, some assumptions can be made about the nineteenth "blessing." It was drafted soon after the destruction of the second temple, when many Jewish Christians still attended the synagogue; therefore, the word *minim* probably was part of the original. Christians would not willingly curse themselves, so their unwillingness or inability to say the benediction served as test of orthodoxy.[23] By the fifteenth and sixteenth centuries, the word had come to mean all Christians, and therefore it is not surprising that it was dropped from the liturgy in some Christian lands. The use of the word *m'shumdim*, apostates, as per Reuchlin and Pfefferkorn, carried its own problems. Converts to Christianity often "informed" on the community, as did Margaritha in his book, or made up slanders, such as the blood libel, to confirm the worst suspicions about Jews. These converts were also *malshinim*. Even if a curse directed at these new Christians was not written in the manuscript prayer books, the Jewish communities may have said the word. The 1580 printing of the epithet in a prayer book is a proof, albeit weak, that it may have had some currency in German synagogues. One important fact indicates that among Ashkenazim at least the blessing was specifically applied to apostates. Naphtali Hirtz Treves, in his commentary on the blessing, is quite clear that the entreaty referred to the *m'shumdim*. He wrote of the *malshinim*, "they are proselytes and apostates (*mishumdim*) who will be held accountable."[24]

How Jews understood their prayers and what they thought about non-Jews is difficult to determine from the prayer book alone. This is especially true because few prayer books contain commentaries. The *Prague Prayer Book* of 1519, for example, has no commentary. Hirtz Treves's extensive discussion is invaluable and reliable. Margaritha's comments on the prayer book, although biased, are also a source for the oral tradition among Jews. As will be seen below, when Margaritha's accuracy can be tested against other sources, he proves reliable. For most prayer books, variations in blessings provide the only clues to the opinion of their users.

The different forms of the benediction against heretics and traitors in the Sephardic and Ashkenazic liturgies provide data on the problems facing those Jews who lived among non-Jewish majorities. The variant forms also show that the worshippers had an understanding of what was meant, even if certain words were not spoken aloud in prayer or written in the prayer book. This point should be abundantly clear from the discussion of the *Aleinu* prayer above. As Margaritha noted, some congregations retained the words omitted from the *Aleinu* in their printed prayer books. Such was the case with the 1519 Prague edition.[25] The insights into the meaning behind certain prayers are a major aspect of the study of Margaritha's translation. Although his *meshumad* status must be borne in mind, his knowledge of liturgy and its interpretation was significant. His comments are a treasure for understanding Jewish attitudes.

III

It is not possible to identify the prayer book Margaritha used for his translation.[26] His German rendering is not precise, so textual nuances that might single out a particular prayer book are absent. Moreover, he translates the daily prayers only, not the prayers unique to Sabbath and festival, reducing the material that can be used to determine his source. He comments on the Sabbath and festival prayers, but only for polemic and informational purposes.

Apparently Margaritha was using a prayer book that thanked God that he "did not make me a heathen," for he used that phrase, which was the normative text and also used in the *Prague Prayer Book* in 1519. This differs from Naphtali Hirtz Treves's "made me an Israelite," which followed the dominant Talmudic reading.

Margaritha's discussion of prayer book printing in Venice in his commentary on the *Aleinu* could, but does not necessarily, lead to the conclusion that his text was from Venice or perhaps elsewhere in Italy. If he used the prayer book from his days as a Jew in Regensburg, the printing would have been before 1521. Between 1490 and 1521, several Ashkenazic prayer books were printed. Moreover, the Regensburg community may have used manuscript prayer books. Such manuscripts served as the basis of the printed prayer books, such as the Prague 1519 edition. Margaritha's family was closely associated with Prague. Certainly most communities retained and used manuscripts with the order of prayer. Some manuscripts were scholarly and encyclopedic, containing all the prayers said throughout the year, as well as instructions. Such manuscripts were called *Kol Bo*, "everything in it." Soncino printed a *Kol Bo* in 1490 (Naples) and a German order of prayer in 1495. Margaritha surely knew the *Kol Bo* in manuscript, if not in print.

A number of printed Ashkenazic prayer books appeared after Margaritha's conversion in 1521. It can be assumed that these editions were based on manuscripts still in use as well as on previous printings. The demand for printed prayer books in the sixteenth century indicates that communities were replacing traditional manuscript books. Margaritha could have based his translation on a printing made after 1521. As the inventory of his books at death mentions only some Hebrew books, without further designation, the question of which and how many prayer books he owned is open; all of the above is mere speculation. What is certain is that Margaritha had an intimate knowledge of the prayer book from years of using it daily and from his training in the rules of prayer and the worship service. He, like his brother the rabbi and his brother the cantor, was taught and studied the contents of the *Kol Bo.* He and other Jews, applying their knowledge and theory of prayer daily, saw their worship as a service to God, which had to be mastered and done properly. His conversion caused him to rethink Jewish prayer and ritual, but not to forget what had become ingrained.

If the exact copy-text of Margaritha's Hebrew prayer book remains a mystery, its structure and probable appearance can be inferred from known editions. The lore surrounding the prayers was a shared tradition of scholars and laymen. What of that tradition influenced Margaritha is seen in his remarks on the various prayers. He had read the teachings of the twelfth-and thirteenth-century pietist rabbis who composed hymns and wrote the *Sefer Hasidim* (Book of the Pious).[27] Chief among them was Judah the Pious, son of Samuel the Holy. They stressed appropriate, reverent behavior during prayer and developed meditations on God's glory and redemption.[28] Margaritha drew on Judah in his commentary on the prayer book.

The appearance of a printed Ashkenazic prayer book is typified by the *Prague Prayer Book* and the one on which Naftali Hirtz Treves commented. Hirtz Treves's source almost certainly was the one used in Frankfurt, where he served as cantor for more than three decades. The fact that his commentary was not printed until 1560 illustrates the relationship between manuscripts used in communities and printed prayer books in the sixteenth century; the year of printing does not necessarily correlate with the book's first use. Like many prayer books, Hirtz Treves's has a name, *Knowledge of the Lord Will Fill the Earth as Water Covers the Sea.*[29] If Treves's long commentary, which was an unusual feature for a prayer book, is disregarded, the structure and appearance are roughly what might be expected for Margaritha's original Hebrew source.

One can infer much about Margaritha's Hebrew prayer book from the Prague and Hirtz Treves examples.[30] Indeed, printed books often followed the form of manuscripts. In both printed prayer books, the blessings, psalms, and prayers are set in large, square type. Instructions and notes in the *Prague Prayer Book*are in smaller type and in Hirtz Treves's in Rashi type, which is the Hebrew equivalent of italics. First words in very large type, sometimes in decorative boxes, mark the divisions of the book. In both works, the first text is the meditation on entering the synagogue, "How goodly are your tents, Oh Jacob." This is followed by the hymn, "Lord of the World," a rhymed statement of God's infinite nature and his uniqueness.[31] The *kaddish* separating sections is not always printed; its inclusion in the oral prayers depended on the congregation's supplying the omitted lines. In the introductory psalms, those to be added or omitted on the Sabbath are marked with Hebrew (Prague) or Judeo-German instructions

(Hirtz Treves). For example, Psalm 100, "a psalm of thanksgiving," was not sung on Saturday, and the Hirtz Treves instruction reads, "One says this in the week and not on Shabbat" (*Das zagt man in der wochn un nit im Sabbath*).[32]

The organization and even the elements of both prayer books correspond to Margaritha's German translation. The differences lie in Margaritha's more complete explanations and instructions. Whereas the Hebrew text was intended for Jews experienced in synagogue worship, Margaritha was addressing Christians, who had little or no understanding of the Jewish service. Both prayer books also included Sabbath and holiday material after the daily prayers, which Margaritha omitted. Because his purpose was polemical and ethnographical, Margaritha did not need to present the complexities of a *Kol Bo* or even those found in a prayer book designed for use for the entire year.

When one reads Margaritha's translation of the prayer book, it is helpful to envision the layout of a Hebrew edition. Margaritha's directions follow the pattern exhibited in them. Margaritha abbreviated many sections to present the German reader with the basic information he would need to understand the Jewish worship service. He also prefaced the psalms and prayers with their first Hebrew words and, to a degree, a transliteration of the Hebrew into German. This would have allowed a reader to find his place in the service, although it is highly unlikely that a German Christian would have visited a synagogue with *Der gantz Jüdisch glaub* in hand.

Margaritha's work also differed from the Hebrew originals in that his critical, anti-Jewish interpretations turned his prayer book into an ethnographic polemic. His presentation of the traditions and motivations behind the prayers, however, served much the same purpose of educating and informing the reader as did the longer, more Jewishly relevant comments of Hirtz Treves. Mieses's criticism notwithstanding, Margaritha created a credible German-Christian edition of the Ashkenazic order of prayer.

IV

Margaritha's prayer book continues his grappling with many of the matters dealt with in the ethnographical section of *Der gantz Jüdisch glaub.*[33] His commentary reveals the conflict between his former Jewish life and learning and his Christianity. The overlap, repetition, and difference in the development of themes give the impression that the two primary parts of *Der gantz Jüdisch glaub* likely were not written at the same time. They seem to have been put together at a later date so that each augmented the other. The details of Margaritha's critique of Judaism and Jews argue that he translated the prayer book before he composed the ethnography. The shorter Refutation may have been written last in order to reinforce his arguments about the falseness of the Jewish faith and its messianic hopes. The following analysis is not necessarily based on this hypothesis, but may indicate why it is tenable.

A

The introduction to the translations reads,

> There follows the Jewish prayer book, [from] which they pray everyday in their synagogue/ and sing/ including the hundred blessings (*Beruchos*)/ that is praises/ translated from the Hebrew language/ Beginning (anfenlich) as they enter the church/ each prays this prayer together.[34]

The prayer recited by the Jews as they enter the synagogue was "How goodly are your tents Oh Jacob." Margaritha follows this with Psalms 25, 26, 95, and 64. These psalms do not follow "How goodly" in Hirtz Treves's prayerbook. They may have reflected local custom, which was a variable in all orders of prayer. Margaritha stated that the hymn "Lord of the World . . ." began the service proper, "This is the beginning of the prayer . . . mornings as the Jews stand in their synagogue."[35] Margaritha was aware that Christians understood what a synagogue was, yet he preferred and more frequently used the word "church." This seems to grow out of some sense that a "church" was more familiar to his audience as a place of worship.

The "Lord of the World . . ." was apparently sung responsively, "now they sit down and sing one verse after another."[36] After singing, the congregation began reciting the hundred benedictions. The form of a benediction was "Blessed Art Thou Our God, Who . . . etc." The first benediction was, "gave us the command of washing the hands."[37] At this point, Margaritha challenged the Jews to demonstrate that God had actually commanded them to wash their hands. He acknowledged that hand washing was a good practice, but that did not make it a commandment. Margaritha does not say so, but it is clear that he believed that Jews, in particular the rabbis, had fabricated such commandments and ascribed them to God.[38] His translation then continues without comment through the blessings "created mankind with wisdom, . . . heals all creatures, . . . has given me a pure soul . . . which you will take . . . and restore again to me." The blessings, beginning with "made the cock, . . . did not make me a heathen (*hayden*)" and ending "removed sleep from my eyes" follow the customary Ashkenazic order.[39]

He wrote, "Next the Jews pray a prayer that God will shield them from all misfortune."[40] This long meditation begins "May it be your will" and ends with "blessed are you," making it one of the hundred benedictions. This blessing is followed by an acknowledgment (*allhie bekent*) that God is the Master of the world and that everything depends on his mercy.[41] Thereafter, the Jews "congratulate themselves" (*beruempt sich*) that God covenanted with Abraham at the offering of Isaac.[42] This section laid the basis for connecting the binding of Isaac with the daily sacrifices in the temple. Before reading the passages dealing with those sacrifices, Margaritha stated that the Jews "praised themselves and God," recited the *Shema,* and recalled the giving of the law on Sinai.[43]

Studying and reciting passages from scripture and the Talmud were considered, as discussed above, to be equivalent to offering sacrifice. Margaritha translated without comment the Talmudic text that presented the rabbinical discussion of the burnt offering, the sin offering, the most holy burned offering, the utensils used in the temple, the offering of the Nazirite, the peace offering, and the sacrifice of the first born.[44] He explained their purpose and disposition in the text. Because the offerings were biblical practices, Margaritha did not question them. Only after the final offering (the paschal offering) did he insert an explanation. Margaritha did not give the temple offerings a Christological exegesis, such as the one in his ethnography. Rather, he chose to comment derisively on the Jewish mythology of the wonders of the temple.

> One might think that there was a foul stink in the Temple courtyard where the offering table stood . . . the Jews, however, set down in their Talmud ten wonders that occurred in their Temple. Among them they place that flesh offered there, which they call holy flesh, never stank . . . whoever does not believe such a thing, may well be saved by it [i.e., unbelief in such foolishness].[45]

Margaritha's repetition of the temple's wonders and his doubt thereof revealed something of the mental conflict that led him to reject Judaism. Surely the temple was also a place of wonders for Christians as well as Jews. Its sacrifices prefigured the sacrifice of Christ. Was it really impossible that it did not have the odor of an abattoir? Was everything in the Talmud of the rabbis suspect? Margaritha's attitude toward the rabbis and their interpretation of scripture, as well as his confidence in his own Jewish education, are made clear in his discussion of Rabbi Ishmael's Thirteen Rules of scriptural exegesis to determine law. The rules end the section of the prayer book that contains the introductory blessings and the sacrifices. The Thirteen Rules were taken from the *Sifra,* an early, probably second-century CE commentary on Leviticus. Reading them fulfilled part of the required daily Torah study and reinforced the hold of the rabbis over the interpretation of the Law. The rules have a certain ex post facto nature, in that the examples of their application seem to demonstrate the known law, not the derivation of a legal concept from the unknown. Margaritha viewed the rules as arcane and confusing. He considered them to be examples of rabbinic obscurantism. They demonstrated the rabbis' desire to maintain power through their possession of special knowledge.

> There follows a very difficult prayer [study text] of the Jews. It is entirely unsuitable and unintelligible to translate into German without certain interpretations and circumlocutions because in it all the principles of the Talmud are understood. One may feel and see how they go about interpreting the scriptures. In truth there is nothing useful to be found in them. I was long moved not to translate them into German. But because the stubborn Jews might [argue] that I am not able to translate [them], I have made them intelligible in German and interpreted them in order that they have no cause to talk. Take note, there is no Christian so learned that he could translate this prayer into German.[46]

Margaritha's translation began, "Rabbi Ishmael said the law is interpreted through 13 ways." He then proceeded to translate each rule and give an illustration. The rules are themselves cryptic, even in the original Hebrew. The first rule is the briefest and, perhaps, the most easily understood. Its treatment exemplifies Margaritha's approach. "The [rule] is that the law should be interpreted [by inferring] from simple to harsh."[47] He gave the example, "One should understand this as when I say a person who had a minor sin and God punished him for it, how much more [will God punish him] if he does a serious sin."[48] Margaritha's explanation, although not wrong, is not absolutely correct, because it adds human behavior to a legal requirement. The Hebrew idea is that one infers from a minor (lenient) law to a major (strict) law. As with all the rules, it applies only to laws that begin "Thou shalt," and "Thou shalt not." It does not apply to interpretations of moral stories and homiletic materials. For example, if some action is forbidden on a lesser holy day, it is also forbidden on Yom Kippur, a major holy day.

Margaritha himself understood that his explanation of the rules was inadequate, and he closes his discussion with an apology.

The difficult prayer goes to here. I have much bestirred myself to make it clear and intelligible with many words. It is, however, very vexing to read. . . . I could have made it clearer, but it would have cost more time and words.[49]

Rabbi Ishmael's rules ended the section of the prayerbook in which the morning sacrifices were recited. Margaritha's overall explanation of that "prayer" unit came a few pages earlier, after the part of the service celebrating the receiving of the Torah. He did not explicitly state that the Gospel had superseded the Law, as he did in the ethnography and in the Refutation; however, he did imply that the construction of the prayer service as a replacement of temple worship was due to the misinterpretation of Hosea.

When the Jews were in the land and had the Temple, they sacrificed according to the five books of Moses. Meanwhile, when they were driven out and cast away for many noteworthy reasons, and the Temple was destroyed and not rebuilt, they could no longer make sacrifices. So they say that they sacrifice with mouth and prayer each and every offering in its time. How and when they offer follows [in the passages which are read that concern the sacrifices]. They command themselves with the passage in Hosea 14[:1–2], "Return Israel to God your Lord, etc. and [say to him] we will pay you the bullocks of our lips, etc."[50]

Every morning the Jews brought the required sacrifices, the prayers written in the prayer book; in Margaritha's view, this was a doubtful endeavor of self-commandment.

B

Before continuing with his translation of the morning service, Margaritha discussed the Regensburg custom of donning *tallit* and *tefillin* after the sacrifices, the general western Ashkenazic custom. He also explained the making and use of these crucial ritual objects. In Regensburg, the senior priest, a descendant of Aaron, led the *tallit* ritual. Margaritha explained that the *tallit*, or prayer shawl, was usually white and about the size of a large four-cornered tablecloth.

Each corner has a tassel, tassels are called ציצת *cicis* [*sic*][each with] eight threads hanging down and five knots above. So the chief priest takes this cloth and wraps it around his head and says, "Blessed are you God . . . who has commanded us to wrap ourselves with this cloth."

> Thereafter all the Jews—over 13 years—who are in the church follow him. And this ceremony is taken from the end of Num. 15.[51]

Following donning the *tallit,* the men put on their own *tefillin,* or "the commandments" as they were called in German. No one led this part of the ritual. Margaritha explained that the *tefillin* were boxes made from kosher cowhide. The boxes were sewn onto an eight-layer leather base. The *tefillin* that would be strapped onto the head contained scriptures from Exodus 13 and Deuteronomy 10 in compartments. The box that was made for strapping on the arm contained a parchment with a passage from Exodus 2. This box was placed on the outside of the arm and the straps were wrapped around the arm and the hand. Margaritha wrote that "much more could be written . . . but for brevity I will cease because they have large books on how to make them."[52] He then explained that the basis for the commandment of binding *tefillin* was Deuteronomy 2, "and you shall bind them [the *shema* and the command to love God] for a sign on your hand." He gave the blessing recited when placing them on the arm, but not the verses used when putting them on the head. He probably omitted it because traditionally it was said only if the actor interrupted the process by speaking after saying the first blessing. Margaritha did not mock the reverence with which the Jews attended to their *tefillin.*

> The tefillin they hold in such honor that if one lets it fall to the ground, he and all those who see it lying must fast the same day. Also, before they put the tefillin on they kiss it and put it up to the eyes—such they take from Dt. X.[53]

Before beginning the morning service proper, participants recited a meditation/prayer for the rebuilding of the temple, speedily and in our days. Its hope of the restoration of God's temple and his people to their land is deeply messianic. It was very much a part of Margaritha's upbringing and daily prayer experience. Thereafter, the congregation rose and blessed God, who had spoken and the world came to be (*Baruch sh'amar*). Margaritha attested to the power of this prayer and the desire among the Jews of Regensburg to acknowledge God as King and Creator. He described the emotion attached to singing of God's praises.

> All stand and sing with great purpose. In Regensburg and other places they have the custom in summertime to sing this prayer for an hour, as I have heard many times from my brother—he has sung this song to exhaustion [*uberfluessig*] as he is a good musician [cantor] among the Jews.[54]

The prayer consists of eighty-seven words. (Margaritha does not mention it, but eighty-seven is the numerical value of *pay zayin,* or pure gold. This *gematria* was well known to scholars.) Singing for ten minutes could lead to rhythmic, emotional states. Repetition for an hour must certainly count as an attempt to reach a state of communal religious ecstasy. Margaritha's participation in such group-worship moments focused him on the Messiah and redemption and the glory of God.

Margaritha coupled his insider's understanding of prayer practices and intentions to his attempt to explain the prayer book to Christians. His work helps modern scholars better comprehend the mindset of his fellow Jews. As noted in the discussion of the *Aleinu* prayer above, his knowledge allowed him to both explain and attack Judaism. He gave examples of Jewish anti-Christian attitudes throughout his translation. One long excursus occurs in his commentary on the verses of Nehemiah 9:6–11, which are recited before the Song of Moses in the prayer unit of psalms that follow the morning blessings and precede the *shema.* The Nehemiah verses quote Ezra, who praised God for choosing Abraham and giving his progeny the Land of Canaan. Margaritha stated that the Jews saw the Christians as Edomites, descendants of Esau, who would eventually be subservient to Israel. He mentioned that in the Babylonian Talmud tractate of *Gittin,* the doctrine concerning the Edomites is expounded.

> In the fifth chapter, called *Nizikin,* the Talmud writes . . . that Titus Vespasian descended from Esau. And it says, A voice spoke from heaven to Titus, "You godless son of a godless [man], a child's child from Esau the godless." Now there are poor, foolish people who believe such lies. . . . It also says that as Titus destroyed the Temple and was a leading Roman, and Rome has long been the head of Christendom, so they reasonably call the Christians Edomites after Titus Vespasian.[55]

Jewish hostility to Christians was a major concern for Margaritha. His statements about Jewish attitudes are probably correct for it is not surprising that a persecuted, disliked minority would resent its oppressors. What may seem surprising is his perception that he is revealing something shocking to Christians. Could Christians, many of whom were willing to believe blood libels and almost all of whom considered Jews complicit in the death of Jesus, nonetheless be shocked and offended that Jews mocked them and their beliefs? Margaritha must have found that to be the case.

Margaritha touched upon the Jewish hope for God's ultimate vindication and punishment of Christians in the blessing against heretics. In that blessing, a certain kingdom (*malchuth*) is called *zedon,* insolent, arrogant.

Margaritha identified that kingdom with the Christian princes and their magistrates. This was consistent with the secret meaning of the *Aleinu.*

> The Jews' commentators, first and foremost R. Solomon [Rashi] the Talmudist who [claimed] that all the [negative statements of the prophets] refer to Christianity. From such talk the prayer [against the arrogant kingdom] is based and also the Christian leaders and government are called arrogant.[56]

Margaritha argued that the word "arrogant" was singular, so that when the word was used in Germany, it could not refer to the Turks or other heathen nations. Therefore, when the German Jews prayed for God to curse the arrogant kingdom, they meant the Christians, who oppressed them. Also, the prayer was found only in liturgies of Jews in the Christian nations. "So the Jews pray only against Christendom or rather those raised in Christendom."[57]

Margaritha, thinking of Jewish hostility to Christianity, attacked those Christians who advocated a more humane treatment for Jews. He argued that this would not help the Jews convert, but rather would solidify them in their beliefs and anti-Christian opinions. Thus any kindness that prevented their acceptance of Jesus was actually misplaced and an eternal cruelty. In order to stop such behavior in Christians, he presented the truth about Jewish attitudes.

> Please God I once was attacked by Christians of little learning because I wrote such things about Jews. I want to find myself, as one will, writing the truth. Also [in disputations] against the Jews, [I would rather argue] with their most learned and not with the ignorant.[58]

C

Related to Margaritha's revelations about Jewish hostility to Christians was his anger about the daily prayer against traitors. In many places in *Der gantz Jüdisch glaub,* he wrote about his status as a *meshumad,* a convert. He knew that the word *malshinim*in the blessing was actually a circumlocution for converts. The Jews prayed for his and their destruction. He entitled the translation and commentary on the blessing, "And to the traitors . . . for destruction: understand baptized Jews."[59] Margaritha, of course, believed that baptized Jews were honorable and that they had made the theologically correct decision in changing religion or, better said, in accepting the Messiah who had come and rejecting rabbinism. When the Jews challenged converts and wished for their destruction, they were demonstrating their own blindness and fallen state.

When pressed, both common Jews and rabbis denied that the negative word referred to converted Jews. They stated that *malshinim* meant the slanderers and bearers of falsehoods from all nations, who should be cursed; it did not refer to honest Christians. Margaritha set out to prove that he, as a convert, was among those the Jews cursed.

> I feel moved to say somewhat more because it applies to me and all baptized Jews. . . . First it should be known that this prayer of the *shemoneh esre,* as the Jews write, was ordered by Rabbi Simeon in the presence of the great Chief Rabbi Gamaliel in the city of Yabneh . . . but after a long time thereafter came one called Rabbi Samuel and added this piece.[60]

Margaritha was correct in stating that Rabbi Samuel composed the blessing-curse after the eighteen benedictions had already been established. His reference to its Talmudic origin is evidence of his knowledge of the *amidah*'s development. From that basis, he demonstrated that the blessing-curse was directed at baptized Jews and not at the generality of the ungodly.

> Now I have shown here that this additional piece did not originally belong in the prayer [*amidah*]. It is an addition primarily against all who are not of their belief and with interpreted words against baptized Jews, against all leaders and all who have a particular belief which opposes their belief.[61]

Margaritha went on, discussing pressures brought against Jews in Venice, which he attributed to official reaction to the anti-Christian elements in the prayer book. Jews were not only required to remove the offending words from the prayer book but also to wear a yellow badge on their clothing. They were enjoined from praying that God curse baptized Jews when they recited the benediction. Circumstances, in other words, forced the Jews to pray against traitors in general and not specific ones. Margaritha had traveled to Venice and knew the restrictions. He was also aware that the Jews found ways to subvert the rules among themselves. As with the *Aleinu,* they maintained a stubborn opposition to Christians and converts in their thoughts while praying.

> There was, by man's opinion, once a learned Christian in Venice [Bernadino da Feltre?], who had written against the Jews, namely their

usury and cursing against Christ and his Christians. He desired the Venetians, for notable reason, to require the Jews to wear a yellow mark and to take less usury and remove and change certain prayers from their prayerbook and specifically this part. Now it is not allowed to single out baptized Jews rather than traitors in general . . . but I know that they do not do [what is required by Christian authorities]—I have indeed prayed in Venice.[62]

Allowing that Margaritha conflated events in Venetian Jewish history that occurred over the period of a century, his eyewitness account is likely correct as to the prayer against traitors and its interpretation. It is unlikely that pressure and legislation would actually change beliefs.

Margaritha ended his challenge to the blessing with an emotional argument that would have moved Christians. The Jewish hatred of baptized Christians extended to the holy apostles of the Christian Lord, who were themselves baptized Jews.

I make known that the dear apostles were baptized and the Jews call them *Taschmidim* instead of the correct name *Thalmidim. Taschmidim* means destroyed, and *Thalmidim* means youths or students—they call baptized Jews the same thing *mashumad,* in German a destroyer.[63]

D

Margaritha found fault not only with the blessing against traitors but also with the other eighteen blessings in their entirety. He emphasized that the temple sacrifices had ceased when he commented on that section. He recounted how the Jews had attempted to replace the sacrifices with prayer. He had saved his discussion on the erroneous and ineffectual nature of Jewish prayer until his comments on the *amidah,* the standing prayer. The *amidah* was the central prayer of the liturgy and was repeated three times a day, every day, with variations for Sabbath and holidays. Called the "service of the heart," it corresponded to the morning and afternoon temple sacrifices. Its blessings were the "bullocks of the lips." Margaritha felt that the notion of prayer replacing the rituals of the destroyed temple was the fundamental, irremediable flaw of Jewish worship; the sacrifice of Jesus completed and ended the need for temple sacrifice. This useless substitution, as much or more than anything else in their faith, blinded the Jews to the reality of the Christian Messiah. Margaritha attacked the *amidah* as one who once relied on it, but had now found the Messiah.

> When a Jew prays/ he should direct his heart so that he thinks on the time when the Holy Temple was in Jerusalem, when one could make offerings. In place of the selfsame offering, he makes his prayer. . . . Therefore each Jew . . . should think that he brings a sacrifice before God.[64]

This was pure blindness on the part of the Jews. The temple sacrifice had ended, as the prophets predicted would occur when the Messiah came. The Jews actually did recognize that a sacrifice, and especially the sacrifice by Abraham of his son, known as the binding of Isaac, was a type, a prefiguring, of the sacrifice, by the Father, of his son. By not accepting Christ, who fulfilled the temple sacrifice, and by adhering to powerless prayer, the Jews continued to warrant God's anger.

> Now let each see the blindness which they must acknowledge themselves, that sacrifice ceased and they have nothing more to remove their sins. [They are] under God's anger. . . . What did the prophets write, especially Daniel, that when the sacrifices would cease, the Messiah would come who will be the proper sin offering.[65]

Rather than placing their faith in Christ, the Jews "placed [their faith in] prayer and works"; their prayers "were changed to sins."[66] They comforted themselves with the thought that although God seemed to have turned his face from them, he was actually merely hiding himself, for a time, behind the shadow of his hand, as Isaiah had predicted. Isaiah had also foretold that the shadow would pass away. But Margaritha argued that the Jews were truly blind to the words and the true meaning of the prophets:

> They comfort themselves and speak to each other [thus,] even though God . . . has hidden his face from us, [it] is nothing more than the shadow of his hand over us as he said to us.[67]

Margaritha described Jewish prayer to Christians in order that they might understand its worthlessness. Those Jews who read *Der gantz Jüdisch glaub* would, perhaps, see that his Christian interpretation was the correct reading of the prophets' words about the temple, sacrifice, and prayer. Some might, he thought, come to understand the truth.

E

Margaritha did not always lace his comments on prayer with polemic. He presented, without vitriol, the Jewish explanations for the proper prayerful intentions and the choreography for individual and group prayer. Margaritha's commentary also reveals the spiritual yearnings of his former fellows, yearnings that he once shared. This is evident in his remarks about the recitation of "holy, holy, holy are you" from Isaiah 6 in the paragraphs leading to the *Shema*. He wrote, "Here all the Jews sing 'sanctified' (*einhelligklich*) with a loud voice as if they were angels."[68] The striving for sanctity is an essential characteristic of Jewish prayer.

For Jews, holiness grew out of dedication to the commandments given by the Creator of Heaven and Earth. When they were obedient, especially in prayer, they felt profoundly connected to both the world of matter and the empyrean realm. This was symbolized in the paragraph immediately preceding the *Shema*. Each man took the "tassels" or fringes of the *tallit* into his hand. This unified the congregation with the commandments, the earth, and heaven. Margaritha explained the theurgy of this action as a rabbi might.

> So as you look at them [the fringes], you should think of all the commandments of the Lord, and do [them] and you should not turn your heart after lust. . . . In this . . . personal prayer the Jews have much reverence, they direct their eyes to heaven and the four corners of the world.[69]

The fringes represented all the commandments because of their construction. The eight threads and five knots were treated as numbers. Indeed, the Hebrew word *tzizit* had a *gematria*. The rabbis had identified 613 commandments in the Torah. The number of the fringes and the numerical value of their name added up to 613. When a Jew recited the blessing and looked at the fringes, it was understood that he was again making a commitment to study and keep the commandments.

> The Jews understand and write that the reason [for] the *zizis* [one of Margaritha's spellings] . . . [is to] admonish [and] remind one of all the commandments of God. Namely that the word *zizis* has the numeric value of 613, including all the eight threads and five knots of the *zizis* . . . so they admonish one to think of all the commandments, which are also 613.[70]

Fulfilling the commandment of fringes required personal reflection. Either at home or in the synagogue, each worshipper was alone with God. Heartfelt meditation was the counterpoint of the cantor's singing, either *sola voce* or with the congregation. The *amidah* encompassed both aspects of worship. Margaritha described it as "where the entire congregation prays together quietly by themselves with great reverence. Thereafter the cantor sings very loudly."[71]

The ecstatic singing of the meditation on the rebuilding the temple discussed above was a preface to singing the *amidah*. The cantorial rendition was based on tunes known to all. Isaiah's vision of the heavenly host of angels declaring to one another "holy, holy, holy" was repeated by the cantor accompanied by the congregation. If done properly, everyone in the congregation became angels, removed from the mundane. Daily prayer created in the worshippers a sense they were God's people, the children and heirs of Abraham, Isaac, and Jacob. The first words of the *amidah* declare, "Blessed are you, Lord our God, God of our fathers, God of Abraham, God of Isaac, and God of Jacob." Margaritha, perhaps in spite of himself, expressed the exalted feelings of Jews at prayer.

The mystical aspects of prayer have been discussed in Appendix B and in the body of this book. The work of the rabbinic mystics, who may also be termed pietists, emphasized not only theurgy and speculation but also physical connections between the prayer service and heaven. This attempt to unify the individual and congregation with the divine realm used not only the power of divine names but also a mythology of unseen forces present during prayer. The idea that the worshippers were attempting to emulate the angels in serving God pointed to a spiritual yearning in the congregation. The *Kol Nidre* prayer, the community prayer before Yom Kippur, although not mentioned by Margaritha, is an example of this connection between heaven and earth, for it is addressed to the court above as well as the court below.

Margaritha's mention of the 1,800 angels that were believed to attend the *amidah* gives a glimpse of a myth that emphasized the nearness of the celestial kingdom to God's servants on earth. Those who prayed were participating in a sacrificial service. Their petitions, which were not limited to the printed words of the prayer book, were meant to ascend to the Throne of Glory. Angels carried specific parts of the prayers to heaven. The origin of the prayer angels is uncertain. An early mention is in a *piyut*, a post-temple hymn, attributed to Rabbi Elazar Kalir. His *piyut* is often found in the Rosh Hashanah liturgy. It describes how 1,800 angels receive heartfelt petitions and carry them back to heaven. The 1,800 angels are also mentioned by Rabbi Elazar ben Yehudah of Worms (1160–1237), a member of the school of Rabbi Judah the Pious, in his mystical-theological work, *Sodei Razayya*, even yet known mainly in manuscript. Margaritha probably had access to both sources, but most certainly to Kalir's hymn. Having this background, Margaritha reported on the 1,800 angels and how their number was determined from the letters of the *amidah.*

> Now the Jews have a great secret and superstition in all their writings. The numbers and sum of the first letters of the words [of the eighteen benedictions] . . . is 1770 [the blessing of Rabbi Samuel against the traitors] is 30. [When they] are added, the sum is [1,800], filling out the number of angels.[72]

The secret was no secret to the Jews. All or most knew that God would hear their prayers if they said them from the heart. How did the Holy One, Blessed be He, receive prayers? His celestial servants went down and brought them to him. This mystery was fundamental to the efficacy of prayer. The question was not, "Are there prayer-angels?" but, "How does one pray in such a way as to have access to them?" The question was dealt with by mystics, such as Judah the Pious, who created a choreography of prayer and a psychology of intention. Margaritha knew these aspects of prayer. He discussed them and their sources in some detail.

A pious Jew knew that inner thoughts and passions could deflect him from the divine during prayer. Heartfelt communication with God not only depended upon angels but also upon discipline. *Mussar* is a word meaning rigorous, ethical discipline. Judah the Pious and the pietistic movement of the Hasidei Ashkenaz, mentioned above in the discussion of the *Aleinu,* were *mussar*-oriented mystics. Kabbalistic prayer was only possible when the one who prayed exercised mental and physical self-control. Margaritha knew that every Jew had been taught from childhood that

> when one begins to pray, each Jew should hold his feet together and deport himself (as they take from Ezec. 1) so do the angels who pray to God who stand with their feet in like manner.[73]

Margaritha explained that this posture helped Jews resist great temptations, "that [might] move them to transgress the law and not pray reverently.[74] No one could say in his heart, "I know for sure that God heard my prayer."[75] Only time would tell if a request would be fulfilled. During prayer, as noted above, the Jew needed to remove himself to the temple of old and offer sacrifice. These statements all reflect the teachings of the Hasidei Ashkenaz, which had such a profound effect on the spiritual life of German Jewry. As a resident of Regensburg, Margaritha knew a great deal about its thirteenth-century rabbi, Judah the Pious. He was aware that Judah had instructed Jews and organized those rules of prayer that he was now sharing with Christians in *Der gantz Jüdisch glaub.* He made his reliance on the practices of Rabbi Judah explicit.

> The Jews write about a rabbi called Rabbi Judah the Pious, whom they consider very holy. He was born in Speyer and lived and died in Regensburg. . . . [H]e taught what a Jew should do to pray reverently that God might hear him. Namely, he should stand with bowed head; the great toes of both feet should grip the ground but not completely, that he not err in prayer. Should he do this, he can direct his heart diligently and reverently to God.[76]

Before assuming the appropriate prayer posture, the Jew stepped forward three steps in order to encounter God. The model of Jewish prayer was always Abraham, who conversed with God, even bargaining with the Divine in an effort to save the cities of Sodom and Gomorrah. Each Jew stood in the posture suggested [mandated?] by Rabbi Judah through the eighteen benedictions. At certain points, one bowed or swayed and at times, such as during the recitation of "holy, holy, holy," stood on tiptoe. Every physical stance was geared to help the words reach heaven, or rather, heaven's prayer angels. Margaritha wrote, "They travel with their feet in the air and make themselves like the angels." Margaritha also detailed how one withdrew from the presence of the king of kings after the *amidah.* Upon finishing the personal *amidah,* one would take three steps back, bow to each side and the center and then could walk away. Good manners and custom dictated the actions.

> After this verse, the Jew takes three steps back like a crab and bows before him then lowers the head to the left side, then the right, then bows again before him. The bowing means that he wants peace in all places, the last bow . . . is toward God. He steps backward in order that he not show God his rear—this is the custom of the knowledgeable.[77]

Margaritha drew attention to the practice of knowledgeable Jews, such as his family. This comment implies that there were less scrupulous worshippers who did not follow the most pious custom. He stated that the three-step practice was drawn from comments in the Talmud.

> That he makes three steps back, no more nor less, they derive from an imagined, fantastic Talmudic comment on Ex. 20:[15] at the end. There the text says, "Moses went up the mountain, etc. and the people

> stood afar, etc. About this they write that a great wonder occurred, as God gave the law, the entire people of Israel were so very terrified and greatly frightened that they were by a great wonder moved back three miles from Mt. Sinai in the blink of an eye. Because of these three miles, they arranged the three steps back as a remembrance.[78]

Margaritha's story of the three-mile miracle is not exactly as found in the Talmud. His account combined two passages and required a rabbinic interpretation of a word. In the Talmud (*Shabbath* 88b), Rabbi Joshua ben Levi states that the people of Israel retreated twelve *mil* at every word God spoke from Sinai. The linear measure system in the Talmud is a hybrid of Jewish and non-Jewish units. A *mil* is about seven and a half stadia (*ris*); a Hebrew *parsah* contained about thirty stadia (*Yoma* 6:4); twelve *mil*, therefore, was three *parasoth*. Margaritha interprets three *parasoth* as three miles. Margaritha's understanding of Exodus 20 is given in Zedekiah ben Abraham Anav's (thirteenth-century) *Shibbolei ha-Leket*.

Another Talmudic passage, attributed to Rabbi Joshua ben Levi, dictates that one take three steps back after prayer to honor God. He said that one should not withdraw quickly like a "dog running to its vomit." Margaritha referred to that analogy like a "dog to his vomit" after citing the Talmudic statement on three miles.[79]

This study has repeatedly drawn attention to Margaritha's education and his understanding of things Jewish. The three-mile story and its use of several texts demonstrate yet again that Margaritha was not unlearned. He was capable of teaching Christians a great deal about Judaism and Hebrew in spite of his lack of Latin. The most reasonable judgment must be that he was an acceptable but not great Hebraist and Talmudist. Although not an Elias Levita, he could have served as a rabbi in the Jewish community. Certainly, he could have been a teacher (something less than a rabbi), as his family suggested when they tried to entice him to return to Judaism.

Margaritha gave a further explanation about the practice of bowing during prayer. As background to his comments, the Hebrew word *baruch*, translated "bless" or "blessed be," has its origin in bending the knees. In the *amidah*, after each of his first two blessings and after the final two, the person praying bent the knees, straightened, and then bowed at the waist. Margaritha describes the bows, backing and bending in three directions, after the last blessing. Whenever one bowed, it had to conform to convention.

> To begin, they write how one should bow the head . . . thereafter the body . . . he should not bow further than that he might see the heart

> and not so deeply that he may see his legs, and thus come think about his private parts [*schame*].[80]

A sense of modesty was part of the prayer lore taught by the pietists and passed down through the centuries.

Heartfelt petitions to the Holy One, Blessed be He, could suffer no distractions in mind or body. These aspects of prayer, if not the myths supporting them, Margaritha reported respectfully. He tended to discuss the movements of the cantor and other prayer leaders matter-of-factly. Such actions, however, were essential to the spirituality and decorum of services as well as to their mechanical progress. "Cantor" was both a professional office and a position that could be filled by a layman. For example, Margaritha's brother, who led the ecstatic singing discussed above, was a professional and probably was paid by the congregation. An example of the nonprofessional cantor was a man recently bereaved, or one observing the anniversary of his parent's death, who would be called upon to lead services, for he "must be cantor in the synagogue."[81]

A regular, trained cantor usually led services, and it was to such a person that Margaritha generally referred. The cantor held an honored and crucial position as the representative before God of the congregation. His lead and words set the tone for prayer. Margaritha described the cantor's place at the beginning of the services, before the Holy Ark, which contained the scrolls of the Law. The prayer book or manuscript rested on a stand before him. With his posture and voice, he set the mood of the petitions, standing before and facing the Ark of the Covenant, which was represented by the ark in the synagogue.

> Now a cantor stands up and goes and faces east because Jerusalem lies in the east . . . and this cantor places himself over a book, which is on a pillar or a stand. Which stand is directly opposite their ark, in which ark lie the five books of Moses. And this cantor must stand deep as in a grave and this they take from the 30th Psalm which says, "From the deep, O God have I called you," and he also sings.[82]

The cantor set the pace of the service and took the lead as each new section began. One of the most important prayer units was the *tachanun* (Margaritha transliterated the Hebrew in his dialect as *Thechino*), or plea for mercy. A short form was read on Sunday, Tuesday, Wednesday, and Friday. Margaritha wrote that a longer form was recited on Monday and Thursday, when passages from the Torah were read. The persecutions and daily indignities of Jewish life in hostile societies ensured that *tachanun* was recited with the deepest feeling. Individuals and the congregation asked God to change his anger to mercy and preserve his people, who sanctify him three times a day with prayer and the *shema.* Margaritha described the scene:

> The following prayer is named *Thechino.* It is a prayer for mercy, it is prayed only on Monday and Thursday during the week . . . the cantor goes behind the stand and sits on the steps which are in front of the Ark. And [he] falls with his entire face on his left hand and prays personally with great pain the following prayer. Each Jew does likewise.[83]

The Jews prayed with their faces on the left arm because the heart was on that side, the same reason that they usually placed the *tefillin* on the left arm. This led to "more reverence."[84]

Jewish prayer, as Margaritha described it, was emotionally intense, at least in theory, certainly often in practice. He was not reticent to make known its futility, because any sacrifice of lips had already been fulfilled in the Messiah who had come.

In various places, Margaritha acknowledged that the faith of the Jews attracted some Christians. In the *amidah*'s blessing for scholars and converts to Judaism, he stated that the Jews were "very industrious to try and move a Christian to convert to their belief."[85] Apparently, Margaritha knew of some converts who had embraced the Torah and the heartfelt prayers, and were willing to suffer the persecutions the Jews endured. According to Margaritha's testimony, the worship service was a factor in conversion to Judaism. When a Christian converted, Margaritha declared that he was given "money and sent to Turkey or Russia." (If his conversion were discovered, he would be forced to recant or be executed.) Margaritha lamented, "for such is this daily prayer [for converts], how can a Christian establishment suffer and tolerate it."[86] Margaritha's comments give a firsthand account of the powerful nature of Jewish prayer in reaching the heart of the non-Jew.

F

Margaritha not only discussed the theory, intentions, and choreography of prayer but also the differences among various orders of prayer (*nusachoth*). He suggested that the customs of Regensburg and the Rhineland were derived from those of French Jews. That connection was of interest to Leopold Zunz in his nineteenth-century study of the German liturgies.[87] Margaritha mentions the liturgies of Germany, Eastern Europe, France, Italy, Spain, and Turkey in the context of the blessing-curse against the arrogant kingdom in the *amidah.* He attempted to demonstrate that only the European Jews prayed those words; hence, they must be directed against Christendom. His analysis, which is subject here, was based upon liturgical differences between the *nusachoth.*

> Know that the Jews in Germany, Bohemia, Moravia, Silesia, also the Jews in Poland, Russia, and Hungary all have one way and order in their churches and prayer. The Jews who were in France agree for the most part with the Jews mentioned above. But the Jews of Rome, which are most of the Jews in Italy who are not of German heritage, have a very different order in their churches. The Jews who lived in Spain and Sicily have yet another order. Also the Jews who were always in Turkey and especially those in Constantinople and Salonika have another order. . . . I say that only the Jews in Christendom pray this prayer.[88]

Margaritha was correct about the differences in *nusachoth.* Sephardic Jews and others of non-German origin prayed against an "evil kingdom," which means one that did not follow moral rules. Christians and Moslems would find little of offence in such a general statement, for they did not want to live in an evil kingdom either. Many Jews living outside Germany would have identified their own non-Jewish, oppressive rulers as evil or arrogant. Margaritha surely knew this from his travels, but it did not advance his argument against German Jews. The Jews themselves were aware that such passages might offend Christians, so they had denials for common charges ready. Margaritha was amazed that Christians would believe "Jews [who] come and say on all grounds and declare it is a lie,"[89] rather than believe converted Christians.

Margaritha added the passages on different orders of prayer and on gullible Christians believing dissembling Jews to the second edition of *Der gantz Jüdisch glaub.* His astonishment at Christian credulity reflects his reaction to the outcome of his debate with Rabbi Josel of Rosheim. He never really got over the fact that Christian leaders ignored the "truths" about Jewish attitudes that he revealed.

One aspect of Jewish life that Margaritha often noted was communal strife. In his prayer book commentary, he wrote about the politics of worship, the source of much ill feeling in the Jewish community. In order to meet the financial requirements of the community, the custom of "auctioning honors" had grown up. Margaritha told how the honors for the year were auctioned off to the highest bidder during the festival of *Simchath Torah,* which began the Torah reading cycle. These honors included the right to say certain blessings connected with the reading of the Torah, called *aliyahs.*

The offices were auctioned by the *schulklopffer* (sexton, *shamesh*) who stood at the raised platform on which the Torah reading service occurred. If offices were not bought for the entire year, they were sold at each service. In all cases, the money raised went to maintain the synagogue and help the poor. In his discussion, Margaritha mentioned the honors of *gelila* (the Torah scroll roller); *Etz Chaim* (the holder of the wooden handles to which the scroll is attached); *hagboho* (one strong enough to lift the Torah); the candlelighter for each day; the provider of wine for sanctification; and the *segen*, an assistant to the cantor. Margaritha said that the *segen* had to be a *prelat* (a member of the tribe of Levi?). The *segen* called people up to bless the Torah and stood in for the cantor.[90]

At the point when the Torah was read, the auction began. "The sexton goes to the . . . *almemor* . . . and calls, 'Who buys *Gelila, Etz Chaim* and also *Hagboho* . . . ?' [The *segen*'s] office was to stand near the cantor on the left side."[91] As the Torah was read, the blessings were sold. Each purchaser was blessed by the *segen* after the reading. These *aliyahs* usually cost two pfennigs on a weekday, and a creutzer or five pfennigs on a Sabbath or holiday. Margaritha saw wealthy men bid up to "a gulden more or less."[92]

Competition for blessings and honors and disappointment in not receiving them was a major problem in a congregation, especially for those charged with dispensing them.

> Note here Christian reader, that at this point during the Torah [reading] by the Jews concerning this *segen* there occurs more animosity, envy and disgraceful [behavior] also profanation of God than in all Christendom, in all our ceremonies and customs. When the leader called the *segen* has called a Jew, the others complain and murmur among themselves and say [sarcastically] that this is a fine *segen*. He [the *segen*] seeks advantage and notice of the person called. [He chooses] a rich [man] before a poor, a young before an old, an ignorant before a learned, a bad before a pious, etc. Also, this one and that one he calls often in the year, but me and mine, he never calls, etc.[93]

Margaritha described the kind of behavior, only at a lesser level, that he and Josel said led to the destruction of the Regensburg community. The sniping among men in the synagogue probably remained at a low level unless real political gain was at sake, as in the Moses Wolf affair.

Of more interest for Margaritha's discussion of the prayer book and Jewish worship is his analysis of the connection between the vocabulary used in the Regensburg synagogue and that of the lost Jewish community of France:

> The Jews have very many foreign words that are neither Hebrew nor German, but rather French. This is because all Jews in the German nation and especially those living on the Rhine, were driven out of France. [They] have retained such words among themselves as will be shown hereafter.[94]

Margaritha chose to illustrate his point with technical words for articles necessary to the function of the synagogue, such as *almemor* and *mappa.* He defined each word and its usage.

> That this word *almemor* is also French is proved from their Talmud from the last chapter of *Succoth.* There they write about the *almemor,* the text calls the *almemor* "*bimah*"... a wooden elevation. Their commentator Rabbi Solomon [Rashi], who was not German but rather French, writes [in his comments on the Talmud passage], It is an *Almemor.* In German this means "Memory." From this [word] the Memory Book [also] gets its name.[95]

Margaritha derived *almemor* from the Latin word "memoria."[96] "The Jews in Italy, Sicily, Naples, Spain, etc. do not call this construction an *almemor,* rather *Tevah,* in German 'Ark' [as in Noah's Ark]."[97]

The Jews recorded the names of the dead in a special book, the Memory Book, and the cantor honored the departed by reading from it three times each year.[98] Margaritha claimed that no name was entered into the book unless "a sum of money" was given.[99] Margaritha found this practice especially reprehensible, because inclusion in the book was tied to helping the souls of the departed gain paradise by reminding the living to pray for them.[100] Margaritha did not compare the practice to the Roman Catholic sale of indulgences and offering special prayers to shorten the time the dead spend in purgatory. As with the second coming of the Messiah, Margaritha often demonstrated a more analytical and judgmental attitude toward Jewish practices and beliefs than he did toward analogous practices and ideas he found, or should have found, in Christianity.

Margaritha discussed the French word *mappa* at length. He said that the simplest description of a *mappa* was "cloth." A decorated *mappa* covered the Torah scrolls and differently colored and decorated *mappas* were used on special occasions. Over the *mappa* was hung a silver breastplate. Another *mappa* covered the reading table to protect the Torah while it was unrolled and read.

> And this mantle the Jews call... *mappa* as noted above. And not only these mantles but also all the clothes that are upon the stand on which

> they need to lay books . . . that one not touch the book with an exposed hand.[101]

Other French words used in Regensburg were *repetier* and *ertorn.*

> They also have a word that a schoolmaster uses when he wants to speak to his student, *repetier.* [When he wants to say], get up and come forward, he says *ertorn,* which also comes from French.[102]

The names of synagogue furnishings and words used in the teacher-student relationship tend to be conservative and stable; thus, Margaritha's tracing the French words found in the German Jewish community to emigrants who came from France and settled in the Rhineland seems plausible. Finding evidence of French influence in the prayer book itself is more difficult, because it was manifest in vocabulary that is not used in the prayer book. Given his firsthand account and the fact that his knowledge checks out in so many other areas, it is reasonable to assume that in Regensburg and in the Rhineland, Jews had retained much from their sojourn in France.

The *almemor* and *mappa* were furnishings related to the Torah reading ceremony. The actual reading was central to congregational worship. Men and women in the congregation observed the removal of the scrolls from the Holy Ark, listened to the reading from the scroll, and then watched its return. Margaritha discussed how the women, separated from the men either by a screen (*mehizah*) or by sitting in a balcony, in their "church," prayed quietly and listened to the cantor's singing, until the Torah service. When the Torah was taken out or replaced, the men chanted psalms and kissed the mantels covering the scrolls.

> When the Jew carries the law from the *almemor,* the women make a big scuffle and press around the peepholes which are made from their church into the men's church because they are not able to kiss it, they look at it with pleasure.[103]

Margaritha explained to his Christian readers why men and women had separate "churches." This was an exotic aspect of the synagogue that required commentary.

> Why must the women and the men have their own special church? They write in their Talmud in the last chapter of *Succoth* that men and women were together at first. They carried on much roguery. Because of this, they made a rule that women were below and men above in the

church. That did not help, so they tried another rule. That also did not help. Because of this, they were moved to protect against such whoredoms, [therefore] each [sex] must have its own separate church. And this they get from Zach. 12[:12, where] the text speaks of the lament for the Messiah and says, The women will lament separately and the men separately. Here one sees what great reverence this people had in the Temple and still has.[104]

Margaritha's brief account of the passage in the Talmud tractate *Succoth* 51b is basically correct, but it skews the wording there to make the ancient Jews appear more sexual than the text warrants. *Succoth* deals not with synagogue worship, but with the fall festival in the temple. Rabbi Eleazar states that at "first the walls [of the women's court] were smooth."[105] This statement is traditionally understood to mean that men and women were together. The rabbis also taught that women were in the court and men outside, but this caused *kaloth rosh,* levity or light-minded behavior. The men then were required to be inside the courtyard, with the women outside. There was still *kaloth rosh.* Finally, a balcony was constructed and the women sat separately above, out of the men's view. This solved the problem. *Succoth* 52a goes on with a citation to Zechariah 12:12, in which the families of the land mourn, the House of David [is] apart, and their wives apart. The *kaloth rosh,* the term used to describe the reason given for the separation of the men and women, does not mean "whoredoms," but rather chatting that detracts from reverence. In the Talmud account, it seems that the men were more likely to cause irreverence than were the women. The solution to the problem was not to erect a screen, but to construct a balcony, which created a separation. Margaritha's interpretation of Zechariah 12:12 is rooted in the idea that Israel is not properly focused in worship. The scripture is a proof text for the separation of women. Men are not part of the quotation, as Margaritha implied. Still, his knowledge of the Talmud, especially *Succoth,* from which he quotes more often than other Talmudic tractates in *Der gantz Jüdisch glaub,* is solid. His subtle and not so subtle skewing of Jewish sources, which he uses to put Jews and Judaism in a bad light, does not much diminish his value as a source for what Jews thought.

Each major transition in the prayer service was marked by a doxology, *kaddish.* Its purpose was threefold: to end a section, to give a mourner a chance to acknowledge God's judgment as just, and, even in the absence of any mourner, it gave a congregation the opportunity to sanctify God. In his commentary on the *kaddish* that preceded the *Aleinu,* Margaritha told an Elijah story. The story illustrated the piety that was required of Jews in prayer and contrasted that piety to the human frailty shown in the chatting that took place at inappropriate moments.

> They write that once two angels encountered the prophet Elijah. They had many sacks filled with fury and anger. Elijah asked toward whom they wanted to direct the anger. They answered him, Over all who chat in the synagogue when one prays the *kaddish.*[106]

The story is a variant of one in the *Shibbolei ha-Leket* of Zedekiah ben Abraham Anav. Zedekiah relates that Rabbi Hama bar Hanina met the prophet Elijah, who was leading two laden camels. He asked Elijah what the camels carried. Elijah answered, "Anger and contempt for those who speak during Kaddish." The *Shibbolei ha-Leket* was famous and part of the Hasidei Ashkenaz corpus, so Margaritha was probably acquainted with this story, which he either knew in a different version or misremembered. Nonetheless, he presented his readers with a tale exhibiting the Jewish desire that people behave appropriately during prayer. It was a fitting finale to his commentary on the prayer book.

Conclusion

Most of the conclusions and inferences that can be drawn from Margaritha's translation of the prayer book are noted above. At root, he presented the daily Ashkenazic *siddur.* His text differed little from other Hebrew prayer books. The translation suited his purpose and is useful to scholars in its presentation of basic content. His commentary went through two phases. The first edition presented a briefer discussion of the text. It evinced Margaritha's polemical-ethnographic mindset. The second edition was obviously influenced by Margaritha's unsuccessful debate with Rabbi Josel of Rosheim. He knew that his arguments had been truthful, yet he was the one who was imprisoned. The second edition gave him the opportunity to strengthen his arguments and add factual details that disproved Josel without having to face him.

Margaritha's commentary to the prayer book in the second edition is a more important text because of its additions. The customs, stories, and "snapshots" of prayer life make it a richer source for scholars of ethnography and liturgy. Unlike the ethnography and the Refutation, the second edition of the prayer book commentary largely superseded its predecessor. It was the second edition that was most often reprinted. The final state of the commentary is essential in evaluating Margaritha's influence on Christians. That influence is well documented with regard to Martin Luther and

Johann Buxtorf. Margaritha's explanation and citations of the Talmud and other Jewish texts prove him to have been a reliable informant.

Without Margaritha's conversion, there would have been no *Der gantz Jüdisch glaub,* let alone the prayer book translation and commentaries. It may be that he originally envisioned the prayer book as a separate work. His conversion and his birth into a learned Jewish family were the central events in his spiritual life. The commentaries and translations should be read with these facts in mind. Every story, passage, and explanation reveals something about Margaritha's discomfort with Judaism and reason for converting. His Messiah consciousness grew out of the learning and prayer experiences in Regensburg and his travels to other Jewish communities. Jews, as the commentary, kabbalah, and Refutation abundantly demonstrate, lived in a heightened and sometimes ecstatic expectation of the Messiah. Margaritha not only came to accept a Messiah but also to see his Jewish education and the texts he studied as rabbinic structures intended to obfuscate the truth. His heartfelt prayers recited daily were inadequate utterances to the divine. The prayer book commentary was part of Margaritha's retrospective falsification of the religious, spiritual dimensions of Judaism. He also used it to reveal Jewish private and secret practices. Except obliquely, he did not say that Judaism, nor his rejection of it, led him to Christianity. When he remarked that Jews should see the truth of scriptures, he described something of his own experience. Margaritha's prayer book is a multilayered source of data. It offers scholars opportunities for analysis that go beyond the material presented here.

Notes

Preface

1. Margaritha's date of birth is not known. In *Der gantz Jüdisch glaub* (Augsburg, 1530), Kiii-L, he mentions a Jewish communal conflict in Regensburg with an imperial official named Rohrbach. He notes that he was about fourteen when this occurred. Rohrbach died in 1511. From this it can be inferred that Margaritha was born in the 1490s.

2. Leopold Zunz, *Die Ritus des synagogalen Gottesdienstes, geschichtlich entwickelt* (Berlin: J. Spinger, 1859); Leopold Geiger, "Die Juden in die deutsche Literatur," *Zeitschrift für die Geschichte der Juden in Deutschland* 2 (1888): 297–374 at 324–25; Heinrich Graetz, *Geschichte der Juden,* vol. 9 (Leipzig, 1877); H. Bresslau, "Aus Strassburger Judenakten," *Zeitschrift für die Geschichte der Juden in Deutschland* 5 (1892): 307–34 at 310–12.

3. Josef Mieses, *Die älteste gedruckte deutsche Uebersetzung das jüdischen Gebetbuches a.d. Jahre 1530 und ihr autor Anthonius Margaritha* (Wien: Löwit, 1916).

4. Raphael Straus, *Regensburg and Augsburg,* translated from German by Felix N. Gerson (Philadelphia: Jewish Publication Society, 1939), 67, 69, 156.

5. Selma Stern, *Josel of Rosheim* (Philadelphia: Jewish Publication Society, 1965).

6. Chava Fraenkel-Goldschmidt, *Joseph of Rosheim, Historical Writings* (Hebrew) (Jerusalem: Magnes Press, 1996).

7. Hans-Martin Kirn, *Das Bild vom Juden im Deutschland des frühen 16. Jahrhunderts* (Tübingen: J. C. B. Mohr, 1989); R. Pochia Hsia, *The Myth of Ritual Murder: Jews and Magic in Reformation Germany* (New Haven, CT: Yale University Press, 1988).

8. See Stephen G. Burnett, "Distorted Mirrors: Anthonius Margaritha, Johann Buxtorf and Christian Ethnographies of the Jews," *Sixteenth Century Journal* 25 (1994): 275–87.

9. Elisheva Carlebach, *Divided Souls: Converts from Judaism in Germany, 1500–1750* (New Haven, CT: Yale University Press, 2001).

10. Peter von der Osten-Sacken, *Martin Luther und die Juden—Neu untersucht anhand von Anton Margaritas* "Der gantz Jüdisch Glaub" *(1530/31)* (Stuttgart: Kohlhammer, 2002).

11. Maria Diemling, "Christliche Ethnographien über Juden und Judentum in der Frühen Neuzeit: Die Konvertiten Victor von Carben und Antonius Margaritha und ihre Darstellung jüdischen Lebens und jüdischer Religion" (PhD diss., Universität Wien, 1999).

12. Maria Diemling, "Chonuko-Kirchweyhe," *Kalonymos* 3 (2000): 1–3; Maria Diemling, "Antonius Margaritha on the 'Whole Jewish Faith'; A Sixteenth-Century Convert from Judaism and the Depiction of the Jewish Religion," in *Jews, Judaism, and the Reformation in Sixteenth-Century Germany,* ed. Dean Phillip Bell and Stephen G. Burnett (Leiden: Brill, 2006), 303–34.

13. Yaacov Deutsch, "Polemical Ethnographies: Descriptions of Yom Kippur in the Writings of Christian Hebraists and Jewish Converts to Christianity in Early Modern Europe," in *Hebraica Veritas? Christian Hebraists and the Study of Judaism in Early Modern Europe,* ed. Allison P. Coudert and Jeffrey S. Shoulson (Philadelphia: University of Pennsylvania Press, 2004), 202–33; Yaacov Deutsch, "Von der Juden Ceremonien: Representations of Jews in Sixteenth Century Germany," in Bell and Burnett, eds. *Jews, Judaism, and the Reformation,* 335–56. Andrew Colin Gow had earlier used the term "hostile ethnography." See, for example, his *The Red Jews: Antisemitism in an Apocalyptic Age, 1200–1600* (Leiden: Brill, 1995), 47.

14. Michael T. Walton, "Anthonius Margaritha—Honest Reporter?" *Sixteenth Century Journal* 36 (Spring 2005): 129–41.

Chapter 1

1. Arye Maimon, *Germania Judaica, bd. III, 1350–1519* (Tübingen: Mohr, 1987) is the primary assembly of sources concerning German Jewry. Jacob's genealogy is noted on page 1036. The use of matronymics is mentioned there. The outline of Jacob's life presented above is largely drawn from this text. The identification of Jacob's parents is from Z. Baruchson, "R. Jacob Margolis, His Life and Work" (Hebrew master's thesis, Bar-Ilan University, 1978). The names Moses and Margoles are from later sources, such as David Gans, *Tzemah David,* ed. Mordechai Breuer (Jerusalem, 1983), original Prague, 1633. Josef Mieses in *Die älteste gedruckte deutsche Uebersetzung das jüdischen Gebetbuches a.d. Jahre 1530* (Wien: Löwit, 1916), 15, presents the opinions of Leopold Zunz and Heinrich Grätz regarding Jacob's origins.

2. Dean Phillip Bell, *Jewish Identity in Early Modern Germany* (Aldershot, England: Ashgate, 2007), discusses the memory book and the social structure, 76–81.

3. Maimon, *Germania Judaica,* III, 1016.

4. Henry Wasserman, "Ulm," *Encyclopaedia Judaica,* 15: 1524.

5. Maimon, *Germania Judaica,* III, 1016.

6. Ibid.

7. Ibid., 1036.

8. Ibid.

9. Ibid.

10. Ibid.

11. Ibid.

12. Ibid.

13. Ibid., 1016, and Baruchson, "R. Jacob Margolis," 186–93.

14. Anthonius Margaritha, *Wie aus dem heylligen 53 Capittal* (Wien, 1534) (hereafter *Isaiah Commentary*), 16–17. The discussion here is based on his account and that of Josef Mieses, *Die älteste gedruckte Uebersetzung des jüdischen Gebetbuches a.d. Jahre 1530* (Wien: Löwit, 1916), 18–21.

15. R. Judah Mintz, *Sh'aloth vT'shuvoth* (Hebrew) (Venice, 1553), in Mieses, *Die älteste gedruckte Uebersetzung des jüdischen Gebetbuches a.d. Jahre 1530,* 19.

16. Christopher Ocker, "German Theologians and the Jews in the Fifteenth Century," in *Jews, Judaism, and the Reformation in Sixteenth-Century Germany,* ed. Dean Phillip Bell and Stephen G. Burnett (Leiden: Brill, 2006), 46.

17. Hans Folz, "Ein Spil von dem Herzogen von Bufgund," in *Fastnachtspiele aus dem fünfzehnten Jahrhundert 1,* ed. A. Von Keller (Stuttgart, 1853), 169–90. This translation is from Andrew Colin Gow, *The Red Jews: Antisemitism in an Apocalyptic Age, 1200–1600* (Leiden: Brill, 1995), 375.

18. Maimon, *Germania Judaica,* III, 1037.

19. Johannes Reuchlin's *De Verbo Mirifico* (1494) focused on the power of divine names and finding Jesus at the root of kabbalah. His *De Arte Cabalistica* (1517) is a dialogue discussing the kabbalah as a tradition that confirms Christianity as well as conferring metaphysical and theological knowledge.

20. Eric Zimmer, "Jewish and Christian Hebraist Collaboration in Sixteenth Century Germany," *Jewish Quarterly Review* n.s. 71, no. 2 (1980): 73–74.

21. Some suggest that Saidia's son, Isaac, was Samuel's father-in-law. Isaac's age and apparent identification as Samuel's brother-in-law support the argument that Saidia was Samuel's father-in-law. See Maimon, *Germania Judaica,* III, 1220.

22. The Veiflin-Straubing family is discussed in Raphael Straus, *Regensburg and Augsburg,* translated from German by Felix N. Gerson (Philadelphia: Jewish Publication Society, 1939), 132–33.

23. Ibid., 132.

24. Ibid., 87–117.

25. The decline was related to many factors, including the changing attitude toward allowing Christian lenders to take interest on loans. Rethinking usury reached a high point under Pope Leo X (1517–25), who allowed Christians, especially charitable institutions that granted loans, such as the Monti di Pietà, to collect interest. The rise of Christian bankers, like the Fuggers at the end of the fifteenth century, increased competition with Jews for large loans. Of

course, Jews still made loans and were blamed for the evil of usury. A point of departure for the analysis of the economic situation of Jews in the fifteenth and sixteenth centuries is Georg Caro, *Sozial-und Wirtschaftsgeschichte der Juden im Mittelalter und der Neuzeit,* 2 vols. (Leipzig: Fock, 1908–20). Volume 2 covers the period discussed in this study. There is a limited discussion in H. H. Ben-Sasson, ed., *A History of the Jewish People* (Cambridge, MA: Harvard University Press, 1976), 628–45. See also Salo Wittmayer Baron, *A Social and Religious History of the Jews,* vol. 11 (Philadelphia: Jewish Publication Society, 1952).

26. Ibid., 113–14.

27. Ibid., 145.

28. See Heinrich Schmidt, "Die deutschen Städtechroniken als Spiegel des bügerlichen Selbstverständnisses im Spätmittelalter," Schriftenreihe der historischen Kommission bei der Bayerischen Akademie der Wissenschaften, 3 (PhD diss., University of Göttingen, 1958), 89–97. This is also discussed in Kristen E. S. Zapalac, "'With a morsel of bread': Delineating Differences in the Jewish and Christian Communities of Regensburg before the Pogrom of 1519," in *Infinite Boundaries: Order, Disorder, and Reorder in Early Modern German Culture,* ed. Max Reinhart, Sixteenth Century Essays and Studies, No. 40 (Kirksville, MO: Sixteenth Century Journal Publishers, 1998), 271–90.

29. Cited in Ocker, "German Theologians," 51.

30. Ibid.

31. Yacob Guggenheim, "Meeting on the Road: Encounters between German Jews and Christians on the Margins of Society," in *In and Out of the Ghetto,* ed. R. Po-chia Hsia and Hartmut Lehmann (Cambridge: University of Cambridge Press, 1995), 125.

32. Ibid.

33. Ibid.

34. Margaritha, *Der gantz Jüdisch glaub,* Kii.

35. Ibid., Kiii r., translated in Guggenheim, "Meeting on the Road," 124. The customs of Regensburg were like those of Austria. *Der gantz Jüdisch glaub* is an important source for those customs. Rabbi Isaac (Eisik) Stein (d. 1495) discussed the local customs in Hebrew. Several manuscripts exist and much was printed in his posthumously published *Sefer Mitzvot Gadol* (Venice, 1547).

36. Maimon, *Germania Judaica,* III, 1189. Wolf's activities were similar to those of the Horowitz family in its move to Prague, where it became a communal power. The Horowitzes' story is briefly noted in *Encyclopaedia Judaica* 8: 983–84 s.v. "Horowitz." Rabbi Joseph of Rosheim mentions disputes that he mediated; see Chava Fraenkel-Goldschmidt, *Joseph of Rosheim, Historical Writings* (Hebrew) (Jerusalem: Magnes Press, 1996), 204–12. Selma Stern, *Josel of Rosheim* (Philadelphia: Jewish Publication Society, 1965), 144–45, tells the story of Josel and the Horowitzers, who tried to have the authorities kill him.

37. Margaritha, *Der gantz Jüdisch glaub,* Kiii and ff., and Maimon, *Germania Judaica,* III, 1189.

38. Dean Phillip Bell in *Jewish Identity* mentions similar conflicts in other communities, see, e.g., 112–15.

39. Straus, *Regensburg,* 146.

40. Raphael Straus, ed., *Urkunden und aktenstücke zur Geschichte der Juden in Regensburg, 1453–1738,* in *Quellen und Eröterungen zur bayerischen Geschichte,* N.F. 18 (Munich: Beck, 1960), no. 693, translated in Zapalac, "With a morsel of bread," 280.

41. Ibid., no. 695, translated in Zapalec, "With a morsel of bread," 280.

42. Ibid., no. 708, translated in Zapalec, "With a morsel of bread," 280.

43. Melanchthon cited in Ludwig Geiger, *Das Studium der Hebräischen Sprache in Deutschland* (Breslau, 1870), 52. Translation mine. Boeschenstein is noted for his transcription of Askenazic chants, which were published in Johannes Reuchlin, *De accentibus et orthographia lingue Hebraicae* (Hagenau, 1518). He also translated some Hebrew prayers into German that were printed in 1523 or 1525, *Viel gutter ermanungen zu Gott dem hymlischen vater, Ermahnungen auss hebreyscher Sprach in Teutsch gebrach.* This was not a translation of the entire prayer book. Boeschenstein advertised his teaching of Hebrew in Regensburg in 1518, see Jean Baumgarten and Jerold C. Frakes, *Introduction to Old Yiddish Literature* (Oxford: Oxford University Press, 2005), 10.

44. David Gans, *Tzemah David,* ed. Mordechai Breuer (Jerusalem, 1983) 137, #1530. Cf. the translation in Abba Hillel Silver, *A History of Messianic Speculation in Israel from the First through the Seventeenth Centuries* (New York: Macmillan, 1927 reprinted Gloucester, MA: 1978), 144, cited in Elisheva Carlebach, *Between History and Hope: Jewish Messianism in Ashkenaz and Sepharad* (New York: Graduate School of Jewish Studies, Touro College, 1998), 6. Carlebach treats the Lemlein affair in detail.

45. Maimon, *Germania Judaica,* III, 1188.

46. Ibid., 1188.

47. Ibid., 1216.

48. Johannes Pfefferkorn, *Der Juden Spiegel* (Nürnberg: Huber, 1507), L v., translation mine. For a study of Pfefferkorn, see Hans-Martin Kirn, *Das Bild vom Juden im Deutschland des frühen 16. Jahrhunderts* (Tübingen: J. C. B. Mohr, 1989). The issue of converts is explicated in Elisheva Carlebach, *Divided Souls: Converts from Judaism in Germany, 1500–1750* (New Haven, CT: Yale University Press, 2001). She discusses Pfefferkorn throughout; Lemlein at 74–75.

49. Straus, *Urkunden . . . der Juden Regensburg-,* nos. 762 and 833, cited in Zapalac, "With a morsel of bread," 280.

50. Crackerlike *matzo* was baked in special ovens at Passover. See Gans, *Tzemah David,* 137.

51. Alfred Haverkamp, "The Jewish Quarters in German Towns during the Late Middles Ages," in *In and Out of the Ghetto,* ed. Hsia and Lehmann, 19–20. On expulsions, see also Salo Wittmayer Baron, *A Social and Religious History of the Jews,* 2nd ed. (Philadelphia: Jewish Publication Society, 1952–), 11: 275.

Although he deals with a later period, Jonathan Israel, *European Jewry in the Age of Mercantilism, 1550–1750* (Oxford: Clarendon Press; New York: Oxford University Press, 1985) offers data and insights into economics and Jewish expulsions. The Jews of Regensburg hired the lawyer Johann Zasius to present their case. Steven Rowan, "Johann Zasius, Attorney for the Jewish Community of Regensburg, 1519 C.E.," *Jewish Quarterly Review* n.s. 72, no. 3 (1982): 198–201.

52. The letter is quoted in Leonhard Widmann, "Chronik von Regensburg," in *Chroniken der deutschen Städte* 15: 31. See also Johannes Heil, "Beyond 'History and Memory,' Traces of Jewish Historiography in the Middle Ages," *Medieval Jewish Studies Online* 1 (2007/8), at http://www.medieval-jewish-studies.com/Journal/Vol1/article02.html, translation by Andrew Gow of Heil's original "Jenseits von 'History and Memory.' Spuren jüdischer Geschichtsschreibung im Mittelalter," *Zeitschrift für Geschichtswisenschaft* 55 (December 2007): 989–1019.

53. The synagogue was depicted in two 1519 prints by Albrecht Altdorfer, see Richard I. Cohen, *Jewish Icons* (Berkeley: University of California Press, 1998), 24–25. David Landau and Peter Parshall, *The Renaissance Print* (New Haven, CT: Yale University Press, 1994), 338–39, discuss Altdorfer's prints and the destruction of the Regensburg synagogue in some detail. They date the prints to a few days before the building's destruction. There is also a copy of an old sketch of the "medieval synagogue" in Straus, *Regensburg and Augsburg*, following p. 98. Margaritha noted that there were two marble stones engraved with the name of God in the synagogue. Margaritha, *Der gantz Jüdisch glaub*, Xii v.

54. Margaritha, *Der gantz Jüdisch glaub*, Kiii–L. The Jewish perspective on the Regensburg expulsion and the relevant documents are found in Heinrich Graetz, *Geschichte der Juden* (Leipzig, 1877), vol. 9, Appendix 4. See also Elisheva Carlebach, "Between History and Myth: The Regensburg Expulsion in Josel of Rosheim's *Sefer Ha-Miknah*," in *Jewish History and Jewish Memory*, ed. Elisheva Carlebach, John M. Efron, and Davis M. Myers (Hanover, NH: Brandeis University Press, 1998), 40–53. There is a Christian account of the Regensburg expulsion. Christoph Hoffman (Christophorus Ostrofrancus), a Benedictine, published *De Ratisbona metropoli boioariae et subita ibidem judaeorum proscriptione* (Augsburg, 1519) in which he discussed the care with which the Jews abandoned their synagogue and prepared it to avoid defilement. Hoffman's report is remarkably neutral.

55. "Das ain solche unainigkeit zu Regenspurg under ynen entsprungen ist/ dar durch sy vertriben worden seind/ dann weñ sy ains gewesenn werenn/ weren sye sollicher vertreibunng wol furkommen." Margaritha, *Der gantz Jüdisch glaub*, L r. Translation mine.

56. R. Joseph of Rosheim, *Sefer ha-miknah* (MS Bodleian 2240), in Graetz, *Geschichte der Juden*, 9: 1084. The *Sefer* has been edited and printed, Chava

Fraenkel-Goldschmitt, *Sefer ha-miknah* (Jerusalem, 1970). The passages cited above are found on pages 14–15. The passage I have here translated reads, "ראה על החורבן רעגינשפורק ההתחלה אינה אלא בסיבת שני מוסרים."

57. Ibid., 1089. The text reads,
בעבירה יצאו לתרבות רעה האחד עם כל זרעו והאחר עם ארוסתו ואף שמבני גדולים היו אביהם . . .
לא הועיל להן זכות אביהן אותו שני מוסרים שהתחילו.

58. Ibid., 1086. The text reads,
כל בני הגולה בדפוס העמיק ספרי מינות להוציא עלילות דברים בשלשה דברים לאמר להם :
ואותו האיש האחד ציער היהודים מקללים האומות ומזלזלים ישו בעלינו לשבח ומילם גרים.

59. An editor's note in the *Encyclopaedia Judaica*, "Leipzig," 10: 1592, states that Margaritha's father-in-law was the Leipzig publisher Melchior Lotther. This seems highly unlikely given that (1) Margaritha published with another printer in Augsburg, (2) he was married before he published with Lotther, (3) he did not publish his later works with Lotther, and (4) when he left Leipzig, his wife and children were impoverished (see chapter 4). It is doubtful that a successful publisher would allow his daughter and grandchildren to live in poverty.

60. Carlebach, "Between History and Myth," 44.

61. Bell, *Jewish Identity*, 59.

62. Maimon, *Judaica Germanica*, III, 1227.

63. See Israel, *European Jewry*.

Chapter 2

1. For example, Margaritha mentions different circumcision practices in Hungary, Italy, and German in *Der gantz Jüdisch glaub* (1530), Hiii r. (All citations are to the 1530 edition unless otherwise noted.)

2. The importance of community customs in Judaism is seen in many texts and commentaries, e.g., B. T. *Pesachim* 50a, which allows work until midday on the eve of Passover if it is the community custom, but not if it is against the custom. A person had to observe the customs of the place from which he came, rather than those of his destination. Authoritative rabbinic decisions were widely known by scholars; see Irving A. Agus, *Rabbi Meir of Rothenburg* (New York: KTAV, 1970).

3. Yacob Guggenheim, "Meeting on the Road: Encounters between German Jews and Christians on the Margins of Society," in *In and Out of the Ghetto*, ed. R. Po-chia Hsia and Hartmut Lehmann (Cambridge: University of Cambridge Press, 1995), 131.

4. The family of Cantor Kalman did not convert. Maimon, *Germania Judaica*, III, 1225.

5. Ibid., 1188.

6. Ibid., 1187. In Christian theology one baptism was sufficient. Repeated baptisms were viewed as sacrilegious.

7. An example of this is Margaritha's criticism regarding the failure to observe Levirate marriage, *Der gantz Jüdisch glaub,* Iiiii v., and throughout his refutation of Judaism (Appendix A of this book).

8. Maimon, *Germania Judaica,* III, 1183.

9. The discussion of Jewish life in *Der gantz Jüdisch glaub* is taken from the first eighty-nine pages. Where I use other sources for Jewish life, they will be cited.

10. Margaritha, *Der gantz Jüdisch glaub,* B r. The book, probably in manuscript, cannot be identified with certainty. There was a Yiddish book of customs printed in Venice in 1590, see Hans-Martin Kirn, *Das Bild vom Juden im Deutschland des frühen 16. Jahrhunderts* (Tübingen: J. C. B. Mohr, 1989), 39 n. 102. The source of the hundred blessing rule was Rabbi Meir, B. T. *Menachth* 43b. The benediction against the *minim* is found at *Berakot* 28b–29a.

11. There are many contemporary pictures of the doorpost box (*mezuza*) such as Jerusalem, Israel Museum, MS Rothschild 24, folio 126 v. This and other scenes of Jewish life are collected in Thérèse Metzger and Mendel Metzger, *Jewish Life in the Middle Ages* (New York: Alpine Fine Arts Collection, 1982), 88.

12. Metzger and Metzger, *Jewish Life,* 97, 104–5. Diane Wolfthal, *Picturing Yiddish: Gender, Identity, and Memory in the Illustrated Yiddish Books of Renaissance Italy* (Leiden: Brill, 2004), mentions Pfefferkorn's and Margaritha's illustrations.

13. Elisheva Baumgarten, *Mothers and Children, Jewish Family Life in Medieval Europe* (Princeton, NJ: Princeton University Press, 2004) discusses *mikveh,* childbirth, and marriage in various chapters.

14. Margaritha, *Der gantz Jüdisch glaub,* Hiii. Baumgarten, *Mothers and Children* discusses the *Wachnacht* (Night of waiting) in detail, 99ff. Baumgarten makes extensive use of *Sefer Hasidim,* part of which was written by Judah the Pious, a thirteenth-century rabbi in Regensburg.

15. Baumgarten, *Mothers and Children,* 101–5, notes that the period of impurity originally ended a short time after giving birth but that another immersion was required forty or eighty days later. Margaritha's text reflects this custom. Later the immersion took place only after forty (for male child) or eighty days (for female child).

16. Elisheva Carlebach, *Divided Souls: Converts from Judaism in Germany, 1500–1750* (New Haven, CT: Yale University Press, 2001), 249, cites Margoles. She also discusses women who threatened to convert on pages 30–31.

17. This same point was made by the author of *Voice of a Fool,* discussed below.

18. Margaritha, *Der gantz Jüdisch glaub,* Iii r; 1544 edition, Lii v. The Jewish mouse was a delicious superstition that caught the attention of Christian Friedrich Garmann (1640–1708). In his *De Miraculis Mortuorum* (Leipzig, 1670), 32. (There is a facsimile with German translation by Silvio Benstello and Berne Hermann [Göttingen: Universitat Göttingen, 2003].) Garmann referred

to Margaritha, but not to Carben (see note 29), as a source for information about the superstition.

> Eiusdem farinae est mus ille Judaicus, quem Cadaver statim ut Terrae concreditum tam crudeliter mordere afferunt, ut etiam clamare, (risum teneatis amici) cogatur. . . . ex Antonio Margarita: Scissione vestimenti super sepulchro facta cuncti magno cum strepitu & vociferatione è Coemiterio diffugiunt, ne Lethiferum defuncti: andiant clamorem, quem terra obrutus atq́; à mure nares ad morsus edere creditur, & quo audito intra trigesimum diem mori itidem cogatur animadvertens.
>
> Of the same kind is the Jewish mouse which according to their claim bites the body most horribly as soon as it is covered with earth—please do not laugh friend—so that it is forced to scream . . . according to Antonius Margarita, as soon as the vestment is torn over the grave [Jewish mourning custom] everyone flees the cemetery, frightened and screaming so that they do not hear the yell of the dead which brings death . . . for that person who hears it dies within thirty days. (Translation mine)

19. The tradition comes from B. T. *Shabbat,* 119b.

20. See Jacob Katz, *The "Shabbas Goy": A Study in Halakhic Flexibility* (Philadelphia: Jewish Publication Society, 1989), especially 9–68.

21. R. Yosef Yuzpah Halmo, *Yosef Ometz* (Frankfurt am Main, 1928), 172, para. 788, and R. Yair Hayyim Bachrach, *Mekor Hayyim* (Jerusalem, 1984), 2: 464 (both in Hebrew). The entrance of Elijah described in *Der gantz Jüdisch glaub* is mentioned in many studies, see Israel Jacob Yuval, *Two Nations in Your Womb,* trans. Barbara Harshav and Jonathan Chipman (Berkeley: University of California Press, 2006), 124.

22. See Yaacov Deutsch, "Polemical Ethnographies: Descriptions of Yom Kippur in the Writings of Christian Hebraists and Jewish Converts to Christianity in Early Modern Europe," in *Hebraica Veritas? Christian Hebraists and the Study of Judaism in Early Modern Europe,* ed. Allison P. Coudert and Jeffrey S. Shoulson (Philadelphia: University of Pennsylvania Press, 2004), 202–33.

23. This idea was derived from a divination practice described in B. T. *Horayoth* 12a.

24. Margaritha, *Der gantz Jüdisch glaub,* K v.–Kii r., "sye sollich ding ihm Thalmude schreyben darmit das die armen einfelftigen Judenn nicht darhin komen sollen das sy gedechten freylich . . . das unser vater den rechten Moschiach nicht hab'n woellen annemen."

25. See Stephen G. Burnett, "Distorted Mirrors: Anthonius Margaritha, Johann Buxtorf, and Christian Ethnographies of the Jews," *Sixteenth Century Journal* 25 (1994): 275–87, and Yaacov Deutsch, "Von der Juden Ceremonien: Representations of Jews in Sixteenth Century Germany," in Bell and Burnett, eds., *Jews, Judaism, and the Reformation,* 335–56, for discussions of *kapporoth.*

26. *Encyclopaedia Judaica* 10: 756, s.v.

27. The issues of the concealed society of the Jews and the revelation of its secrets are treated in Elisheva Carlebach, "Attribution of Secrecy and Perceptions of Jewry," *Jewish Social Studies* n.s. 2, no. 3 (1996): 115–36. Yaacov Deutsch, "Jewish Anti-Christian Invectives and Christian Awareness: An Unstudied Form of Interaction in the Early Modern Period," *Leo Baeck Institute Year Book* 55 (2010): 41–61, also discusses texts that revealed Jewish secrets.

28. Some see Margaritha's work as highly derivative of Victor von Carben's anti-Jewish work, *Juden Buechlein* (Cologne, 1508/9) translated into Latin by O. Gratius as *Opus aureum ac novum* (Cologne, 1509), and published again in German, *Juden Buechlein* (Cunitz, 1550). Although treating many of the same topics as Margaritha, Carben devotes much of the work to the Virgin Mary and the doctrine of the Trinity, two topics Margaritha virtually ignores. Mieses, *Jüdischen Gebetbuches,* thought Carben was the source for Margaritha, but Burnett, "Distorted Mirrors," minimizes Carben's influence. I agree with Burnett. It is true that most of the themes for anti-Jewish polemics, but not the description of customs, were set by the *Pugio fidei* of Raymond Martini (thirteenth century). Carben's discussion of *kapporoth* is original to him.

29. All chapters cited are from part I of the 1550 edition of *Juden Buchlein.* He mentions the "sambation" in chapter 18.

30. See Yaacov Deutsch, "Polemical Ethnographies," 215–16.

31. Carben, *Juden Buechlein,* part III, chapter 21.

32. Kirn, *Das Bild vom Juden im Deutschland des frühen 16. Jahrhunderts,* 147, discusses this story from *Toldoth Jesu.*

33. Carben, *Juden Buechlein,* part I, chapter 19.

34. See Talya Fishman, *Shaking the Pillars of Exile, "Voice of a Fool": An Early Modern Jewish Critique of Rabbinic Culture* (Stanford, CA: Stanford University Press, 1997), 92. Leon's autobiography has been translated and discussed in Mark R. Cohen, *The Autobiography of a Seventeenth-Century Venetian Rabbi: Leon Modena's "Life of Judah"* (Princeton, NJ: Princeton University Press, 1988).

35. Fishman, *Shaking the Pillars of Exile,* Essay 2, 103–6. The idea that Ezra restored the lost Torah was held by Irenaeus, Tertullian, Clement of Alexandria, Eusebius, and Jerome. It was a doctrine mentioned by Pererius in his biblical commentary (1589) and by Pareus in his (1609). Arnold Williams, *The Common Expositor* (Chapel Hill: University of North Carolina Press, 1948), 23–24.

36. Fishman, *Shaking the Pillars of Exile,* 107.

37. Ibid., 117.

38. Ibid., 125–41.

39. Another sixteenth-century Jew who criticized Judaism was Eliezer Eilburg. He was born about 1530 and wrote the "Ten Questions" about 1575. The unique manuscript has been discussed by Joseph M. Davis, "The 'Ten Questions' of Eliezer Eilburg and the Problem of Jewish Unbelief in the 16th Century," *Jewish Quarterly Review* 91 (January–April 2001): 293–336. Among

other things, Eilburg called into question the accuracy of the Masoretic text, the Talmudic multiplication of commandments, and Jewish chosenness. Davis associates Eilburg with the tradition of challenging Talmudic stories found in R. Azariah ben Moses De' Rossi (c. 1511–c. 1578), *Me'or Einayim* (Light of the eyes) (Mantua, 1573–75) as well as the philosophical tradition of Jewish Aristotelianism seen in Maimonides.

Chapter 3

1. For sources on Lemlein, see Ephraim Kupfer, "Hezyonotav shel R. Asher b'r Meir ha-Mekhuneh Lemlein Reutlingen" (Hebrew), *Kobez al Yad* 8/18 (1975): 285–423. Elisheva Carlebach presents an insightful view in *Between History and Hope: Jewish Messianism in Ashkenaz and Sepharad* (New York: Graduate School of Jewish Studies, Touro College, 1998).

2. See Harris Lenowitz, *The Jewish Messiahs: From the Galilee to Crown Heights* (New York: Oxford University Press, 1998).

3. *Megillah* 29A, cited in Joseph Klausner, *The Messianic Idea in Israel,* trans. W. F. Stinespring (New York: Macmillan, 1955), 471. Klausner treats the history of Messianism to the formulation of the *Mishnah,* the basic text of the Talmud. He sees a development from the idea of a restoration under a Davidic king to a spiritualized king and kingdom.

4. Sukkah 52a, cited in Klausner, *Messianic Idea in Israel,* 489. Klausner sees the origin of the Messiah ben Joseph in a division of the traditional warrior and spiritual aspects of the Messiah ben David.

5. Lenowitz, *Jewish Messiahs,* has demonstrated that each succeeding Messiah tended to incorporate aspects of his predecessors, thus meeting the evolving expectations of his followers.

6. See Elisheva Carlebach, "The Sabbatean Posture of German Jewry," *Jerusalem Studies in Jewish Thought,* nos. 16 and 17 (2001): 1–29, especially 24 and works cited therein, and Gerson Cohen, "Messianic Postures of Ashkenazim and Sephardim," Leo Baeck Memorial Lecture 9 (1967), in *Studies of the Leo Baeck Institute,* ed. Max Kreutzberger (New York: 1967), 117–56, reprinted in Marc Saperstein, ed., *Essential Papers on Messianic Movements and Personalities in Jewish History* (New York: New York University Press, 1992), 202–33. Carlebach and Cohen document continual messianic movements and speculations in Europe, demonstrating the background of Margaritha's early life.

7. Johannes Pfefferkorn, *Der Juden Spiegel* (Nürnberg: Huber, 1507), "Die vored" (unpaginated). Translation mine.

8. Ibid., B r.

9. Ibid., next to last page.

10. Carben, *Juden Buechlein,* part 2, chapter 19.

11. Ludwig Geiger, *Johann Reuchlin, Sein Leben und Seine Werke* (Leipzig, 1871), 212, noted this. It was reiterated by Samuel Abraham Hirsch, *The*

Cabbalists and Other Essays (London: W. Heinemann, 1922), 199. Richard I. Cohen, *Jewish Icons* (Berkeley: University of California Press, 1998), reproduced Pfefferkorn's illustrations and noted Margaritha's use of them.

12. The following discussion is based on the 1550 German edition and the 1509 Latin text, *Opus aureum.*

13. Carben, *Juden Buechlein* (1550), B r.

14. Ibid., part 1, chapters 8 and 12; part 2, chapter 10.

15. Ibid., part 1, chapter 11; part 3, chapter 8.

16. For a discussion of Rabbi Abraham's contacts in Germany and elsewhere, see Ira Robinson, "Messianic Prayer Vigils in Jerusalem in the Early Sixteenth Century," *Jewish Quarterly Review* n.s. 72 (July 1981): 32–42.

17. Ibid., 35.

18. Ibid.

19. Margaritha, *Der gantz Jüdisch glaub,* 1544, Rii.

20. The "wider den gantzen glauben der juden" runs from Ziii v. to *b*iii v. in the 1530 edition and from *g* to *i*iii in the 1544 edition. My commentary more or less follows the order of Margaritha's arguments. My translation of the entire text is found in Appendix A. The facsimile pages are from the 1544 edition.

21. See Klausner, *Messianic Idea in Israel,* 483–501.

22. Ibid.; Sukka 52a, discussed in *Der gantz Jüdisch glaub,* Ziii v.

23. *Der gantz Jüdisch glaub,* Ziiii v.

24. Ibid.

25. Ibid., *a*ii r.

26. Ibid., *a*ii v.

27. Ibid., *b* v. The idea that the Jews were so assimilated as to have lost their status as God's chosen people is similar to that of Eliezer Eilburg; see Joseph Davis, "The 'Ten Questions' of Eliezer Eilburg and the Problems of Jewish Unbelief in the 16th Century," *Jewish Quarterly Review* 91 (January–April 2001): 293–336.

28. Ovadiah's remarks are printed in A. Yaari, *Iggerot Eretz Yisrael* (1940), 140, and translated in "Messianic Movements," *Encyclopedia Judaica,* 1426. See also Simcha Shtull-Trauring, ed., *Letters from Beyond the Sambatyon: The Myth of the Ten Lost Tribes* (New York: Maxima New Media, 1997).

29. See Lenowitz, *Jewish Messiahs,* and Andrew Gow, *The Red Jews: Antisemitism in an Apocalyptic Age, 1200–1600* (Leiden: Brill, 1995).

30. Margaritha, *Der gantz Jüdisch glaub, b*ii–*b*iii. The ideas that the Jews bribe Christians, then mock them, and need to be turned to honest labor, which will soften their hearts, are all mentioned in Luther's *On the Jews and Their Lies* (*Von den Juden und ihren Lügen*) (Wittemberg: H. Lust, 1543). Margaritha's *Der gantz Jüdisch glaub* was well known to Luther.

31. Margaritha, *Der gantz Jüdisch glaub, b*ii–*b*iiii.

32. Leopold Zunz used Margaritha's translation in his study of the liturgy, *Die Ritus des synagogalen Gottesdienstes, geschichtlich entwickelt* (Berlin: J. Springer, 1859).

33. Josef Mieses, *Die älteste gedruckte deutsche Uebersetzung des jüdischen Gebetbuches, a.d. Jahre 1530 und ihr Autor Anthonius Margaritha* (Wien: R Löwit, 1916), 51. Translation mine.

34. As noted above, some works that present a picture of Margaritha without adopting Mieses's negative perspective are: Stephen G. Burnett, "Distorted Mirrors: Antonius Margaritha, Johann Buxtorf, and Christian Ethnographies of the Jews," *Sixteenth Century Journal* 25 (1994): 275–87; Maria Diemling, "Christliche Ethnographien über Juden und Judentum in der Frühen Neuzeit: Die Konvertiten Victor von Carben und Antonius Margaritha und ihre Darstellung jüdischen Lebens und jüdischer Religion"(PhD diss., Universität Wien, 1999); Maria Diemling, "Chonuko-Kirchweyhe" *Kalonymos* 3 (2000): 1–3; Maria Diemling, "Antonius Margaritha on the 'Whole Jewish Faith': A Sixteenth-Century Convert from Judaism and the Depiction of the Jewish Religion," in *Jews, Judaism, and the Reformation in Sixteenth-Century Germany,* ed. Phillip Bell and Stephen G. Burnett (Leiden: Brill, 2006), 303–34; Yaacov Deutsch, "Polemical Ethnographies: Descriptions of Yom Kippur in the Writings of Christian Hebraists and Jewish Converts to Christianity in Early Modern Europe," in *Hebrew Veritas? Christian Hebraists and the Study of Judaism in Early Modern Europe,* ed. Allison R. Coudert and Jeffrey S. Shoulson (Philadelphia: University of Pennsylvania Press, 2004); Yaacov Deutsch, "Von der Juden Ceremonien: Representations of Jews in Sixteenth-Century Germany," in Bell and Burnett, *Jews, Judaism, and the Reformation,* 335–56.

35. Margaritha, *Der gantz Jüdisch glaub,* Lii v.

36. See Appendix D for a more detailed analysis.

37. Margaritha, *Der gantz Jüdisch glaub,* Q r., 1530 edition.

38. Ibid., 1530 edition, Qiiii and 1544 edition, X v.

39. B. T. *Berakth* 60 a–b.

40. Regensburg Jews claimed that their community existed prior to the time of Jesus, while other German Jewish communities claimed descent from the scholars set adrift by Vespasian after the fall of Jerusalem. See Johannes Heil, "Beyond 'History and Memory,' Traces of Jewish Historiography in the Middle Ages, *Medieval Jewish Studies Online* 1 (2007/8), at http://www.medieval-jewish-studies.com/Journal/Vol1/article02.html, translation by Andrew Gow of the original "Jenseits von 'History and Memory.' Spuren jüdischer Geschichtsschreibung im Mittelalter," in *Zeitschrift für Geschichtswisenschaft* 55 (December 2007): 989–1019.

41. Margaritha, *Der gantz Jüdisch glaub,* Oiiii.

42. Ibid., Vii r. The passage reads, "Was ein Jude thun soll/ das er andechtig bete/ und Gott ihn erhoere."

43. Moses Isserles, *Sefer Torah ha-Olah* (Prague, 1570), 3: 4, quoted in *The Wisdom of the Zohar: An Anthology of Texts,* arranged and rendered into Hebrew by Fischel Lachower and Isaiah Tishby with introduction and explanations by Isaiah Tishby, English translation by David Goldstein (Oxford: For The Littman Library by Oxford University Press, 1989), 1: 111 n. 182.

44. Tishby, *The Wisdom of the Zohar,* 1: 97–98.

45. Moshe Idel, *Kabbalah: New Perspectives* (New Haven, CT: Yale University Press, 1988), 160.

46. Ibid., xiii, 28–29.

47. Ibid., 50.

48. Abraham ben Eliezer, *Nebri'ot haYeled,* translated in Ira Robinson, "Messianic Prayer Vigils in Jerusalem in the Early Sixteenth Century," *Jewish Quarterly Review* n.s. 72 (July 1981): 50. For a more detailed discussion of Margaritha's kabbalah and a translation, see Appendix B.

49. Margaritha, *Der gantz Jüdisch glaub,* V v., translation mine. See Appendix B for a translation of Margaritha on the kabbalah from *Der gantz Jüdisch glaub.*

50. See B. T. *Avoda Zara* 18b.

51. Margaritha, *Der gantz Jüdisch glaub,* Vii, translation mine.

52. Ibid.

53. Ibid.

54. Naftali Hirtz Treves, עם פיר'... ועוד פי' ע"ד הקבלה / אשר חיבר ולוקט... מה"ר [נפתלי] הירץ [טריביש] ש"ץ מלאה הארץ דעה:... תפילה מכל השנה referred to as *Sefer Dikduk Tefillah* (A Commentary on the Prayer Book. Malah ha-Aretz Da'th) (Thiengen, 1560). Hirtz Treves (the family name is often not used and Hirtz is transliterated Herz, "Naphtali Herz") died sometime before 1556. His sons issued the commentary as a book of 235 folios. Hirtz Treves cites many sources for his explanations. The pages cited are from the numbering of the copy at the Jewish National and University Library, which is digitized online.

55. Ibid., fol. 39.

56. Ibid., fol. 202.

57. Anthonius Margaritha, *Wie aus dem heylligen 53 Capittel des fürnemigsten prophetan Esaie grüntlich ausgefürt/probliert/das der verhaischen Moschiach (welcher Christus is) schon khomen...* (Wien: Sigrenium, 1534) (hereafter *Isaiah Commentary*).

58. Wilhelm Rotscheidt, *Stephan Isaak... Sein Leben* (Leipzig: Nachfolger, 1910), 7–11.

59. Stephan Isaac, *Wahre und einfaeltige Historia Stephani Isaaci (1586)* in Selma Stern, *Josel of Rosheim, Commander of Jewry in the Holy Roman Empire,* trans. Gertrude Hirschler (Philadelphia: Jewish Publication Society, 1965), 228–29.

60. The best available discussion of *Nizzahon* is Ora Limor and Israel Jacob Yuval, "Skepticism and Conversion: Jews, Christians, and Doubters in *Sefer ha-Nizzahon,*" in Coudert and Shoulson, *Hebrew Veritas?,* 159–80. My discussion of its context comes from this study.

61. Stephen G. Burnett, "Spokesmen for Judaism: Medieval Jewish Polemicists and Their Christian Readers in the Reformation Era," in *Reuchlin und seine Erben,* ed. Peter Schaefer and I. Wandrey, *Pforzheiner Reuchlinschriften* 7 (Stuttgart: Jan Thorbecke, 2005), 41–51, discusses the role of the *Toldoth Jesu* and the *Nizzahon* in the context of Christian Reformation thought.

62. Hans-Martin Kirn, *Das Bild vom Juden im Deutschland des frühen 16. Jahrhunderts* (Tübingen: J. C. B. Mohr, 1989), 122, notes Pfefferkorn's citation of *Nizzahon* but seems to think that Pfefferkorn referred to the much earlier *Nizzahon Vetus,* which, based upon the few extant manuscripts, would have been much less available. It is difficult to know which *Nizzahon* is referred to unless its specific contents are mentioned. See David Berger, *The Jewish Christian Debate in the High Middle Ages: A Critical Edition of the* Nizzahon Vetus(Philadelphia: Jewish Publication Society, 1979).

63. Margaritha, *Isaiah Commentary,* 20.

64. R. Yom Tov Lippman Mühlhausen, *Sepher HaNizzahon,* ed. Frank Talmage (Jerusalem: Mercaz Dinur, 1983).

65. Margaritha, *Isaiah Commentary,* 18. Margaritha referred again to *Nizzahon* at page 76 of his *Isaiah Commentary* without mentioning any specific doctrine.

66. Eck wrote *Ains Judenbuechlins Verlegung* (Against the defense of the Jews)(Ingolstadt, 1541), a pamphlet, in German rather than his usual Latin. There he reported that as a young man in 1503 he had seen the corpse of a victim of ritual murder. He is apparently referring to a case in which the father of the slain Christian child was convicted of the crime and executed and the local Jews released. Heiko Oberman, *The Roots of Anti-Semitism in the Age of Renaissance and Reformation,* trans. James I. Porter (Philadelphia: Fortress Press, 1984), 36–37. Eck wrote his tract in response to Andreas Osiander, *Ob es wahr und glaublich sey, dass die juden der christen kinder heymlich erwürgen und jr blut gebrauchen ein treffenliche schrifft auff eines yeden urteil gestalt* (1529?), bl v.–b2 r. (Whether it be true and credible that Jews secretly strangulate Christian children and make use of their blood.) Osiander, a prominent Lutheran theologian and Hebraist who also saw Copernicus's *De Revolutionibus* through the press, decried the blood libel, as did Margaritha.

67. Letter, February 19, 1535, Johannes Eck to Nikolaus Ellenbog, Paris BN MS lot 8643, 2, fol. 132, reproduced in *Briefwechsel Eck* in *Übersicht Reformationsgeschichte* no. 294; http://ivv7srv15.uni-muenster.de/mnkg/pfnuer/Eckbriefe/N294.html.

68. Ibid., translation mine. The Latin reads:

> Antonius Margarita contra Iudaeos aedidit, sed hui, quam hallucinatur in verbis, in personis, in adfixis. Asserit Isa. 63 textum corruptum per Iudaeos, qui pro "*lo*" (cum waw) reposuerint "*lo*" (cum aleph), et ita contenditt affirmative legi, cum sicc etiam nostra byblia et Septuaginta esset falsa, quia legit negative. Non est bonum cathecuminos seu neophitos aedere libros nisi bene revisos.

69. Isaiah 63:9. Hebrew translation mine. The Hebrew text reads, בכל צרתם לא צר. "In all their afflictions there is no affliction." The Vulgate reads: "In omni tribulatione eorum non est tribulatus." This follows the Hebrew. The marginal

marking changes לו to לא. This reads: In all their afflictions to him there is no affliction.

70. Margaritha, *Isaiah Commentary,* xii, translation mine. "Juden hie an diesem ort gar ain boesen possen reissen/ nemblich das sy an die stat/ lo mit der vof/ welches zu im haist/ lo mit de olef/ welches nicht hairst setzen/ so wierde dan das Text also lauten In all jrem laid ist zu im nicht laid."

71. The status and importance of the Masoretic markings in sixteenth-century Bible studies is worth a long note. Margaritha's early rabbinic training is revealed in his *Isaiah Commentary.* He understood that the Masoretic markings written in the margins of the Hebrew texts and known as *keri* and *kethiv* ("read" and "written") were corrections. He was able to enlighten his Christian readers. Perhaps naively, he did not see that importing Jewish traditional readings could undermine the Church's role as interpreter of scripture.

During much of Margaritha's adult life, *The Great Rabbis Bible* (often called the Bomberg Bible), edited by Jacob ben Chaim ibn Adonijah and Elias Levita, was being published in Venice (1525–48). It contained the marginal note to Isaiah 63:9, giving the "to him" reading. See Michael T. Walton and Phyllis J. Walton, "In Defense of the Church Militant: The Censorship of the Rashi Commentary in the *Magna Biblia Rabbinica,*" *Sixteenth Century Journal* 22 (Fall 1990): 385–400, esp. 386 and note. An earlier Bible, published by Bomberg (1517), was edited by Felix Pratensis, who was not versed in the Masoretic tradition. Elias Levita criticized Pratensis's work and warned readers not to pay attention "to the false remarks printed in the margin, in the form of keri and ketiv" in that edition; see Harry M. Orlinsky, ed., *The Library of Biblical Studies; Jacob ben Chajim ibn Adonijah's Introduction to the Rabbinic Bible* by Christian D. Ginsburg; and *The Massoreth Ha Massoreth of Elias Levita* by Christian D. Ginsburg, Prolegomenon by Norman H. Sneath (New York: KTAV, 1968), 2 vols. in 1, *Levita,* 115. Levita (1468–1549), a preeminent Hebraist, was educated In Germany. He and Margaritha shared a context, although his distinction in Hebrew cannot be imputed to his younger contemporary. Levita would certainly have disagreed with Margaritha's view that the rabbis deliberately altered the established text. Such a position flew in the face of Jewish learning. *Nizzachon Vetus* noted that both Rashi and Ibn Ezra read "to him" לו according to the marginal notes.

The initial editor of the Bomberg Bible, Jacob ben Chaim, chastised "the heretics who dared to accuse us of willfully altering and changing passages in our holy law." "Heretics" was a code word for Christians, which could also apply to Jewish converts, such as Margaritha. (Ginsberg in *Jacob ben Chajim,* 42.) Jacob ben Chaim explained, in his introduction to the Bomberg Bible, that there were several possible reasons for the addition of the Masoretic markings. R. David Kimchi and other Jewish Hebrew scholars and grammarians taught that *keri* and *kethiv* arose from the differences in manuscripts used by Ezra the Scribe in establishing the biblical text after the return from Babylon (ibid., 42–43). Ben Chaim repeated the explanation of Don Isaac Abravanel (1437–1508) that although Ezra used perfect writings, some of the words in the narrative appeared "irregular," so he corrected them in the margin (ibid., 44–46). Ben Chaim taught that both the *keri* and the *kethiv* transmitted the Law of Moses:

> From this then, it is evident that the whole of it is a law of Moses from Mount Sinai, and that Ezra the Scribe did not put *the Keri* in the margin to explain ungrammatical phrases; nothing appeared anomalous to Ezra, nor did he meet with any uncertainties and confusions, for the whole of it is the law of Moses from Mount Sinai. (Ibid., 50)

72. Anthonius Margaritha, *Psalterium Hebraicum* (Lipsiae: Melchior Lottheri, 1533). Margaritha's translation of Matthew went unnoticed until Maria Diemling identified the *Psalter* and its Matthew as his composition. This identification brings to eight the number of known Hebrew translations of Matthew, in print or manuscript, made before the end of the sixteenth century. Sebastian Münster's 1537 edition, printed four years after Margaritha's work, has been thought to be the earliest printing of any Hebrew Matthew. Münster stated that he had compiled his translation from several Jewish Hebrew manuscripts. Münster's Hebrew text shares its stilted characteristics with that of Margaritha. Neither Münster's nor Margaritha's Matthew is as idiomatic or literary a Hebrew as that in the two *Nizzachons* nor that of Shem Tov ibn Shaprut. The existence of the *Psalter* has been known for some time, see A. Marx, *Studies in Jewish History and Booklore* (New York: Jewish Theological Seminary, 1944), 332. The Matthew section seems to have eluded scholars before Maria Diemling. Melchior Lotther, the printer, had a son of the same name who was also a printer. Lotther the Elder worked in Leipzig; the son published works by Luther in Wittenberg, including his translation of the New Testament in 1522.

73. For a discussion of Hebrew translations of Matthew, see George Howard, "The Textual Nature of Shem-Tob's Hebrew Matthew," *Journal of Biblical Literature* 108 (Summer 1989): 239–57, and William L. Petersen, "The Vorlage of Shem-Tob's Hebrew Matthew," *New Testament Studies* 44 (1998): 491. This is discussed in Stephen Burnett, "Spokesmen for Judaism: Medieval Jewish Polemicists and Their Christian Readers in the Reformation Era," in *Reuchlin und sein Erben. Pforzheimer Reuchlinschriften,* vol. 11, ed. Peter Schaefer and I. Wandrey (Stuttgart: Jan Thorbecke, 2005), 41–51. Pinchas E. Lapide, *Hebrew in the Church: The Foundations of Jewish-Christian Dialogue,* translated from German by Erroll F. Rhodes; foreword by Helmut Gollwitzer (Grand Rapids, MI: Eerdmans, 1984), also discusses Hebrew Matthew translations, but not that of Margaritha.

74. Margaritha, *Psalterium Hebraicum,* colophon.

75. Ibid., Latin introduction. This reads, "ministri [et] praeceptoris adolenscentum, antonij Margaritae."

76. Mieses, *Die älteste . . . Uebersetzung* (Vienna, 1916).

77. Margaritha, *Der gantz Jüdisch glaub,* Ziii. See Appendix C for a discussion of its evolution and printing history.

78. Margaritha, *Psalterium Hebraicum,* pii. שלום לכל אהבי תורתך יהוה.

79. Ibid., Latin introduction, "Haec sunt verba amici vestri . . . Antonij Margaritae." Margaritha certainly had access to the Latin Bible through his colleagues. He may also have read a German translation, for German translations of the Vulgate had been printed eighteen times by 1522.

80. Ibid., pii in Hebrew and piiii in Latin.

81. Ibid., pv. זה ספר מתולדות המושח אשר בן דוד.

82. Ibid.

83. Margaritha's partial Matthew poses many questions regarding its place in the Hebrew Matthew tradition. The Standard English version translates the first verse of Matthew as, "The book of the generation of Jesus Christ, the son of David, the son of Abraham." Luther renders the verse as, "Dies ist das Buch von der Geburt Jesu Christi, der da ist ein Sohn Davids, des Sohnes Abrahams (This is the book of the history of Jesus Christ, the son of David, the son of Abraham)." The Vulgate begins, "liber generationis Iesu Christi filii David filii Abraham (The book of the generations of Jesus Christ, the son of David, the son of Abraham)." Margaritha translated, "This is the book from [*mem*] the generations of Joshua [Jesus] יהושע the Messiah who was the son of David his son of Abraham." In choosing "from," Margaritha followed the model of Genesis 16 and 17, where *mem* is used to indicate the source from which a person comes.

Margaritha's use of "Joshua" was consistent with his identification of the Hebrew name for the Messiah in *Der gantz Jüdisch glaub.* Margaritha's Hebrew name for Jesus differed from Münster's *Yeshua* (ישוע) and Du Tillet's and *Nizzachon Vetus*'s *Yeshu* (ישו). (Du Tillet betrays the Jewish origin of his translation by his use of *Yeshu,* the "meaningless" word, according to Margaritha, that Jews substituted for the real name.) Margaritha may or may not have known Shem Tov ibn Shaprut's *Even Bohan,* a Jewish Hebrew Matthew.

Margaritha followed Isaiah and Jewish tradition by using the word for "a young woman" (*almah* עלמה) rather than the word for "virgin" (*betulah* בתולה) when he translates verses 21 and 22 of the first chapter. (English rendering: "Now all this was done, that it might be fulfilled which was spoken of the Lord by the prophet, saying, Behold, *a virgin* shall be with child." The Vulgate is "hoc autem totum factum est ut adimpleretur id quod dictum est a Domino per prophetam dicentem ecce *virgo* in utero habebit.") Margaritha's translation is consistent with the manuscript tradition used by Shem Tov and differed from Christian theology based on the Greek Isaiah and Matthew. In the year following the Matthew publication, Margaritha changed his position. In his *Isaiah Commentary* (p. 43), he used the German word for virgin, *jungfrau,* in the context of the Isaiah prophecy.

What exposure Margaritha had to the Hebrew Matthew manuscript tradition is difficult to say. His citation of *Nizzachon Mülhausen* indicates that he had probably seen it and presumably the passages of Matthew therein. He apparently did not carry a copy of the manuscript with him into Christianity. Had he done so, his Hebrew renderings of Matthew might have been more literary. Those works he did have, such as the rabbinic commentaries, he cited correctly and extensively. There is a passage in the Matthew that bears some resemblance to the Shem Tov tradition. At the end of chapter 1, Shem Tov criticized the manuscript from which he took his Matthew, writing that it read, "A young woman is conceiving (הוה) and will bear (תלד) a son." Shem Tov noted that the Matthew used by Christians states, "She is conceiving and *is* bearing a son (יולדת) (George Howard, "Shem-Tob's Hebrew Matthew," *Journal of Biblical Literature* 108 [Summer 1989]: 239–57 at 240 n. 6). Margaritha translated the word as "bearing," and not as "will bear." He spelled "bearing" defectively ילדת, without the *waw* Shem Tov used. He may have achieved his translation without reference to Shem Tov, by following the German, which reads "wird schwanger sein und einen Sohn gebären." (*Gebären* is a participial form analogous to that suggested by Shem Tov and used by Margaritha.)

Students of early modern Hebrew and of the Hebrew translations of Matthew can profit from the study of Margaritha's fragment and his Hebrew introduction. The indications are that Margaritha did not use other Hebrew translations and made his own translation from the Christian New Testaments available to him. He seems to have known something of the rabbinic polemic tradition and its Matthew fragments. The Hebrew renderings of Shem Tov, Münster, Du Tillets, and now Margaritha differ from one another. (George Howard has examined the translations of Shem Tov, Münster, and Du Tillet and made that judgment. Ibid., 239. Margaritha's Matthew was unknown to him.) Margaritha, like the others, was able to produce an original, albeit incomplete, Matthew.

84. Ibid., piii. שהיא שנית התורה.

85. Margaritha, *Der gantz Jüdisch glaub*, Riii.

86. For a detailed discussion, see Michael T. Walton, "Anthonius Margaritha—Honest Reporter?" *Sixteenth Century Journal* 36 (Spring 2005): 129–41. Zunz in *Die Ritus*, p. 148, noted the *Aleinu* and Margaritha's description of printings leaving out ten words. Amnon Raz-Krakotzkin, *The Censor, the Editor, and the Text: The Catholic Church and the Shaping of the Jewish Canon in the Sixteenth Century*, trans. Jackie Feldman (Philadelphia: University of Pennsylvania Press, 2007), 163–69, notes that Italian Jewish editors began to censor phrases from prayer books before legally required to do so.

87. See Ya'akov Elbaum, "Concerning Two Textual Emendations in the *Aleinu* Prayer" (Hebrew), *Tarbiz* 42 (1972–73): 204–8. Elbaum discusses and rejects the idea that forgers introduced some emendations in the *Aleinu;* he also reports on Urbach's work on the *Siddur Hasidei Ashkenaz.* See also Naphtali Wieder, "Investigation into the Anti-Christian and Anti-Islamic Gematria (in the Prayer Aleynu L'Shabeach)" (Hebrew), *Sinai* 76 (1998): 1–14. Wieder discusses the Hasidei Ashkenaz and the censorship of prayer books. This article

can also be found in a collection on Jewish liturgy, *Hitgavshut Nusach Hatefilah be Mizrach u va'Ma'ariv* (Jerusalem, 1997), 453–67. Yaacov Deutsch, "Jewish Anti-Christian Invectives and Christian Awareness: An Unstudied Form of Interaction in the Early Modern Period," *Leo Baeck Institute Year Book* 55 (2010): 55–56, adds to the understanding of *gematria* and the *Aleinu*, showing its early use by Mühlhausen and others.

88. Margaritha, *Der gantz Jüdisch glaub* (1544), Vii. The section on Rabbi Judah does not appear in the 1530 edition.

89. Margaritha, *Der gantz Jüdisch glaub* (1530), Viiii v.

90. Ibid., Viiii r.

91. Ibid., Viiii v.

92. Ibid.

93. Ibid., Viiii r.

94. Wieder, "Investigation into the Anti-Christian and Anti-Islamic Gematria," 453–54. See note 47 above.

95. Margaritha, *Der gantz Jüdisch glaub*, Qiiii v and Viiii r.

96. Ibid., Viiii r.

97. Among all of Margaritha's charges against the Jews, it is interesting that he does not note anti-Christian attitudes and acts on *Purim*. He did mention that Moses Wolfe said that the Jews of Regensburg called the Christian leader Haman, but the context does not suggest Purim. His omissions, if such they are, are interesting in light of the anti-Christian practices Elliot Horowitz describes in "The Rite to Be Reckless: On the Perception and Interpretation of Purim Violence," *Poetics Today* 15 (1994): 9–54. Horowitz expanded this article into a book, *Reckless Rites: Purim and the Legacy of Jewish Violence* (Princeton, NJ: Princeton University Press, 2006).

98. Luther used Margaritha's testimony concerning the *gematria* of Jesus's name in the *Aleinu* in his *On the Jews and Their Lies* (1543). He wrote,

> Then "Jesus" is savior or helper in Hebrew. . . . To vex, the Jews use "Jesu" which is no word or name in Hebrew, rather its letters, which according to the *sifra* or sum of the letters . . . is 316. Such a sum yields another word "*Hebel Vork.*" You can read more about this in Anthonius Margaritha. (Martin Luther, *Von den Juden und Irhren Lügen* in *Werke*, Kritische Gesamtausgave v. 53 [Weimar: Nachfolger, 1920], 513ff. Translation mine.)

Margaritha gave ammunition to Luther's prescription of "fiery mercy" to humble the Jews.

Johann Christoph Wagenseil (1633–1705) also used *Der gantz Jüdisch glaub* to demonstrate Jewish anti-Christian attitudes:

> Antonius Margarita brought this mystery forth in the German book on the Jewish faith among other things, but [the use of the *Aleinu* prayer

to criticize Jesus was presented] in his true, negligent awkwardness. (*Tela ignea Satanae,* 216. Translation mine of "Mysterium istud Antonius Margarita in libello Germanico de Fide Judaica, juxta cum alio, sed in quo meram oscitantiam suam ineptiasque prodidit.")

99. This agrees with the judgment of Yaacov Deutsch in "*Von der Juden Ceremoniem:* Representations of Jews in Sixteenth-Century Germany," in *Jews, Judaism, and the Reformation in Sixteenth-Century Germany,* ed. Dean Phillip Bell and Stephen G. Burnett (Leiden: Brill, 2006), 335–56. This agrees with the judgment of Yaacov Deutsch in "*Von der Juden Ceremoniem:* Representations of Jews in Sixteenth-Century Germany," in *Jews, Judaism, and the Reformation in Sixteenth-Century Germany,* ed. Dean Phillip Bell and Stephen G. Burnett (Leiden: Brill, 2006), 335–56.

Chapter 4

1. Maria Diemling's research has added a great deal of data on Margaritha's activities. Like all previous scholars, she has been unable to detail his early Christian years. See her valuable doctoral thesis, "Christliche Ethnographien" über Juden und Judentum in der Frühen Neuzeit: Die Konvertiten Victor von Carben und Anthonius Margaritha und ihre Darstellung jüdischen Lebens und jüdischer Religion" (PhD diss., Universität Wien, 1999). This thesis may soon be published in English. I thank Dr. Diemling for kindly providing me with a copy of her valuable work.

2. D. Hermann Jordan, *Reformation und gelehrte Bildung in der Markgraphschaft Ansbach-Bayreuth, Quellen und Forschungen zur bayerischen Kirchengeschichte,* no. 1 (Leipzig: Werner Scholl, 1917) provides the essential data on Margaritha. There are a few errors, where he relies on others, such as identifying Margaritha as the son of Jacob not Samuel, but it is reliable in those details he himself seems to have researched.

3. Jordon, *Reformation und gelehrte,* 134–36, discusses Margaritha, Ziegler, and Ziegler's carrier.

4. Robert Rosen, "Valentin Trotzendorf," in *The Oxford Encyclopedia of the Reformation,* ed. Hans J. Hillerbrand (New York: Oxford University Press, 1996), 1: 179.

5. Jordan, *Reformation und gelehrte,* 128–29.

6. Diemling, "Christliche Ethnographien," 20, suggests that Margaritha married about 1524. She does not appear to have taken into account Rabbi Joseph of Rosheim's statements.

7. Anthonius Margaritha, *Wie aus dem heylligen 53 Capittel des fünemigsten prophetan Esaie grüntlich ausgefürt/probliert/das der verhaischen Moschiach (welcher Christus is) schon khomen . . .* (Wien, 1535) (hereafter *Isaiah Commentary*), Zii r.

8. Heinrich Graetz, *Geschichte der Juden* (Leipzig, 1877), 9: 290.

9. Georg Buchwald, *Kleine Notizen aus Rechnungbüchern des Thüringischen Staatsarchivs. II. In: Archiv für Reformationsgeschichte* 31 (1934): 201, cited in Diemling, "Christliche Ethnographien," 21. The passage reads "1534. Leipzig. Ostermarkt.—ij gulden aus gnaden Anthonius Margarita weibe, der ein ebreischer lector und itzt zu wien sein soll, welchem hievor zu Augsburg als der Churfürst zu Sachsen hochloblicher gedechtnus des ortes gewest, ein kint aus der tauff gehoben worden, und solch sein weib itzt mit cleinenkindern zu leipzigk in armut gelassen."

10. Ibid.

11. Margaritha, *Isaiah Commentary,* Z v. Translation mine.

12. Margaritha's report of Jews living in Leipzig and Tübingen is particularly interesting because they had ostensibly been expelled from those cities. This suggests that the reality of Jewish presence and life in sixteenth-century Germany differed from civic pronouncements.

13. Ibid., xix r., "Mit solcher außlegūg khan noch magen Jud nicht hinumb / dan ich hab selbst zu Tübingen / die weil ich auch daselbst lesete mit jnē auf dise weiß v[er]sucht." Margaritha also mentioned meeting and discussing religious issues with Rabbi Joseph von Presse in Worms. Ibid., xxviii r.

14. Ibid., iii–iiii.

15. Margaritha, *Der gantz Jüdisch glaub* (1530), *b*iii v. "Auch waiss ich das gantz wol/ als bald die Juden ynnalt dises büchleins ynnen werden/ werden sy ein versamlung haben dennck aber wol/ sy werde zu Wormbs sein/ dann daselbs ist yetz zumal ir oberster Rabi/ Rabi Samuel genandt."

16. Continuing contact between converts and Jews is indicated by questions posed to rabbis about whether Jews could hire converts to work on the Sabbath, give converts unkosher meat, charge them interest, and such. Elisheva Carlebach discusses this in *Divided Souls: Converts from Judaism in Germany, 1500–1750* (New Haven, CT: Yale University Press, 2001), 26. She sees contact as tied to a desire to have converts return. In many ways, converts and Jews could not avoid meeting in towns and cities. The Italian convert Immanuel Tremellius wrote about seeing his brother again after twenty-four years; see Kenneth Austin, *From Judaism to Calvinism: The Life and Writings of Immanuel Tremellius (c. 1510–1580)* (Aldershot, England: Ashgate, 2007), 11. Kenneth Stow, *Jewish Life in Early Modern Rome: Challenge, Conversion, and Private Life* (Aldershot, England: Ashgate, 2007), 260–81, describes the strictures on recent converts, *neofiti,* to Catholicism in Italy, who were ordered to break contact with family and friends. The papacy, however, supported the claims of the converts to inherit from their Jewish kin.

17. Margaritha, *Der gantz Jüdisch glaub* (1530), Rii v.

18. Margaritha, *Der gantz Jüdisch glaub* (1544), xiii v. This does not appear in the 1530 edition.

19. Archiv der Universität Wien: Superintendenbuch, 114vf, cited in Diemling, "Christliche Ethnographien,"21.

20. Margaritha, *Isaiah Commentary,* v, "so es sein goetlicher wil waere/ das ich armer grosser sunder/ hie auf erden leben moechte/ biß meine unerzogne

khindl/ zum vorstand khaemen/ und etwas studieren und lernen/ dardurch sie Gott und den menschen nutz sein moechten. Amen."

21. Diemling suggests that Margaritha died of plague, "Christliche Ethnographien," 23. She reproduces the inventory of his apartment made by the university at his death, Nachlasverzeichness, ibid., 247–49.

22. Joseph Davis, "The 'Ten Questions' of Eliezer Eilburg and the Problem of Jewish Unbelief in the 16th Century," *Jewish Quarterly Review* 91 (January–April 2001): at 331.

23. H. H. Ben-Sasson, "The Reformation in Contemporary Jewish Eyes," *Israel Academy of Sciences and Humanities, Proceedings* 4 (1970): 239–26; Jerome Friedman, "The Reformation in Alien Eyes: Jewish Perceptions of Christian Troubles," *Sixteenth Century Journal* 14 (Spring 1983): 23–40. Jewish-Christian interaction in the Reformation is outlined in Debra Kaplan and Magda Teter, "Out of the (Historiographic) Ghetto: European Jews and Reformation Narratives," *Sixteenth Century Journal* 40 (Summer 2009): 365–94.

24. Molcho's story is recounted in many studies. The primary documents and the basic details are given in Harris Lenowitz, *The Jewish Messiahs: From the Galilee to Crown Heights* (New York: Oxford University Press, 1998), 103–23.

25. For the life of Josel, see Selma Stern, *Josel of Rosheim,* trans. Gertrude Hirschler (Philadelphia: Jewish Publication Society, 1965); Hava (Chava) Fraenkel-Goldschmidt, *Joseph of Rosheim, Historical Writings* (Hebrew) (Jerusalem: Magnes Press, Hebrew University, 1975); *The Historical Writings of Joseph of Rosheim, Leader of Jewry in Early Modern Germany,* edited with an introduction, commentary, and translations by Chava Fraenkel-Goldshmidt, translated by Naomi Schendowich (Leiden: Brill, 2006).

26. Fraenkel-Goldshmidt, *Joseph of Rosheim,* 169 and 345.

27. The arguments are listed in Stern, *Josel of Rosheim,* 101–2.

28. Joseph of Rosheim, *Trostschrift* 23, "Contra Margaretham baptizatum Judeum," in Fraenkel-Goldschmidt, *Joseph of Rosheim,* 345, translation mine.

> Doch durch die gnaden Gottes, hab ich zu Augspurgk vor unserm allergn. Herren Rom. Keyser und Konig, auch allen Stenden des Reichs im dreißigsten Jar, dem tauften Juden Margaretha genant, drey Artickel uns armen benachlaßart, die ich jme kingelegt. was das der Artickel einer uß den drei, sie bitten um den friden der Königen etc. uns zu leidt werden von ettl. unverstendigen oder von den abtrünnigen lügen ufgeredet. Als ob wir verfluchen solten die frembdling dorunder wir gefangen weren. darumben er die Stadt Augspurg verschweren muest, Wie das E Ers, Rath zu Augsprug wißen tregt, dartzu der hochgelert Doctor Mathias Helldt, Ro. Keys. Mt jetziger Cantzler, und Doctor Brandtner solche disputation uffgeeben mußten.

29. See Buchwald, *Kleine Notizen,* 201 for the official appointment of Margaritha for the summer semester, 1531.

30. Margaritha, *Der gantz Jüdisch glaub* (Leipzig: Lottheri, 1531), Ki v., translation mine. This is noted in Diemling, "Christliche Ethnographien," 244. The German reads:

> Auch hat jetzt ynn gar kurtzten tagen/ ein geborner Christ/ auch nicht vngelert mit synen höchsten eyde bezeuget/ bey beywesens des Achtbarn wirdige Herrn Magister Johannes Stramburck/ Rector der Löblichen Vniuersitet zu Leyptzigk/ wie es sich durch etliche mittel/ zwüschen yhm vnd den Jüden/ zugetragen habe/ das sie sich vndersntaden haben/ yhn zuberreden das ehr sich beschneiden ließ/ vnd zu eynem Juden würde.

Lotther evinced an interest in Hebrew works as early as 1516 when he printed Barptholomeus Caesar, *Elementale hebraicum.*

31. Margaritha, *Isaiah Commentary,* cxvi v.–cxvii, translation mine. The text reads, as punctuated and transcribed by Maria Diemling, "Christliche Ethnographien," 18:

> Also und auff dise weiß haben sie zu Augspurg auch ain listigen buoben und lauren wider mich auffgericht, wellicher zu oder umb Pfreim neulich begriffen und erfunden worden ist, das er falsche müntz gemacht hat, und ist entlossen und entrunnen, summa da ich zuverhor wider und gegen jm vor Kayserlicher Mayestat Marschalch mit namen Caspar Khünigl unnd vor seiner genaden beysitzer khumen bin, hat mich bemelter Marschalch on alle mittel gantz ledig erkhant, und mein widerparthey auff das höchst gehandelt und gantz ubel zugeredt und gesprochen, Du und alle Juden sollen von wegen dieser hanndlung höchlich gestrafft werden etc. Derhalben so bitt ich ain yede Christliche obrigkhait, das man den dückhischen yetzuermainten Juden nicht so gar gerincklich und on allen grund wider mich hinderruckh, und one meine verantwortung glauben solle, wenn ich aber verhört worden bin, und zuuerantworttung khumen, haben sie dann ain recht sach wider mich, und ich ain unrechte, nicht unbillich das man dann handt an mich lege. [. . .] summa sie haben mich durch obbemelten listigen buoben hinderruckh dargeben, ich wolte wider zu jrem glauben fallen, ich were auffuerisch, ich hette Kayserlich Mayestat Rät vbel nachgeredt und auch gefluocht.

32. Joseph of Rosheim, *Sefer ha-Miknah* (Hebrew), ed. Chava Fraenkel-Goldschmidt (Jerusalem, 1970).

33. Dan Diner, *Synchrone Welten: Zeitenräume jüdischer Geschichte, Toldot,* vol. 1 (Göttingen: Vandenhoeck und Ruprecht, 2005), 74. See also H. Bresslau, "Aus Strassburger Judenakten," *Zeitschrift für die Geschichte der Juden in Deutschland* 5 (1892): 307–34, at 310.

34. The history of Leipzig and its shift to reform religion in 1539 is told in the classic works, H. G. Hasse, *Abriss der meissnisch-albertinisch-sächsischen Kirchengeschichte* (Leipzig: Engelmann, 1847), and Friedrich Seifert, *Die Reformation in Leipzig* (Leipzig: Hinrichs, 1883).

35. Diemling, "Christliche Ethnographien," citing *Acta rectorum universitatis studii Lipsiensis inde ab anno MDXXIIII usque ad annum MDLVIIII* (Leipzig, 1859), 41.

36. See Geiger, *Das Studium der Hebraischen Sprache in Deuschland,* 41–55, and Isaac, *Wahre . . . Historia.*

37. For example, Oxford, Rostock, and Hebrew Union College.

38. Maria Diemling's research on Margaritha, especially on his life in Vienna, is fundamental to sketching his life. She traces him through civic and university records. Of major importance is her presentation of the accounting of his apartment and possessions at his death. She also positions him within the struggling university and life in sixteenth-century Vienna. See Diemling, "Christliche Ethnographien," 20–24 and 247–48. All citations to Haus-, Hof-, und Staatsarchiv Wien: Österreichische Akten, are from her work.

39. R. Kink, *Geschichte der Kaiserlichen Universität zu Wien* (Vienna, 1854), 1: 254ff. The university went from 661 students in 1519 to fewer than 30 after 1529. See also http://www.univie.ac.at/archiv/tour/8.htm.

40. Haus-, Hof-und Staatsarchiv Wien: Österreichische Akten. NÖ, fasc. 3, fol. 27 r. This and other sources for the university are cited and the salient quotations are given in Diemling, "Christliche Ethnographien."

41. Superintendentenbuch, 136 v., Kink, *Geschichte,* 1: 270. A. Goldmen, *Die Wiener Universität, 1519–1740* (Vienna, 1977), 22. See also Diemling, "Christliche Ethnographien," 21.

42. Maria Diemling has shown that Faber loaned a book on Jewish ceremonies and foolishness to Margaritha. "Christliche Ethnographien," 41 n. 240, citing Haus-, Hof-, und Staatsarchiv Wien; Österreichische Akten, NÖ, fasc. 3, fol. 27.

43. Ludwig Geiger, ed., *Johann Reuchlin's Briefwechsel* (Bibliothek des Litteraischen Vereins Stuttgart, 126) (Tübingen, 1875), 296.

44. Superintendentenbuch, 107 r., 137 r., 153 r.–v., 161 r., and 178 r.; Diemling, "Christliche Ethnographien," 20.

45. Österreichische Akten, NÖ, fasc. 3, fol. 47; Diemling, "Christliche Ethnographien," 21.

46. Diemling, "Christliche Ethnographien," 21. "Ungarn. Böhemen und Walhen."

47. Superintendentenbuch, 117 r.–v.

48. Superintendentenbuch, 117 r.–v., 118 r., 170 v., and 175 v.; Diemling, "Christliche Ethnographien," 22.

49. Margaritha, *Isaiah Commentary,* lxii v., "Juden uber reden/ dann sie wissen minder grammatick dañ ayn schueller/ . . . bey den Christen seyen/ Wellicher nur ayn jar bey mir oder ain andern Hebraisch studiert hat. . . . Ich

wolt wetten ob man im gantzen Teutschē lannd zehen Juden fende/ die nur disen ainigen punctē/ dises Commentators recht unnd grüntlich grammaticaliter verstienden."

50. Ibid., lxxix–lxxx. The dialectical, scripturally centered teaching of Hebrew is represented in Sebastian Münster's *Institutiones Grammaticae* (Basel: Froben, 1524). Münster relied heavily on David Kimchi, whom he called "of blessed memory (*memoria benedicto*)," a Jewish term of honor for the dead. Münster related words and their grammatical forms to scriptural passages and rabbinic commentators, such as Rashi.

51. Margaritha, *Isaiah Commentary,* xiii v. discusses the Hitpael verb form.

52. Johann Christian Wolf, *Bibliotheca Hebraea* (Hamburg, 1717), 1: 202–4; see Diemling, "Christliche Ethnographien," 26.

53. Margaritha, *Der gantz Jüdisch glaub* (1530), *b*iii and Superintentenbuch, 161 v. ff.; Diemling, "Christliche Ethnographien," 26–27.

54. Anthonius Margaritha, *Ain Kurtzer Bericht und Anzaigung wo die Christlich ceremonien vom Balmesel in boyden Testementen gegründt sei* (Vienna, 1541), Aii r.–v. The German reads, "Gelobet sey Got der heyllig geyst/ der mich von solchem/ und anderin irthumb erloesat hat/ Laut aber die lugen also/ Wann der Moschiach kombt/ werde er auff ainē Esel reyten/ uñ wer de alle Juden auf den Esel setzē. Aber alle Christen werden auf des Esels schwantz sitzen."

55. Margaritha, *Kurtze ausslegunу uber das Wort Halleliua,* final page. The German reads, "Ein yede seel wirtlobē jah/ halleluiah/ daz ist das alle selē Christum loben. Lobet Christū."

56. Goldman, *Wiener Universität,* 3f; see *Nachlassverzeichms,* 24.

57. Ibid.; see Diemling, "Christliche Ethnographien," 247–49.

58. Margaritha, *Der gantz Jüdisch glaub,* L.

59. *Midrash Rabbah,* "Ruth," VI: 4, trans. R. Dr. L. Rabinowitz (London: Soncino Press, 1983), 79.

Appendix A

1. Solomon ibn Verga's account, *Shevat Yehuda,* translated by Hyam Maccoby in *Judaism on Trial* (London: Littman Library of Jewish Civilization, 1982); Daniel J. Lasker, *Jewish Philosophical Polemics against Christianity in the Middle Ages* (London: Littman Library of Jewish Civilization, 2007); Jeremy Cohen, *The Friars and the Jews* (Ithaca, NY: Cornell University Press, 1989); Amos Funkenstein, "Changes in the Pattern of Anti-Jewish Polemics in the Twelfth Century," *Viator* 13 (1982): 203–23.

2. Funkenstein, "Changes in the Pattern of Anti-Jewish Polemics in the Twelfth Century," 170.

3. Ibid., 205. Translation of Latin protocols in Antonio Pacios López, *La Disputa de Tortosa* (Madrid, Barcelona: CSIC, 1957).

4. Maccoby, *Judaism on Trial,* 119, translation of Nachmanides's *Vikuah.*

5. Joseph Albo, ספר עקרים [*Sefer Ikkarim*]: *Buch Ikkarim, Grund= und Glaubenslehren der Mosaischen Religion von Rab. Joseph Albo,* translated into German by Ward Schlessinger and Ludwig Schlesinger (Frankfurt: n.p., 1844). Chapter 42, translation mine. Joseph Albo, *Sefer ha-ikkarim; Book of Principles,* ed. and trans. Isaac Husik, Hebrew and English on facing pages in 5 volumes (Philadelphia: Jewish Publication Society, 1946).

6. All quotations that follow are taken from my translation of the Refutation in this appendix.

7. In *Der gantz Jüdisch glaub* (1544), *d*ii v. and r., Margaritha refers to a book in Hebrew "in a place not far away which is thought believable by the Jews. Therein is described the entire life, death, and martyrdom of Christ with some stories of the Apostles. A good friend promised to bring it to me if I am willing to translate it." This is not a reference to the *Toldoth Jesu,* but to some kind of counter-*Toldoth.* The German reads: "Es ist an einem ort nicht weet ein Hebreisch buechlein/ wird von den Juden glaubwirdig gehalton/ darinn das gantz leben/ tod und marter Christi beschribē wird/ sampt etlichen geschichten der Aposteln/ hat mir ein gut freund verheissen dasselbige zu wegen zubringen/ bin ich willens zuverteuschen.

8. This literally means the dedication of churches. Although he may mean the rare event of a building's dedication, Margaritha uses the term in the ethnography to refer to Channukah. It seems more likely that he is referring to a yearly event, such as New Year's and the other Christian holidays mentioned rather than the building of churches.

9. *Af* in Hebrew means "also" or "even so." Margaritha implies a double meaning because *affe* means "ape" in German.

Appendix B

1. For a discussion of the composition of the *Zohar* see Yehuda Liebes, *Studies in the Zohar,* trans. Arnold Schwartz, Stephanie Nakache, and Penina Peli (Albany: State University of New York Press, 1993), 85–138. Moshe Idel discusses name kabbalah and Eleazar of Worms as a practitioner in *Mystical Experience in Abraham Abulafia* (Albany: State University of New Press, 1988), 14–23.

2. The ten utterances (*maamarim*) are also mentioned in the Talmudic tractates *Rosh Hashanah* 32a and *Megillah* 21b.

3. The indispensible work on Pico's kabbalah is Chaim Wirszubski, *Pico della Mirandola's Encounter with Jewish Mysticism* (Cambridge, MA: Harvard University Press, 1989).

4. Ibid., 29.

5. Menachem ben Benjamin Recanati, *Menachem Recanati Commentary on the Daily Prayers: Flavius Mithridates' Latin Translation, the Hebrew Text, and an English Version,* ed. Giacomo Corazzol (Turin: Nina Aragno Editore, 2008), II: 428–29.

6. Wirszubski, *Pico della Mirandola's Encounter with Jewish Mysticism*, 34.

7. Ibid., 38.

8. Ibid., 73. Pico's use of Flavius's translations was not limited to those from the works of Recanati and Gikatilla. Those authors, however, loomed large in his "Cabalistic Theses." They were also crucial to Johannes Reuchlin's later work, *De Arte Cabalistica* (1517). One important source for Pico was the Jewish scholar Johannes (Yohanan) Alemanno. Pico studied personally with Alemanno, as he did with Flavius. Alemanno was deeply committed to kabbalistic magic, as will be discussed below.

9. Johannes Reuchlin, *De Verbo Mirifico* (1494), II: 57 in the facsimile published Stuttgart-Bad Connstatt: Frommann, 1984. The original text is unpaginated.

10. Ibid., 60.

11. Ibid.

12. Ibid., 79.

13. Ibid., 90–91.

14. Ibid., 94.

15. Ibid., 96.

16. Victor von Carben, *Juden Buechlein* (1550), I: 11. The passage reads, "von Christo sagt/ wie und durch . . . er seine wunder werck gethan hab/ der Talmut sagt/ wie in dem Tempel zu Jerusalem sey in einem gewelb beschlossen gewesst ein kostlicher stein/ darinne der groeste namen Gottes Thetragrammathon (welicher Hebraisch Schemhamforras genant werde)."

17. Anthonius Margaritha, *Der gantz Jüdisch glaub* (1530), Xii. The passage reads, "Nun bekennen sy auch von Christo das er alle seine wunderwerk . . . aber nit durch die krafft das ein gothait in ym were gewesen/ sender er habe den שם המורש [*sic*] Schem hamuqrasch [*sic*]." On folio Y verso, Margaritha transliterates the Hebrew as *schem hamphorasch*. The 1544 edition corrects the typographical errors.

18. Anthonius Margaritha, *Isaiah Commentary*, xxv r. The passage reads, "nemilich mit den vier buechstaben Adonai/ oder Jehoua/ welche Kriechisch tetragrāmaton genēt werde/ Das sind die vier buechstabē/ welche vier buechstabē khainer creatur noch geschepff im himel noch auff erden mügen zugelegt werden."

19. One of the most important practitioners of kabbalistic meditation and magic was Abraham Abulafia (fl. thirteenth century) whose works were known to Pico and Reuchlin. His brand of ecstatic kabbalah was of a different nature than Margaritha's, and a discussion of his doctrines is not very relevant to the present study, but see Moshe Idel, *Studies in Ecstatic Kabbalah* (Albany: State University of New York Press, 1988) for information on Abulafia and other practitioners. Abulafia's ecstatic practices can be distinguished from the techniques of Recanti and Gikatilla.

20. MS Oxford 2234, fol. 8b. Moshe Idel, trans., *Kabbalah: New Perspectives* (New Haven, CT: Yale University Press, 1988), 204.

21. Idel, *Kabbalah: New Perspectives*, 204.

22. Ibid. Idel's chapter, "Kabbalistic Hermeneutics," and his *Studies in Ecstatic Kabbalah* provide an appreciation of Moses's role as the model kabbalist.

23. Idel, *Kabbalah: New Perspectives,* 160, citing *Dikduk Tefillah* (Tiengen, 1560), fol. 202 v.

24. Ibid., fol. 202 r.

25. He does not give a second name.

26. The Hebrew and its transliteration are found in the 1544 printing but not in that of 1530. From this kabbalah and Margaritha's discussion of the *Aleinu* in chapter 3, it is clear that the name of the Messiah and the Tetragrammaton were associated in that each had four letters. This was a Jewish doctrine that Reuchlin popularized among Christians. In his *De arte cabalistica* (Hagenau, 1517), Reuchlin detailed his belief that Pythagoras learned his philosophy from studying the kabbalah. Pythagoras took the "Tetragrammaton or the four letters from the Savior's name and changed it to the tetractys" (Book II, xxx).

Appendix C

1. "Argument oder innhalt dises Büchleins. . . . wie sie Key. Mayestet/ mit außgedruckten worten nennen/ unnd/ gleich darauff sein Key. Maiestet/ mit sampt seinnen gantzen Kayserthumb auff das hoechste verfluechen/ und verdammē. *Der gantz Jüdisch glaub* (Frankfurt: 1544), A v.–Aii r. This is an obvious attack on Josel's arguments against Margaritha. I have noted several such throughout this book. There are many more subtle refutations of Josel, and I have tried to draw attention to them but undoubtedly have overlooked others.

2. Ibid., folio Liii v. See Appendix B for the entire text.

3. See Johannes Pfefferkorn, *Libellus de Iudaica confessione, sive sabbato afflictionis* (Cologne: Landen, 1508), and Johannes Pfefferkorn, *Ich heyß ein buchlijn der iudenbeicht, In allen orten vint man mich beicht . . .* (Cologne: Landen, 1508; Augsburg: Froschauer, 1508).

4. Maria Diemling, "Christliche Etnographien über Juden und Judentum in der Frühen Neuzeit: Die Konvertiten Victor von Carben und Antonius Margaritha und ihre Darstellung jüdischen Lebens und jüdischer Religion" (PhD diss., Universität Wien, 1999), 238. R. Po-chia Hsia, "Jews as Magicians in Reformation Germany," in *Anti-Semitism in Times of Crisis,* ed. Sander L. Gilman and Steven T. Katz (New York: New York University Press, 1993), 136.

5. I discovered as I researched this topic that cataloging errors created the appearance of two printings that do not exist. Harvard (Andover-Harvard Theological Library) lists a 1531 Vienna printing by Johannes Singrenius. The cataloger failed to recognize that a known 1531 Augsburg second edition was bound with the 1534 *Isaiah Commentary* printed by Singrenius. The University of Chicago catalog lists a 1551 Frankfurt printing, which is in fact a 1561 Frankfurt printing.

6. Paul F. Grendler, "Venice, Science, and the Index of Prohibited Books," in *The Nature of Scientific Discovery,* ed. Owen Gingerich (Washington, DC:

Smithsonian Institution Press, 1975), 336. Grendler states that the average press run in sixteenth-century Venice was 1,000 copies, and highly in demand titles could reach runs of 2,000 or 3,000. Owen Gingerich, in *The Book Nobody Read* (New York: Walker, 2004), 121–29, discusses how many copies of Copernicus's *De Revolutionibus* were printed. He evaluates printing practices and the extant records of Plantin of Antwerp (not Copernicus's printer). He notes that Plantin made printing runs of a few hundred to 2,500 copies, with a favorite run of 1,250. He concludes that due to its size, complexity, and limited audience, about 500 copies of Copernicus's masterwork were issued. Gingerich relied on Plantin data in Leon Voet, *The Golden Compasses: A History and Evaluation of the Printing and Publishing Activities of the Officina Plantiniana at Antwerp* (Amsterdam: Van Gendt, 1969). Given such data, 500 seems a conservative estimate of the printings of *Der gantz Jüdisch glaub.*

7. Elisheva Carlebach, "Attribution of Secrecy and Perceptions of Jewry," *Jewish Social Studies* 2, no. 3 (1996): 115–36 at 120–21.

8. The 1540 Köln (Cologne) edition is so rare that I have found reference to only one extant copy, which is in the Austrian National Library. I have examined a microfilm of that copy.

9. The Frankfurt Jewish community managed to survive the sixteenth century and numbered about forty-three families in 1543. At the time of the publication, Frankfurt was a member of the Lutheran Schmalkaldic League.

10. Holy arks in Jewish art are discussed in Thérèse Metzger and Mendel Metzger, *Jewish Life in the Middle Ages: Illuminated Hebrew Manuscripts* (New York: Alpine Fine Arts Collection, 1982), 65–69.

11. Ibid., 69, illustration 96.

12. Ibid., 65.

13. Scholars continued to be interested in *Der gantz Jüdisch glaub* throughout the seventeenth and into the eighteenth century, and it was reprinted in 1651, 1689, 1705, and 1713: *Der gantze Jüdische Glaube* (Frankfurt am Main, 1651 and 1689) and *Der gantz jüdische Glaube* (Leipzig, 1705 and 1713).

Appendix D

1. It is difficult to determine what constituted liturgy before and immediately after the destruction of the second temple. The Talmud records blessings and practices that will be discussed in detail in the text. The sect at Qumran had a place of worship, the "house of prostration," and various blessings and prayers for daily and festival use, but no prayer book as such has been found. Lawrence H. Schiffman, *Reclaiming the Dead Sea Scrolls* (Philadelphia: Jewish Publication Society, 1994), 289–312. The Christian scripture notes that it was Jesus's custom to go to synagogue and gives an instance of his reading what would now be the Haftorah, or lesson from the prophets. Luke 4:16–17. Sketchy as the data are, a basic form of prayer and study is discernable.

2. The most complete discussion of the Jewish liturgy was written in Germany in 1913 and was updated and translated into English in 1993. Ismar Elbogen, *Jewish Liturgy: a Comprehensive History,* trans. Raymond P. Scheindlin (Philadelphia: Jewish Publication Society, 1993). Elbogen treats blessing and prayer in his introduction, 6–7. Elbogen's study presents the liturgy as fragments and is not suited for those who want to understand the Jewish prayer book as a literary whole. The brief discussion here will become more intelligible if one studies Jeremy Schonfield, *Undercurrents of Jewish Prayer* (Oxford: Littman Library of Jewish Civilization, 2006).

3. B. T. *Berakoth* 60a, translation Maurice Simon (London: Soncino Press, 1984).

4. B. T. *Menachoth,* 43b, translation mine.

5. Ibid.

6. B. T. *Berakoth* 4b, translation mine.

7. Ibid., 6a.

8. Ibid., 28b.

9. Ibid., translation Maurice Simon.

10. B. T. *Berakoth* 60b, translation mine.

11. Such boxes were found at Qumron with almost identical passages. See Schiffman, *Reclaiming the Dead Sea Scrolls,* 305–11.

12. B. T. *Berakot* 60b, translation mine.

13. B. T. *Menachoth* 43b, translation Eli Cashdan (London: Soncino Press, 1984), stresses the importance of these precepts:

> [He] surrounded them with precepts: *tefillin* on their heads, *tefillin* on their arms, *zizith* on their garments, and *mezuzoth* on their doorposts; concerning these David said, *Seven times a day do I praise Thee, because of they righteous ordinances.* And as David entered the bath and saw himself standing naked, he exclaimed "Woe is me that I stand naked without any precepts about me." But when he reminded himself of the circumcision in his flesh his mind was set at ease.

14. I am indebted to Elbogen's *Jewish Liturgy,* 8–11, for details of the development of the basic prayer tradition.

15. Ibid., 9.

16. Ibid., 7–8.

17. The prayer book of the present Seattle, Washington, Sephardic community notes the differences in the various Sephardic traditions. *The Seattle Sephardic Community Daily and Sabbath Siddur,* ed. Isaac Azose (Seattle: Sephardic Traditions Foundation, 2002) (hereafter Azose, *Seattle Sepharic Siddur*). For example, the Turkish Jews in the daily supplication say, "What can we say before you who dwells on high," but the Spanish and Moroccans request, "May it be your will Lord our god and god of our fathers" (ibid., 44–45). Where

the Rhodians pray, "Turn from your fierce wrath," the others continue "Our Father our King" (ibid., 45–46).

18. Ibid., 18–19.

19. The discussion of the blessing against heretics is in part drawn from Elbogen, *Jewish Liturgy,* 45–46.

20. Ibid., 45.

21. Azose, *The Seattle Sephardic Siddur,* 37.

22. תפלות מכל השנה. *Tefilloth Mikol Hashana* (Prague: Gershom ben Shlomo ha Cohen, 1519), 35, hereafter *Prague Prayer Book.* This prayer book is available online from the Jewish National Library.

23. The test may also have been used against Gnostics and other heterodox groups.

24. Naftali Hirtz Treves, *Sefer Dikduk Tefillah* (Thiengen, 1560), fol. 69, translation mine. This book has been reprinted as *Siddur R. Hirtz* (Hebrew) (Bnei Brak, Israel: Julius Klugmann and Sons, 2004).

25. *Prague Prayer Book,* 45.

26. A prayer book printed with parallel columns of Hebrew and its Judeo-German translation (German as spoken by Jews written in Hebrew letters) was printed in 1562–63 in Mantua. It is attributed to the noted Hebraist, Elias Levita (Behur ben Asher ha Levi Askenazi) although the text itself does not mention him. The title page states that it was intended for both men and women. The German translation was an aid to those who were not knowledgable in Hebrew. The issue of female prayer is beyond the scope of this study, but, in brief, it is likely that some women had access to vernacular prayer texts. For many, German was their language of prayer. The 1562 prayer book gives instructions for women as well as men in the German, but no instruction in the Hebrew. Of interest is its treatment of the blessing "made me an Israelite." The Hebrew follows the Talmud, as does Hirtz Trevis, but the German reads, "did not make me a *goy* [for men], *goyah* [for women]." Probably, "Israelite" was read aloud and "goy" spoken in one's personal blessing. The 1562 prayer book also censors the blessing against traitors and omits the ten words from the *Aleinu,* as Margaritha claimed Italian printings did. Spaces were left so that the missing text could be added by hand.

The fact that many Jews prayed in German gives rise to the question of the availability of vernacular manuscript prayer texts. That question relates possible influences on Margaritha's translation as well as the Yiddish edition of 1562. Both translations could have made use of long-established material. Margaritha's German rendering compares favorably to that of 1562. See *Tefilah Kol haShanah* (Prayer for the entire year) (Mantua, 1562).

27. There is no published translation of the *Sefer Hasidim.* Elisheva Baumgarten has shown it to be an important source for information on medieval Jewish life.

28. The role of the Hasidei Ashkenaz in establishing prayer behavior and developing the litury is discussed in Elbogen, *Jewish Liturgy,* 288–90.

29. Isaiah 11:9. Not all printed prayer books had distinctive titles. A Constantinople printing of 1510 is called merely *Book of Prayers for the Year.*

30. See Malachi Beit-Arie, "The Affinity between Early Hebrew printing and Manuscripts" (Hebrew), in M. Nabav and J. Rothschild, eds. *Essays and Studies in Librarianship Presented to Curt David Wormann on his 75th Birthday* (Jerusalem: Magnus Press, 1975), 27–39.

31. Hirtz Treves, *Sefer Dikduk Tefillah,* 4.

32. Ibid., 16.

33. The analysis and translations from Margaritha's translation of the Hebrew prayer book (*Siddur*) come from the 1544 Frankfurt printing of *Der gantz Jüdisch glaub,* with comparisons to the 1530 and 1531 editions. The 1544 printing represents the text of the 2nd edition, as discussed in Appendix C. Margaritha wrote additional commentary to the 2nd edition of the prayer book. Much of this will be noted in the discussion. For reference, major additions were attached to his discussion of converted Jews (1544, xii v.), about Judah the Pious and behavior in prayer (1544, vii r. and v.), and against Jewish belief and attempts to convert Christians (1544, xiii r.–xiiii v.).

34. Volgt der Juden Betbuechlein/ das sie alle tag in irer synagoge beten/ und singen/ samt hundert ברכות Beruchos/ das ist lobsprechungen/ nach Hebreischer sprach gründlich teütscht/ Anfenglich/ so sie in die kirchen geen/ bett ein jeder diss gebett gemeynlich. *Der gantz Jüdisch glaub* (1544), Oii r.

35. Diss ist ein anfang der gebet/ so die Judē zu morgens in irer Synagoge. Ibid., Oii v.

36. Jetz sitzen sie nider und singen einen Vers umb dē anderen. Ibid.

37. . . . und uns ein gepott geben von waschung der hende. Ibid., Oiii r.

38. Ich woelt aber gerne das mir ein Jude anzeigete wo Gott solliches gepotten habe. Ibid. This was discussed in chapter 3.

39. Ibid., Oiii r.–Oiiii r. This order is still followed.

40. Hernach betten die Judē ein gebet/ das sie Gott vor allem unglueck beheuten woelle. Ibid., Oiiii r.

41. Ibid., Oiiii v.–P r.

42. Ibid., P r.

43. Ibid., Pi r.–Pii r.

44. B. T. *Zevachim* v, using Leviticus and Numbers.

45. Es moechte einer gedencken/ es hat gar eyndtlich in disem Vortempel darinnen der opffer tisch gestanden ist/ gestuncken . . . / setzen aber die Juden in irē Thalmudt/ zehen wunderzeichen/ die in ihrem tempel geschehen seindt/ und under denen setzen sie/ dass das fleisch—weliches man geopffert hat/ welliches sie dz heilig fleisch nennen/ nie gestuncken habe . . . wer solchs aber nit glaubt/ mag dennocht wol selig werden. Ibid., Q r.

46. Hie nachfolgendt kompt ein vast schweres gebet der Juden/ und das gantz unbreuchlich/ und unverstentlich in das deutsch zubringen ist/ ohn sonderliche ausslegungen und umbredungē/ dē darinnen werden zumal schier alle griff des Thalmuds begriffen/ und allhie man wol spüren und sehen mag/

wie sie mit der schrift und irer ausslegung umbgeen/ wirt aber in der warheit nichts nutzlichs darinnen befundē/ mich solchs bewegt hat/ lang nicht zuverdeutschen/ aber von der verstockten Juden wegē/ die mir etwaan vor nicht fast guenstig seind/ habe ichs auffs verstendlich est verdeutshet unnd ausgeleget/ das sie ja nicht ursach hetten/ zu sprechen/ Sihe es ist noch kein Christ so gelert/ der diss gebett verdeutschē küde. Ibid., Q r. and v.

47. Die Erste/ wirdt das gesetz auss gelegt vom geringen und herben etc. Ibid., Q v.

48. Das verstehet man also/ als wenn ich spreche/ der hat ein geringe suende gethan/ unnd Gott hat ihn darumb gestrafft wie vil denn mer/ so er ein schwere suende thet. Ibid.

49. Biss hieher gehet das schwere gebet/ darinnen ich mich auffs hoechst bemuehet hab/ mit vil wortē/ deutlich und verstaentlich zu redden/ ist aber seer vast verdriesslich zulesen/ . . . wolt es wol klaerer herfuer bracht haben/ aber es hette mer zeit unnd wort gekostet. Ibid., R r.

50. Dazumal da die Judē im land gewesen seind/ uñ haben den tempel gehabt/ da haben sie geopffert/ wie in den fuenf buecherin Mose steet/ dieweil sie aber von viler mercklicher ursachen wegen vertriben und verstossen/ der tempel zerstoert/ unnd nicht mehr erbawt wirt/ der halben auch sie daselbst nicht mehr opffern künden/ so sagen sie/ unnd bekennen doch mit dem mund unnd gebet/ ein jedes opffer auff seine zeit/ und wie und wo die selben opffer geopffert worden seind/ wie hernach volgt. Bafelhē sich aber mit dem spruch Hose am xiiii. Kere dich Israel zu Gott deinem Hern etc. und wir woellen dir bezalen die Stier mit unsern lesstzen etc. Ibid., Pii r.

51. Tales aber ist gemeynklich ein weiss . . . tuch . . . und hat an einer jeglichen egkē einzoten/ welche zoten . . . *cicis* genant/ mit acht faedem hangen und oben ein jeder zot hat fünff knoepff/ so nimpt denn der oeberst Priester dises tuch/ und wicklet es umb den koepff uñspricht Gelobet seisest du Gott . . . und hast uns gepotten um zuwicklen dises tuch/ und darnach volgē im alle Juden nach/ die uber dreitzehn jar unnd in der kirchen seind und dise Ceremonien/ Nemen sie aus dem XV Capi. Nume. am end. Ibid., R r.

52. Aber von kürtze wegen/ will ichs under wegen lassen/ deñ wie man sie machen soll/ haben sie grosse buecher davon geschriben. Ibid., R v.

53. Diese Tephilin halten sie so in grossen eerē/ das wo sie einem auff die erde felt/ muss er den selben tag mit allē/ die sy es darauff sehen ligen/ fastē/ Auch wenn sie die Tephilin anziehen/ kussen sy es zuvor/ unnd stossen es auf die augen/ und solchs nemen sie Deut am x. Ibid., R v.

54. Jetz stehē sie alle auff/ und singē mit grossem fleiss zu Regenspurg und auch anderswo/ haben sie den gebrauch/ das sie diss gebett in summers zeit ein gantze stunde lang syngen/ wie ich denn solliches manches mal von meinem bruder gehoert ab/ das er disses gesang uber fluessig wol gesunen hat/ denn er ist ein gutter Musicus bei den Juden. Ibid., Rii r. This material is not in the 1530 edition.

55. In dem fünfsten Capital . . . der Thalmudt schreibet . . . dz der Titus Vespasianus vom Esau buertig sei. Uñspricht: Und es kam ein stymm von himel

und sprach zu Tito/ Du gottloser Sun eines gottlosen/ ein kinds kind von Esau dem gottlosen . . . Nun seind es jha arme torechte leut/ das sie sollicher lugen glauben geben . . . Sprechē auch/ dieweil der Titus den tempel zerstoeret habe/ uñsei ein oeberster Roemer gewest/ und nun Rom ein lange zeit in der Christenheit das haupt/ so nennē sie billich die Christen Edomiter nach dem Tito Vespasiano. Ibid. Sii v.

56. . . . und auch das Coment der Juden/ und fuernemlich/ Rabi Salomon/ den Talmudischē/ den denselben gantzen Propheten ziehen sie auff die Christenheit . . . Auss sollichem spruch ist solches gebebet fundiert/ und auch das sie der Christen oeberkest und regiment/ das müttwillige künigreich und Regiment heyssen. Ibid., Xiii v.

57. . . . so beten diss gebett nur die Juden/ die in der Christenheit wonen/ order aber die in der Christenheit erzogen worden seind. Ibid., Xiii v.–Xiiii r.

58. Wolt Got/ das es sich ein mal zutruege/ das ich durch solliches mein schreiben von dē Juden/ vor verminsstigen gelerten Christen angefochten wurde/ Ich woelte mich finden lassen/ wo man wolt/ mein schreiben war zu machen/ auch in gegen der Juden/ uñ nit der ungelerten/ vil lieber bei irē gerlertestē. Ibid., Xiii r.

59. Und zu den veretteren . . . zu den abgetilgten, Verstee die getauften Juden. Ibid., X v.

60. Werd ich bewegt etwas weitters zu redden/ auss ursach/ das es mich und alle getaufffte Juden belanget. Anfenglich ist zu wissen/ das diss gebett . . . wie die Juden schreiben/ Rabi Simeon vor dem angesicht des grossen oeberstē Rabi Gamaliel in der statt Jafna/ also verordnet und eigesetzt hat . . . Aber nach einer langen zeit hernach sei einer kommen/ Rabi Samuel genant/ unnd der habe diss stuck hinein gesetzt. Ibid., X v.

61. Nun aber hab ich hie angezeigt/ dz diss eingesetzte stucke nicht allwegen zu disem gebet gehoert habe. Ist aber das eingesetzte stuck/ fuernemlich wider alle die ihres glaubens nit seind/ und mit aussgetrucktē worten/ widder die getaufften Judē/ wider alle oeberkeit/ unnd wider alle/ die einen besundern glauben haben/ der widder ihren glauben ist. Ibid., Xii r.

62. Es ist bei mans gedencken ein gelerter Christ zu Venedig gewesen/ der hat wider die Juden fast geschriben/ nemlich/ wider iren wucher/ und lesterung/ die sie Christo und seinen Christen anlagen/ Der hat bei den Venedigern erlangt/ das alle Juden inn der Venediger land/ von mercklicher ursach wegen/ gelbe paret tragen muessen/ und einen gantz kleinen wucher nemen/ haben auch etlich gebett aus ihrem bett buechlein thun muessen/ und verendern/ unnd davon ist auch nemlich diser stuck eines/ Wiewol sie es jetzt wider wie vor betē/ alleine anstatt des woertleins/ getauffie Juden/ alle verretter setzen . . . aber ich weiss das sie es nicht lassen/ habe es auch wol selbst in der Venediger land gebetet. Ibid., Xii v.

63. Thu hie auch kundt/ darumb das die lieben Apostel getauft seind/ heissen sie die Juden . . . Taschmidim/ an statt ihres rechten namen . . . Thalmidim/ Taschmidim aber heist die vertilgten/ und Thalmudim/ die Junger or

schuler/ dergleichen heyssen sie ein jheden getaufften Juden/ Meschumad . . . auff teutsch ein abgetilgter. Ibid., Xii v.

64. Wenn der Jude betet/ soll er sein hertz dahin richten/ das er gedencke an die zeit do der heilig tempel zu Jerusalem gewest ist/ do man opffern kunde/ uñ an statt der selben opffer/ sein gebett thuee/ . . . Darumb ein jeder Jud/ . . . soll er gedencken/ als brechte er ein opffer vor Gott. Ibid., Vii v.–Viii r.

65. Nun sehe ein jeder die blindheit/ die weil sie selbs bekennen muessen/ das dass opffer auffgehoert/ uñ nichts haben mehr dadurch ihn die suende verzihen werden moechten/ unnd in dem zorn Gottes seindt . . . was doch die Propheten schreiben/ besonderlich Daniel/ das so die opffer auffhoeren warden/ werde der Moschiach herbei kommē sein/ der do das recht suendopffer sein wird. Ibid., Viii r.

66. Stellen ire gebete unnd wercke . . . wie Psalm cviii. Sein gebett soll bekeret werden inn suende. Ibid.

67. Sie troesten sich aber wol under einander uñ sprechen/ Ob wol Gott sein angesichte . . . vor uns verborgen hat/ nichts destweniger ist der schatte seiner hende uber uns/ wie er uns denn zugesaget hat. Ibid.

68. Diss singen hie alle Juden einhelligklich mit lauter stimme als weren sie die Engel. Ibid., Siiii r.

69. So ir sie ansehen werdet/ solt ihr gedencken aller gebott des Herren/ und thon/ uñ solt ewer hertz nit nach lust abwenden . . . In diesem obgemelten heimlich Gebetten haben die Juden gar grosse andacht/ das sie mit den augen gen himel sehen/ und in alle vier oerter der welt. Ibid., Tii v.

70. Das verstehn aber die Juden also/ und schreiben dise ursache/ warum die Zizis . . . einen aller gepott Gottes ermanen und gedencken machen/ nemlich darumb/ des diss wort Zizis . . . in der ziffer hat/ sechs hundert und dreitzehē/ mit sampt den acht fedem und dē funf knoepffen/ . . . so ermanen sie einen aller gepott zu gedenckē welcher auch seind sechs hundert/ und dreitzehen. Ibid., Tii v.–Tiii r.

71. Do die gantze gemeyn mit einander diss gebett still uñ heimlich/ mit grosser andacht bettet/ darnach singet es der vorsinger gar laut. Ibid., Tiiii r.

72. Nun aber haben die Juden ein grosse heimlichkeit und superstition in allen iren geschrifften/ mit der ziffer unnd zal der ersten buchstaben der woerter . . . Tausent sibē hundert und sibentzig . . . das in der zal dreissig betrifft/ hinein gesetzt/ domit das die zal der tausent achthundert Engel erfuellet wurde. Ibid., X v. and Xii r. At this point, I would like to thank my friend Elie Merken, a rabbinic scholar, for our discussions on prayer, Jewish law, and the sources of Margaritha's comments.

73. Anfenglich/ wenn man diss gebett anhept zu bettē/ so muss und soll ein jeder Jude seine fuesse gleich zusaman halten/ und stellen/ unnd das nemen sie auss Ezech. i. Das die engel/ die da Gott anbeteten/ auch mit gleichen fuessen stunden. Ibid., V v.

74. Das sie gereitzet werden das gesetze zu ubertretten/ und nicht andechtig zu beten. Ibid., Vii r.

75. Ich bins gewiss/ das Gott mein gebett erhoeret hat. Ibid., Vii v.

76. Die Juden schreiben von einē Rabbi, Rabbi Judah/ Chosit genant/ den sie für gantz heilig halten/ von Speyer buertig gewesen/ und zu Regenspurg gewonet/ uñ gestorben/ . . . der hat gelert/ was ein Jude thun solt/ das er andechtig bette/ und Gott yn erhoere. Nemlich/ er sol mit gepucktem haupte steen/ unnd sol die beide grossen zehen an seinem fuessen/ ein wenig inn die erde stecken/ doch nit fast/ das er nit irre werde im gebett/ unnd so er solchs thut/ kan er sein hertz fleissig/ und andechtig zu Gott richten. Ibid., Vii r. This material is not in the 1530 edition.

77. Jetz in dem volgenden verse geet der Jude im gebet drei tritt hinder sich/ gleich wie ein kreps/ und bucket sich am ersten fuer sich/ darnach bucket er dē kopff auf die lincke seiten/ darnach auff die rechte seitten/ darnach bucket er sich wol wider fuer sich/ die buckunge bedeuten/ das er den fride auff alle oert wuenschet/ die letzt buckunge . . . gegen Gott. Das er aber hinder sich geet/ das geschicht/ das er Gott nit also bald den hindern zeige und fuerwende/ wie denn noch auch der gebrauch bei den verstendigen ist. Ibid., Yii v.

78. Das er aber drei tritt/ nit mer noch weniger hinder sich thuet/ haben sie es auss einem erdichten/ fablischen/ Thalmudischen Coment/ das sie schreiben uber das xx Capit. Exo. am ende/ da der Text spricht. Moses gieng auff den berg etc. und das volk stund von fernen etc. durüber schreiben sie also/ das dazumal ein solch gross wunder werck geschehē sei/ da Gott das gesetze gabe/ sei dz gantz volck Israel so hart erschrocken/ unnd durch solliche grosse forcht seien sie durch ein gross wunder in einem augē plick/ drei meil hinder sich vom berg Synai kommē/ und gegen den selben dreien meilen/ haben sie dise drei schrit hinder sich zuthun zugedencken verordnet. Ibid., Yii v.–Yiii r.

79. Wie ein hunde zu seinem gespewe. Ibid., Yiii r. The solution to the problems in Margaritha's explanation of the three steps back was largely due to information provided by Elie Merkin.

80. Anfencklich schreiben sie/ wie man sich mit dem kopff bucken und neigen soll/ und darnach den leib . . . unnd soll sich nicht weitter bucken/ denn das er dz hertz sehen mag/ und soll sich nit tief bucken/ das er die beine sehen moege/ damit das er nicht komme inn solche andacht/ die schame zu sehen. Ibid., Y r.–Y v.

81. Und muss den selben tag der Synagoga vorsingen. Ibid., Cii v.

82. Jetz stehet ein vorsinger auff unnd gehet/ unnd stelt sein angesicht gegen Orient/ darumb das Jerusalem auch gegen Oriēt leyt. . . . Und diser Vorsinger stelt sich uber ein buch/ welches auff einer seülen order stander ligt/ welcher stander gleich gegen irer Arche uber steht/ in welcher Arche die fünff buecher Mose ligen/ unnd dieser vorsinger muss tieff stehn/ gleich wie in einer gruben/ unnd das nemen sie auss dem xxx Psalm da er spricht/ Von der tieffe Gott hab ich dich angeruffen/ unnd singet also. Ibid., Sii v.

83. Heyst aber das volgend gebet bei den Juden . . . Thechino/ dz ist ein barmhertzigklichs gebet/ wirt aber nur am montag unnd dornstag in der wochen gebetet . . . / so geet der vosinger hinder dē stander/ und setzt sich auff

die stapffel/ welche vor der Archa seind/ und feld denn mit seinem ganzen angesicht auff die linke hand/ und betet mit grossem schmertzē heimlich diss nachvolgend gebet/ Der gleichen thut auch ein jeglicher Jude. . . . Ibid., Ziii v. Today Ashkenazic Jews do not place their head on the hand with *tefillin.* The *Shulchan Aruch* in the middle of the sixteenth century saw what Margaritha describes as normative, but the custom changed over time.

84. Das er dester mehr andacht habe von hertzen. Ibid.

85. Wo sie einen Christen kuenden bewegen zu ihrem glauben. . . . Ibid., Xiiii v. The material does not appear in the 1530 edition. It is clearly an answer to Josel, who claimed that Jews did not circumcise Christians.

86. Gebē jn auch gelt/ schicken sie deñ in die Tuerckey order in Reüssen/ und fuer solche betē sie alle tage diss gebett/ . . . kan ein Christliche oeberkeit solliches alles leiden und dulden. Ibid.

87. Leopold Zunz's study of the litury in Gemany made use of Margaritha's *Der gantz Jüdisch glaub* in at least five places. Leopold Zunz, *Die Ritus des synagogalen Gottesdienstes geschichtlich entwickelt* (Berlin, 1859). He noted that the two stones in the Regensburg synagogue contained the Tetragrammaton, 70. Of importance here is his agreement with Margaritha's claim that Ashkenazic ritual was virtually identical to that of the French Jews, 75.

88. Das die Juden in Teütschen landē/ Behem/ Merhern/ Schlesian/ auch alle die Juden in Polen und Reüssen und Ungern/ alle eine weise und ordnunge in ihren kirchen und gebetē haben/ Die Juden die in Franckreich gewesen seind/ stimmen vast gleich mit den obgemelten Juden/ Aber die Juden Romanie/ das ist fast als weit als Italie/ welliche Juden nicht deütsch künden/ haben gar vil ein andere ordnung in ihren kirchen/ Die Juden die in Hispanien/ Sicilien gewonet haben/ haben abermals vil ein andere ordnunge/ auch die Juden die alle mal in der Tuerckey/ und zuvorauss die zu Constantinopel und Salinick/ haben abermals ein andere ordnung . . . / so sage ich/ das nur die Juden in der Christenheit seind/ diss gebett beten. *Der gantz Jüdisch glaub* (1544), Xiiii r. This material does not appear in the 1530 edition.

89. So kompt ein Jude order zwen/ reden on allen grund/ und sprechen es sei alles erlogen/ so glaubt man deñ ihnen solliche lugen. Ibid. This material does not appear in the 1530 text.

90. This discussion is distilled from ibid., *a*i v.–*a*ii v. For a biblical use of *segen,* see Jeremiah 51:23. In rabbinic literature, a *segen* was a suffragen to the high priest.

91. . . . gehet deñ der schulklopfer/ dz ist ir kuster/ gerings um den Almemor . . . und rueff t auss wer do kauffen woell Gelila/ Etz Chaim/ und etwan auch Hagboho . . . Ibid., *a*ii r.

92. Biss sie auff einen guldē mer order weniger kommen seind. Ibid., *a*ii v.

93. Merck aber hiebei Christlicher leser/ das an disem ort bei den Juden/ uber disem segen/ mer feindschaft/ neyd/ und hader/ auch Gottes lesterung geschicht/ denn in der gantzen Christenheit/ inn allen unsern Ceremonien und gebreuchen/ denn wenn der Prelat/ der do segen heisst/ einen Juden berueffen

lest/ so zancken und murren sie alle under einander/ und sprechē/ sich das ist ein feiner segē/ er lasset nach gunst uñ ansehen der person berueffen/ einen reichen vor einem armen/ einen jungen vor einem alten/ ein ungelerten vor einem gelerten/ ein boesen vor einem frommen etc. Auch disen und ihenen berueffet er gahr offt im jar/ aber mich unnd meines gleichen hat er nie berueffen etc. Ibid., *a*iii v.–*a*iiii r.

94. Die Juden haben seer viel frembder vocabel die nicht hebeisch noch deutsch seind/ sonder Frantzoesisch den alle Juden in deutscher nation/ uñ vorauss die an dem Reyn wonen/ seind alle auss Franckreich vertriben worden/ und haben solcher wort noch vil bei jn behalten/ wie denn hernach volgen wirt. Ibid., *a*iii r.

95. Das diss wort Alememor auch ein Frantzoesisch wort ist/ und das ist zu probieren aus jrem Thalmudt/ auss dem letsten Capittel. dz do redt von der lauberhütten/ do schreiben sie von disem Almemor/ und der Text nent den Almemor/ Bima . . . eine hütlzene altane/ darauff schreibet jr Commentator Rabbi/ Solomon/ welcher nicht teutsch/ sonder Frantzoesisch kuendt hat/ es sei ein Almemor/ das ist auff deutsch/ darauff man Memoria helt/ darvon volgt denn das oeber Memor büchlein. Ibid., *a*iii r.

96. Welches vō dem latein kompt/ Memoria. Ibid., *a*ii v.

97. Die Juden in Italia/ Sicilien/ Neapoli/ Hispania etce. Heyssen disen baw nicht Almemor/ sonder . . . Tevo. Ibid.

98. Ibid., *a*ii v.–*a*iii r.

99. Er gebe denn ein summa gelts. Ibid., *a*ii v.

100. Gott woelle irer seelē eingedechtig sein/ unnd sie setzen in das paradeiss . . . Ibid., *a*iii r.

101. Und dises maentelein nennen die Juden . . . Mappa wie oben angezeiget/ und nicht allein dises maentelein/ sonder alle die tuecher die sie auff dem stender darauff sie die Buecher legen brauchen . . . damit mā das Buch nit mit blosser hand anruere. Ibid, *b* r.

102. Auch haben sie ein wort/ das gebrauchet ein schulmeister wenn er zu einem schuler sprechē will, Repetier, hebe wider forne an/ so spricht er/ Ertorn/ das kompt auch von dem Frantzoesischen. Ibid., *b* r.

103. Dieweil der Jud dz gesetz also auff dem Almemor umher tregt/ haben die weiber in irer kirchē ein grossen zanck und gestoess umb die gugkloecher/ welliche gemacht seind auss jrer kirchen in der Maenner kirchen/ umb des willē/ so sie es doch nicht kussen künden/ sehē sie die selbige doch gerne an. Ibid., *b*iii.

104. Das aber die weiber unnd Maener ein jeglichs ein besondere kirchen habē muss/ Schreiben sie in irem Thalmudt also: im letzstē Capitel der lauberhütten/ das Mann und weib im anfang zu einander gegangen seind/ do hab sich viel bueberei zu getragen/ haben sie darnach ein ordnung gemacht/ das die weiber unden in der kirchen weren/ uñ die maenner oben/ hat auch nicht geholffen/ Haben darnach ein andere ordnūg versucht/ hat auch nicht geholffen/ dadurch seind sie bewegt worden das solche hurerei verhuet werde/ das ein

jedes ein besondere kirchen jetz haben muss/ und solche ordnung haben sie auss Zacha. xii genommen/ do der Text redet von der beklagūg des Moschiachs und spricht: Die weiber werden besonder klagen/ und die maenner besonder/ Hie sicht mā wie grosse andacht bei disem volck im tempel gewesen und noch ist. Ibid., *b*iii r.–*b*iii v.

105. B. T. *Succoth* 51b, translation mine. It is interesting that the pages following 51b deal with Messianism, especially the Messiah ben Joseph. Given Margaritha's attack on that doctrine in his Refutation, one wonders why he did not take another swipe at it here. His citation of the Davidic prophecy in Zechariah 12:12 would also have been an excellent point at which to expand his critique of Jewish Messianism.

106. Schreiben/ das auff ein zeit dem Prophetē Helie/ zwen engel bekommen seind/ die haben mit sich viel secke/ vol grimmens und zorns gefueret/ habe der Helias gefraget/ uber wen sie den zorn fueren woellen/ haben sie geantwort/ uber alle die da schwaetzen inn der Synagoga/ so man das Kadesch betet. *Der gantz Jüdisch glaub,* cii v.

Bibliography

This bibliography contains the readily available sources upon which this study is based. Difficult to obtain sources, especially those in Hebrew, are not listed, unless crucial. All relevant materials, including those in Hebrew, are cited in the notes. Many sixteenth-century books can now be found in digitized copies on the Internet. Among these are both editions of *Der gantz Jüdisch glaub* and several later printings as well as the *Isaiah Commentary.* See Münchener Digitalisierungszentrum. Many later studies, such as Mieses's 1916 work on Margaritha, are also available. One can expect even more material to come in the near future.

Albo, Joseph. ספר עקרים (*Sefer Ikkarim*): *Buch Ikkarim, Grund-und Glaubenslehren der Mosaischen Religion von Rab. Joseph Albo.* Translated into German by Ward Schlessinger and Ludwig Schlesinger. Frankfurt: n.p., 1844.

———. *Sefer ha-Ikkarim.* Edited and translated into English by Isaac Husik. 5 vols. Philadelphia: Jewish Publication Society, 1929–30.

Austin, Kenneth. *From Judaism to Calvinism: The Life and Writings of Immanuel Tremellius (c. 1510–1580).* Aldershot, England: Ashgate, 2007.

Baron, Salo Wittmayer. *A Social and Religious History of the Jews.* 2nd ed. Vol. 11. Philadelphia: Jewish Publication Society, 1952.

Baumgarten, Elisheva. *Mothers and Children: Jewish Family Life in Medieval Europe.* Princeton, NJ: Princeton University Press, 2004.

Bell, Dean Phillip. *Jewish Identity in Early Modern Germany: Memory, Power, and Community.* Aldershot, England: Ashgate, 2007.

Bell, Dean Phillip, and Stephen G. Burnett, eds. *Jews, Judaism, and the Reformation in Sixteenth-Century Germany.* Leiden: Brill, 2006.

Berger, David. *The Jewish Christian Debate in the High Middle Ages: A Critical Edition of the* Nizzahon Vetus. Philadelphia: Jewish Publication Society, 1979.

Buchwald, Georg. *Kleine Notizen aus Rechnungbüchern des Thüringischen Staatsarchivs.* II. *Archiv für Reformationsgeschichte.* 31. 1934.

Burnett, Stephen G. "Distorted Mirrors: Antonius Margaritha, Johann Buxtorf, and Christian Ethnographies of the Jews." *Sixteenth Century Journal* 25, no. 2 (1994).

Carben, Victor von. *Juden Büchlein: Hyerinne würt gelesen wie Herr Victor von Carben welcher ein Rabi der Juden gewesst ist zu[m] Christlichem Glauben kommen.* 1550. Originally printed Cologne, 1508–9.

Carlebach, Elisheva. "Attribution of Secrecy and Perceptions of Jewry." *Jewish Social Studies* 2, no. 3 (1996): 115–36.

———. *Between History and Hope: Jewish Messianism in Ashkenaz and Sepharad.* New York: Graduate School of Jewish Studies, Touro College, 1998.

———. *Divided Souls: Converts from Judaism in Germany, 1500–1750.* New Haven, CT: Yale University Press, 2001.

———. "The Sabbatean Posture of German Jewry." *Jerusalem Studies in Jewish Thought* 16 and 17 (2001).

Carlebach, Elisheva, John M. Efron, and David N. Myers. *Jewish History and Jewish Memory: Essays in Honor of Yosef Hayim Yerushalmi.* Hanover, NH: Brandeis University Press, 1998.

Cohen, Richard I. *Jewish Icons: Art and Society in Modern Europe.* Berkeley: University of California Press, 1998.

Coudert, Allison P., and Jeffrey S. Shoulson, eds. *Hebraica Veritas? Christian Hebraists and the Study of Judaism in Early Modern Europe.* Philadelphia: University of Pennsylvania Press, 2004.

Davis, Joseph M. "The 'Ten Questions' of Eliezer Eilburg and the Problem of Jewish Unbelief in the 16th Century." *Jewish Quarterly Review* 91 (January–April 2001).

Deutsch, Yaacov. "Polemical Ethnographies: Descriptions of Yom Kippur in the Writings of Christian Hebraists and Jewish Converts to Christianity in Early Modern Europe." In Coudert and Shoulson, eds. *Hebraica Veritas? Christian Hebraists and the Study of Judaism in Early Modern Europe,* 202–33.

———. "Von der Juden Ceremonien: Representations of Jews in Sixteenth Century Germany." In Bell and Burnett, *Jews, Judaism, and the Reformation,* 335–56.

Diemling, Maria. "Christiche Ethnographien über Juden und Judentum in der Frühen Neuzeit: Die Konverten Victor von Carben und Antonius Margaritha und ihre Darstellung jüdischen Lebens und jüdischer Religion." PhD diss., Universität Wien, 1999.

———. "Chonuko-Kirchweyhe," *Kalonymos* 3 (2000).

Diner, Dan. *Synchrone Welten: Zeitenräume jüdischer Geschichte, Toldot.* Vol. 1. Göttingen: Vandenhoeck and Ruprecht, 2005.

Elbaum, Ya'akov. "Concerning Two Textual Emendations in the Aleinu Prayer" (Hebrew). *Tarbiz* 42 (1972–73).

Fishman, Talia. *Shaking the Pillars of Exile, "Voice of a Fool": An Early Modern Jewish Critique of Rabbinic Culture.* Stanford, CA: Stanford University Press, 1988.

Friedman, Jerome. "The Reformation in Alien Eyes: Jewish Perceptions of Christian Troubles." *Sixteenth Century Journal* 14 (1983): 23–40.

Geiger, Ludwig. *Das Studium der Hebräischen Sprache in Deutschland: Vom Ende des XV. bis zur Mitte des XVI. Jahrhunderts.* Breslau: Skutsch, 1870.

———. *Johann Reuchlin, Sein Leben und Seine Werke.* Leipzig: Duncker and Humblot, 1871.

Geiger, Ludwig, ed. *Johann Reuchlins Briefwechsel.* Tübingen, 1875.

Gingerich, Owen. *The Book Nobody Read.* New York: Walker, 2004.

Gingerich, Owen, ed. *The Nature of Scientific Discovery.* Washington, DC: Smithsonian Institution Press, 1975.

Ginsburg, Christian D. *Jacob ben Chaim ibn Adonijah's Introduction to the Rabbinic Bible. The Library of Biblical Studies.* Edited by Harry M. Orlinsky. New York: KTAV, 1968.

———. *The Massoreth Ha Massoreth of Elias Levita. The Library of Biblical Studies.* Edited by Harry M. Orlinsky. New York: KTAV, 1968.

Gow, Andrew Colin. *The Red Jews: Antisemitism in an Apocalyptic Age, 1200–1600.* Leiden: Brill, 1995.

Graetz, Heinrich. *Geschichte der Juden.* Vol. 9. Leipzig, 1877.

Hasse, H. G. *Abriß der meißnisch-albertinisch-sächsischen Kirchengeschichte.* Leipzig, 1847.

Hirsch, Samuel Abraham. *The Cabbalists and Other Essays.* London: W. Heinemann, 1922.

Hirtz Trevis, Naphtali. מלאה הארץ דעה : . . . תפילה מכל השנה עם פיר' . . . ועוד פי' ע"ד הקבלה / אשר / חיבר ולוקט . . . מה"ר [נפתלי] הירץ [טריביש] ש"ץ referred to as *Sefer Dikduk Tefillah* (A commentary on the Prayer Book. *Malah ha-Aretz Da'th*) (Thiengen, 1560). Scanned at http://aleph500.huji.ac.il/nnl/dig/books/bk001744468.html.

Hoffman, Christoph (Christophorus Ostrofrancus). *Ratisbona metropolis boisarae.* Augsburg, 1519.

Horowitz, Elliot. *Reckless Rites: Purim and the Legacy of Jewish Violence.* Princeton, NJ: Princeton University Press, 2006.

———. "The Rite to Be Reckless: On the Perception and Interpretation of Purim Violence." *Poetics Today* 15 (1994).

Howard, George. "The Textual Nature of Shem-Tob's Hebrew Matthew." *Journal of Biblical Literature* 108 (Summer 1989): 239–57.

Hsia, R. Po-chia, and Hartmut Lehmann. *In and Out of the Ghetto: Jewish-Gentile Relations in Late Medieval and Early Modern Germany.* Cambridge: University of Cambridge Press, 1995.

Idel, Moshe. *Kabbalah: New Perspectives.* New Haven, CT: Yale University Press, 1988.

———. *Mystical Experience in Abraham Abulafia.* Albany: State University of New York Press, 1988.

———. *Studies in Ecstatic Kabbalah.* Albany: State University of New York Press, 1988.

Israel, Jonathan. *European Jewry in the Age of Mercantilism, 1550–1750.* Oxford: Clarendon Press, 1985.

Jordan, D. Hermann. *Reformation und gelehrte Bildung in der Markgrafschaft Ansbach-Bayreuth. Quellen und Forschungen zur bayerischen Kirchengeschichte, 1.* Leipzig: Werner Scholl, 1917.

Joseph ben Gershon of Rosheim. *The Historical Writings of Joseph of Rosheim: Leader of Jewry in Early Modern Germany.* Edited with an introduction, commentary, and translations by Chava Fraenkel-Goldschmidt. Translated from the Hebrew by Naomi Schendowich. English edition edited and an afterword by Adam Shear. Leiden and Boston: Brill, 2006.

———. *Joseph of Rosheim, Historical Writings* (Hebrew). Edited with an introduction and translation by Chava Fraenkel-Goldschmidt. Jerusalem: Magnes Press, 1996.

Kaplan, Debra, and Magda Teter. "Out of the (Historiographic) Ghetto: European Jews and Reformation Narratives." *Sixteenth Century Journal* 40 (Summer 2009): 365–93.

Katz, Jacob. *The "Shabbas Goy": A Study in Halakhic Flexibility.* Philadelphia: Jewish Publication Society, 1989.

Kimhi, Joseph. *The Book of the Covenant (Sefer ha-Brit).* Translated by Frank Talmage. Toronto: Pontifical Institute of Mediaeval Studies, 1971.

Kink, Rudolf. *Geschichte der kaiserlichen Universität zu Wien.* Wien: C. Gerold, 1854.

Kirn, Hans-Martin. *Das Bild vom Juden im Deutschland des frühen 16. Jahrhunderts.* Tübingen: J. C. B. Mohr, 1989.

Klausner, Joseph. *The Messianic Idea in Israel.* Translated by W. F. Stinespring. New York: Macmillan, 1955.

Kupfer, Ephraim. "Hezyonotav shel R. Asher b" r Meir ha-Mekhuneh Lemlein Reutlingen" (Hebrew). *Kobez al Yad* 8, no. 18 (1975): 285–423.

Lapide, Pinchas E. *Hebrew in the Church: The Foundations of Jewish-Christian Dialogue.* Translated from the German by Erroll F. Rhodes. Foreword by Helmut Gollwitzer. Grand Rapids, MI: Eerdmans, 1984.

Lenowitz, Harris. *Jewish Messiahs: From the Galilee to Crown Heights.* New York: Oxford University Press, 1999.

Liebes, Yehuda. *Studies in the Zohar.* Translated by Arnold Schwartz, Stephanie Nakache, and Penina Peli. Albany: State University of New York Press, 1993.

Luther, Martin. *On the Jews and Their Lies.* Translated by Martin H. Bertram. *Luther's Works.* Vol. 47. Philadelphia: Fortress Press, 1971.

———. *Von den Juden und ihren Lügen.* Wittemberg, 1543.

Maccoby, Hyam, ed. and trans. *Judaism on Trial: Jewish-Christian Disputations in the Middle Ages.* London: Littman Library of Jewish Civilization, 1982.

Maimon, Arye. *Germania Judaica, bd. III, 1350–1519.* Tübingen: Mohr, 1987.

Marcus, Ivan G. *Rituals of Childhood: Jewish Acculturation in Medieval Europe.* New Haven, CT: Yale University Press, 1996.

Margaritha, Anthonius. *Der gantz Jüdisch glaub mit sampt ainer gründtlichen und warhafften anzaygunge Aller Satzungen, Ceremonien, Gebetten, Haymliche und offentliche Gebreuch, deren sich dye Juden halten, durch das gantz Jar, Mit schönen und gegründten Argumenten wyder jren Glauben. Durch Anthonium Margaritham Hebrayschen Leser der Löblichen Statt Augspurg, beschriben und an tag gegeben.* Augsburg: Heinrich Steyner, 1530 (2 printings, March and April).

———. *Der gantz Jüdisch glaub mit sampt eyner gründtlichenn und warhafftigen anzeygunge, allersatzungen, Ceremonien, gebetten, heymliche und öffentliche gebreüch, deren sich die Juden halten, durch das gantz Jar, mit schönen unnd gegründten Argumenten wider jren glauben, durch Anthonium Margaritham, Hebreyschen Leser, der löblichen Universitet und Fürstlichen Stat Leyptzigt, beschryben und an tag gegeben.* Augsburg: Heinrich Steyner, 1531 and with variant spelling Lipsiae: Melchior Lottheri, 1531.

———. *Der Judischglaub, Mitallen Ceremoniē, satzūgen, heimliche uñ offentliche gebreüch wie sich die Jüdē haltē, Mit schönen und gegründten argumenten widder jren glauben. Durch Anthoniū Margarithā beschribē.* Cöllen: Jaspar von Gennep, 1540.

———. *Der gantz Jüdisch Glaub. Mit sampt einer gründlichen und warhafftigen anzeigunge, aller satzungen, Ceremoniē, gebetten, heymliche und öffentliche gebreüch, derē sich die Juden haltē, durch das gantz Jar, mit schönen unnd gegründyen Argumenten wider jren glauben, durch Anthonium Margaritham Hebreischen Leser, der löblichen Universitet unnd Fürstlichen Statt Leyptzigt, beschriben unnd an tag gegeben.* Franckfurt am Mayn: Cyriacus Jabobus, 1544, 1556, and 1561. (Title page varies in use of sigla.)

———. *Erklerung Wieausdemheylligen 53. Capittel des fürnemigisten Propheten Esaie grüntlich außgefüer /probiert/ das der verhaischen Moschiach (wellicher Christus ist) schon khomen . . . .* Wien: Singrenium, 1534. (*Isaiah Commentary*). 2010 reprint available from Verlag Classic Editions.

———. *Kurtze ausslegung uber das wort Halleluia.* Wien? n.d.

———. *Ain kurtzer Bericht und anzaigung, wo die christlich Ceremonien vom Balmesel in bayden Testamenten gegründet sei.* Wien, 1541.

———. *Psalterium Hebraicum.* Lipsiae: Melchior Lottheri, 1533.

Metzger, Thérèse, and Mendel Metzger. *Jewish Life in the Middle Ages: Illuminated Hebrew Manuscripts.* New York: Alpine Fine Arts Collection, 1982.

Meyer, Isaak. *Zur Geschichte der Juden in Regensburg.* Berlin: Louis Lamm, 1913.

Mieses, Josef. *Die älteste gedruckte deutsche Uebersetzung des jüdischen Gebetbuches a. d. Jahre 1530.* Vienna: R. Löwit, 1916. Reprint Charleston, SC: Nabu Press, 2010.

Modena, Leone. *The Autobiography of a Seventeenth-Century Venetian Rabbi: Leon of Modena's "Life of Judah."* Translated and edited by Mark R. Cohen. Princeton, NJ: Princeton University Press, 1988.

Mühlhausen, Yom Tov Lippman. *Sepher HaNizzahon.* Edited by Frank Talmage. Jerusalem: Mercaz Dinur, 1983.

Oberman, Heiko. *The Roots of Anti-Semitism in the Age of Renaissance and Reformation.* Translated by James I. Porter. Philadelphia: Fortress Press, 1984.

Osten-Sacken, Peter von der. *Martin Luther und die Juden—neu untersucht anhand von Anton Margaritas* "Der gantz Jüdisch Glaub" *(1530/31).* Stuttgart: Kohlhammer, 2002.

Pacios López, Antonio. *La Disputa de Tortosa.* Madrid: CSIC, 1957.

Petersen, William L. "The Vorlage of Shem-Tob's Hebrew Matthew." *New Testament Studies* 44 (1998): 491.

Pfefferkorn, Johannes. *Der Juden Spiegel.* Nürnberg: Huber, 1507.

———. *Ich heyß ein buchlijn der iuden beicht, In allen orten vint man mich beicht* ... Cologne: Landen and Augsburg; Froschauer, 1508 (Der Judenbeicht).

———. *Libellus de Iudaica confessione, sive sabbato afflictionis.* Cologne: Landen, 1508.

Reinhart, Max, ed. *Infinite Boundaries: Order, Disorder, and Reorder in Early Modern German Culture.* Sixteenth Century Essays and Studies, no. 40. Kirksville, MO: Sixteenth Century Journal Publishers, 1998.

Reuchlin, Johannes. *De Arte Cabalistica.* Hagenau, 1517; reprinted Stuttgart-Bad Connstatt: Fromann, 1964.

———. *De Verbo Mirifico.* 1494.

Robinson, Ira. "Messianic Prayer Vigils in Jerusalem in the Early Sixteenth Century." *Jewish Quarterly Review* n.s. 72 (July 1981): 32–42.

Rotscheidt, Wilhelm. *Stephan Isaak . . . SeinLeben.* Leipzig: Nachfolger, 1910.

Rowan, Steven. "Johann Zasius, Attorney for the Jewish Community of Regensburg, 1519 C.E." *Jewish Quarterly Review* n.s. 72, no. 3 (1982): 198–201.

Saperstein, Mark, ed. *Essential Papers on Messianic Movements and Personalities in Jewish History.* New York: New York University Press, 1992.

Schaefer, Peter, and I. Wandrey, eds. *Reuchlin und seine Erben, Pforzheiner Reuchlinschriften,* VII. Stuttgart: Jan Thorbecke, 2005.

Scribner, Robert W. *Popular Culture and Popular Movements in Reformation Germany.* London: Hambledon Press, 1987.

The Seattle Sephardic Community Daily and Sabbath Siddur. Edited by Isaac Azose. Seattle: Sephardic Traditions Foundation, 2002.

Seifert, F. *Die Reformation in Leipzig.* Leipzig, 1881.

Silver, Abba Hillel. *A History of Messianic Speculation in Israel from the First through the Seventeenth Centuries.* New York: Macmillan, 1927; reprinted Gloucester, MA: 1978.

Stern, Selma. *Josel of Rosheim.* Translated by Gertrude Hirschler. Philadelphia: Jewish Publication Society, 1965.

Stow, Kenneth. *Jewish Life in Early Modern Rome: Challenge, Conversion, and Private Life.* Aldershot, England: Ashgate, 2007.

Straus, Raphael. *Die Judengemeinde Regensburg in ausghenden Mittelalter.* Heidelberg, 1932.

———. *Regensburg and Augburg.* Translated by Felix N. Gerson. Philadelphia: Jewish Publication Society, 1939.

Straus, Raphael, ed. *Urkunden und Aktenstückezur Geschichte der Juden in Regensburg, 1453–1738.* In *Quellen und Eröterungen zur bayerischen Geschichte,* N.F. 18. Munich: Beck, 1960.

Voet, Leon. *The Golden Compasses: A History and Evaluation of the Printing and Publishing Activities of the Officina Plantiniana at Antwerp.* Amsterdam: Van Gendt, 1969.

Walton, Michael T. "Anthonius Margaritha—Honest Reporter?" *Sixteenth Century Journal* 36 (Spring 2005): 129–41.

The Wisdom of the Zohar: An Anthology of Texts. Arranged and rendered into Hebrew by Fischel Lachower and Isaiah Tishby with introduction and explanations by Isaiah Tishby. English translation by David Goldstein. Oxford: For The Littman Library by Oxford University Press, 1989.

Yuval, Israel Jacob. *Two Nations in Your Womb.* Translated by Barbara Harshav and Jonathan Chipman. Berkeley: University of California Press, 2006.

Zimmer, Eric. "Jewish and Christian Hebraist Collaboration in Sixteenth Century Germany." *Jewish Quarterly Review* n.s. 71 (October 1980).

Zunz, Leopold. *Die Ritus des synagogalen Gottesdienstes, geschichtlich entwickelt.* Berlin: J. Springer, 1859.

Index

Page numbers in italics refer to illustrations.

www.ingramcontent.com/pod-product-compliance
Lightning Source LLC
LaVergne TN
LVHW010355080826
844660LV00016B/976/J

* 9 7 8 0 8 1 4 3 3 8 0 0 1 *